THE ART OF LEADERSHIP
Volume 1

D1264494

BY OBA T'SHAKA

*AUTHOR OF THE POLITICAL LEGACY OF
MALCOLM X*

●

**Pan Afrikan Publications, Richmond, California
94804**

THE ART OF LEADERSHIP
Volume 1

First Edition 1990   First Printing 1990
                            Second Printing 1991

ISBN Number:1-878557-00-9 Paper
1-878557-03-3 Cloth

Printed in the United States of America
Pan Afrikan Publications, Richmond, California 94804

CONTENTS

Dedication

This book is dedicated to Raye and Julian Richardson. Raye and Julian Richardson are owners of Marcus Bookstore, a bookstore that has nourished African consciousness for Blacks in the Bay Area and throughout the world. Their bookstore has provided support for the "don't buy where you can't work" jobs campaign in the fifties. They have been supportive of the Civil Rights Movement of the sixties, as well as the independent Black school movement, the Republic of New Africa and many other Black liberation movements.

Personally, as an organizer in the Black liberation movement I was denied employment by the white power structure in San Francisco for ten years. Raye Richardson broke this job boycott by making it possible for me to teach in the Marin school district.

From 1972 to 1987 I had the pleasure of working with Raye in the Black Studies Department at San Francisco State University, where she served as chair and a brilliant professor.

Raye and Julian have been a source of intellectual stimulation for me and many others in the bay area. Julian and I have had many conversations about books and world events that have helped me to grow intellectually. Raye has a way of correcting you when you are wrong, which encourages you to do better.

Introduction

In 1960, my mother's best friend, Ella Hutch, co-founder of the San Francisco Chapter of the Congress of Racial Equality, invited me to attend my first CORE meeting. I left the meeting that night, little realizing how that event would change my entire life.

Since 1960, I have been an active member of San Francisco CORE, serving as chair from 1963 to 1965. I was elected Western Regional chair of CORE in 1964, and treasurer of National CORE in 1965. A year later, I co-founded the Afro-American Institute, later to be known as the Pan Afrikan People's Organization. In 1974, I helped to organize the Pan Afrikan Secretariat, serving as the North American Political Chair of the Sixth Pan African Congress. In 1980 I participated in the formation of the National Black United Front (NBUF), an organization founded by Jitsu Weusi. I serve as National Vice Chair of NBUF and Co-Chair of BUFFER (Black United Front For Educational Reform). Since 1984, I have served as Chair of the Black Studies Department at San Francisaco State University.

My involvement in the Black liberation movement has been the most rewarding part of my life. The Civil Rights, Black Power and Pan Africanists movements of the sixties and seventies taught me who I am and who my enemy is. Through my involvement in a collective mass movement, I received the greatest education of my life. My people taught me more about my history and identity than I could ever learn in college. In fact, the movements of the sixties instilled a sense of purpose and vision in me and taught me that the true purpose of life lies in dedicating yourself to a cause greater than yourself.

This book, *The Art of Leadership*, is my way of returning to my people the gift of purpose that I have received from them. Many brothers and sisters in the Black liberation movement have stressed the importance of training our youth for the task of leadership. Unfortunately, too many promising brothers and sisters have lost their lives in the service of our race, simply because they were not able to benefit from the experience of organizers who had walked the same road before them. These two volumes were written so that promising young African leaders in the future will have a frame of reference to draw from. The ideas presented in this book represent my experiences and the experiences of many freedom fighters throughout the world.

A key assumption of this book is that African people have great leadership traditions that need to be respected and drawn upon. Unfortunately, we have been taught by our masters to imitate their philosophies, religious systems, and methods of leadership and organization. But the legacy of slavery and colonialism has instilled a deep sense of self-hatred in the minds of Blacks, making it extremely difficult to develop a creative leadership. As a result, a great barrier of mistrust has developed between leaders, who have a contempt for the people they are supposed to lead - and followers who are suspicious of their leadership.

Through drawing from some of the great African and African-American leadership traditions of our past, we have an opportunity to shape values and organizations that are rooted in the best of the African philosophical and organizational traditions. It is hoped that these two volumes will play a part in shaping African leaders who place service to African people as their highest goal in life.

I want to acknowledge the support and inspiration that I have received from a number of brothers and sisters along with the encouragement that has come from some key institutions. To brother Howard Quander, Father Earl Neal and the Episcopal Church I want to extend my thanks for the grant that enabled me to publish this book. Brother Howard Quander, a leader in the sixties of Brooklyn CORE deserves special praise, not only for the financial support given for the production of this book but also for encouraging the Episcopal Church to provide financial support to the Malcolm X Liberation University, the African Liberation Support Committee, numerous independent Black schools and other Black liberation organizations.

To the members of the Pan Afrikan People's Organization, thanks to all of you for your consistent work in the Black Liberation Movement. To members of the National Black United Front who have organized a militant national Black organization, under difficult circumstances, thank you for your encouragement in the writing of this book. To BUFFER (Black United Front for Educational reform), thanks to all of you for your commitment and for the many new organizational lessons that you have taught me. To the members of CORE, I extend a special thanks because all of you were my first political teachers. I would like to offer a special tribute in memory of the late Dr. Nathanial Burbridge, who was president of the San Francisco NAACP chapter during the sixties. As one of the key leaders of the San Francisco Civil Rights Movement, he demonstrated the power that noble principles play in uprooting injustice. The Burbridge family have good reason for feeling proud about the great contribution made by Dr. Burbridge. To my good friend Dr. Nathan Hare, who helped edit this book and offered helpful suggestions, I want to thank you for your assistance. To Dr. Omowale Satterwhite, an outstanding organizer, I extend my appreciation for helping me to tighten this book up and make it flow better. To Ed and Alvina Guerro, I extend a special thank you for the special professional editing done on the first draft of this book. To Nina Pohl, the final editor of this book, I express my thanks for your professional work in providing such concise editing. To Sandy Baker, who worked hard in typing this manuscript, I want to extend special thanks. To Mark Jeffries, thanks for your special computer assistance. To African youth everywhere, you are our future. This book is especially written for you.

Special Respect

To my mother Sylvia Bradley, a true African Queen, I want to acknowledge that my skills as an organizer are largely due to the gifts that I have received from you. To my father William H. Bradley, who is no longer with us, a brave fighter for the rights of Black people, from him I always drew the example of courage and wisdom in combat. I am appreciative of the fact that both of you have always been in my corner, providing me with all of your support.

To my wife, Anasa T'Shaka, thank you for your support of my organizing efforts. I am especially proud to have a wife who is dedicated to the liberation of African people.

Most importantly, I want to pay tribute to all African people: the living, the dead, and the unborn, who nurture us and inspire us to achieve greatness today and tomorrow.

About the Cover And Illustrations

Artist Larry Crowe drew the cover for the *Art of Leadership*. The cover depicts several great African leaders. The figure on the top row depicts Pharaoh **Ramses I** of ancient Kemet (Egypt). The first person on the row below Ramses to the right is **Amilcar Cabral**, the greatest organizer/Theoretician of the 20th Century. The lady in the center is **Ella Baker**, Mother of the National Civil Rights Movement, former National Director of branches for the NAACP, Executive Director of the S.C.L.C. (Southern Christian Leadership Conference), and an inspiration for Black youth in S.N.C.C. (Student Nonviolent Coordinating Committee). The figure above her is the great **Marcus Garvey**, leader and organizer of the historic U.N.I.A. (Universal Negro Improvement Association). The figure on the front row left is **Dr. Martin Luther King**, leader of the Southern Christian Leadership Conference. To King's right is **Malcolm X**, head of the Muslim Mosque, Inc., and the Organization of African-American Unity. The historical leader that illustrates Chapter One is Dessalines, the great leader of the Haitian Revolution.

J.J. DESSALINES

CHAPTER ONE

LEADERSHIP

African leaders have a twin role. First they lead through following. The Martin Luther King's and Malcom X's are the true mouthpieces of their people. Their voice is the people's voice. Their musical sounds and poetic rhythms mirror "the souls of Black folks." The truly great African leaders not only voice the people's vision, but they forge a oneness with their people that enables them to improve on the people's vision. Visionary leaders call on their people to be the best that they can be.

Great leaders are created by their people, and they become inspirations to their people. A Frederick Douglass, a Dessaline, a Marcus Garvey, a Martin Luther King, an Ella Baker, a Malcolm X, and an Amilcar Cabral were shaped in the fire of the people's struggle. They lived with their people, learned from them, and in time, shaped a vision of liberation that improved upon the people's vision, inspiring their people to move to greater heights.

To understand leadership traditions among African-Americans and Africans in the diaspora, it is essential that we understand traditional African leadership traditions. This understanding is necessary because African-American and African diaspora leadership

traditions contain strong African carry overs. In ancient West Africa, the ancestral home of many Africans in the disapora, the King was the "servant and shepherd of the people.[1] Among the Mossi, the Emperor, or Moro Naba, inherited the right to power from the family of the previous Mora Naba. However, the King did not simply assume power through hereditary right, the King was selected from a number of royal candidates, by the people's representatives. When the King assumed office, he was invested with authority by the people's representatives. To assure that the people's views were respected, the King's Council of Ministers all came from the common people.[2] The Mossi people held their leadership accountable through a system of royal democracy, where candidates of royal birth were selected by the people's representatives and were held accountable to these representatives.

Chancellor Williams, in his book, *The Destruction of Black Civilization* says, "It was therefore in societies without Chiefs or Kings where African democracy was born, and where the concept the people were sovereign was as natural as breathing."[3] These Chief-less societies were governed by age grades, where people were grouped together according to age, and the elders' deliberations were held in the presence of the community.   In these age grade societies the rights of the community came before the rights of the individual. African democracy was collective, communal, and rooted in the will of the people.

In rural southern Black communities, during the Reconstruction and Post-Reconstruction period, rural Blacks drew on rich African leadership carry overs. These African leadership carry overs were blended into a rural Black folk cultural tradition where community decisions were collectively reached. Nell Irvin Painter, author of *The Exodusters*, describes the democratic tradition of Southern Blacks:

> "In actual fact, when uneducated Blacks needed to take public community action, they invariably reached common sense conclusions hammered out in mass meetings. Ideally, everyone had license to speak, and once participants had expressed and discussed all their options, the meeting would reach a consensus and decide upon a course of action, and select an able speaker or organizer, to execute policy on its behalf. Representative colored men and whites sometimes called the spokesman, organizer, or executor "the leader of the colored people," but the role

of the executor did not at all
imply dictation of policies to
the people without their prior
consent. Executorship was
tenuous and it was strictly
conditional upon the
people's agreeing
beforehand on the actions in
question. Because the
executor's mandate was
exceedingly limited, he
necessarily had to remain in
close contact with his
constituency."4

This democratic system described by
Painter, was a carry over of African
democratic traditions. Rural Blacks made
their decisions collectively after a wide
ranging discussion of different ideas. In the
tradition of African democracy, the
community decision was a consensus
decision.

Rural southern Blacks were also clear
about their definition of leadership. For these
Blacks, leaders were 'mouthpieces' of the
group, much as they were in Africa. If some
spokesperson thought that they exercised
power independent of the community, they
soon discovered that they ceased to be
leaders when they voiced views contrary to
the will of the Black community. Nell Irvin
Painter, describes how William Murrell, who
served as a spokesperson for his community,
thought that he could lead the community

when he advanced views contrary to the will of the community:

> "I went out and made speeches against their going, and tried to reason with them. And then I found out one thing that was very peculiar -- one thing that I would never have believed if I had not seen it -- those who had been leading these colored people in political matters could not lead them anymore when it came to this matter; the colored people would not pay any attention to them whatever." [5]

William Murrell, made the mistake of confusing the role of spokesmen who represented the will of the community, with the role of a leader who dictated to the community even when his position went contrary to the community's will. When Murrell opposed the Madison Parish Black community's decision to leave Louisiana for Kansas, because of white violence against Blacks, he found that he had no influence whatsoever. Murrell's views went contrary to the collective wisdom of the Black community, and the Black community "would not pay any attention to (him) whatever."[6]

In traditional West African societies, and in the rural South, leaders were considered to be mouthpieces or spokespersons for the people. To be a spokesperson, it was necessary for leadership to live among the people, listen to them, and learn from them. Among the Mossi, the ruler (Moro Naba), could not leave the capital Duagadougaa. Among the Dogons of Mali, the Hogan or Chief Priest (who is the leader of the Dogon people), could not leave the village. Leadership was based on the leader living among the people, so he would be sensitive to his people's needs. The requirement that traditional African leaders live among the people, was also tied to religious beliefs. In the case of the Hogon, the people believed that he represented the sun, and if he left the village his feet would scorch the earth.

Rural southern Blacks also required their leaders to live among the people. Leaders were expected to "live among the people, attend their local meetings, speak to them, and listen to them."[7] As Nell Irvin Painter points out, "since leadership depended upon close and constant contact between leaders and people, the idea of a national leader was a contradiction in terms."[8] A Nashville Black man expressed his views on the idea of national Black leaders in this way:

> "Now I have to say, that colored people have no national leaders. The leaders of the colored people are

those who are directly
located and associated with
the colored people....It used
to be, and is yet, represented
in the newspapers of this
country, the Frederick
Douglass and John M.
Langston are the leading
colored men of the United
States. This assertion is not true.
Neither Douglass nor
Langston are leaders; they
are nobody but Douglass
and Langston. Whenever
they go among the colored
people they charge them
well for it. All those fellows that
lay around Washington City
and represent that they are
the power of the colored
nation are frauds and
false....So far as there being
any national leaders among
the colored people, there
are none."9

This opinion at first glance may seem to
go contrary to historical truth. Certainly,
Frederick Douglass, served as a national
spokesperson for Black people North and
South when he spoke out against slavery.
Even Blacks in slavery, who had never heard
the name Frederick Douglass, would have
embraced his anti-slavery views because
Douglass represented their desire to end
slavery. Douglass was an effective anti-

slavery spokesperson for Black people because he had endured the pains of slavery. He had lived among the people he spoke for.

However, the "Post-Reconstruction" Frederick Douglass was very much out of touch with rural southern Blacks. Douglass lived in the comfort of Washington, D.C., away from the Ku Klux Klan violence of the rural South. He was out of touch with the thinking of rural Blacks, who met on their own and hammered out their views collectively

So African and African-American leaders were those who were spokespersons for the community. To represent the will of the people, leaders had to live among the people. This concept of leaders as spokespersons who lived among the people, can also be found in other parts of the African diaspora.

In the Haitian revolution, the greatest leader, Dessaline, was a man of the people who built his revolutionary program on African people's vision for freedom and independence. While the military struggle for liberation required a military discipline that was authoritarian, Dessaline remained true to African people's desire for freedom and independence. As Dr. Jacob Carruthers notes in his book *Race Vindication: The Spirit of the Haitian Reveloution*, when Dessaline assumed leadership of the Haitian nation, Dessaline drew on the pride of the Blacks and decreed that all of the different shades of our people were Black. This was a revolutionary act because the policy of Black identity sought to root out the color caste system of the Caribbean which defined white and light skinned Blacks to be superior to dark skinned Blacks. Dessaline's Black identity policies were not only designed to promote race pride, but they were also designed to destroy the basis for political and economic privileges based on light skin.

During slavery, Dessaline was a field Black who bore the lashes of the slave master. Therefore, he understood the hatred that the Blacks of Haiti felt towards their white oppressors. Dessaline expressed the popular will of Blacks when he proclaimed that all whites who had committed crimes against Blacks had to be punished, and that no white person could own land in Haiti. These two policies showed that Dessaline placed the demand for social and economic justice for the Blacks of Haiti over Western interests. This approach also revealed that Dessaline believed that the Blacks of Haiti could build the national economy without white leadership or white technical skills.

While these measures were extremely important, Dessaline's most important decree was that the land of Haiti would be shared equitably, among the Haitian people.[10] This idea of equal ownership of the land, grew out of the tradition of African communalism, where no one could own the land. The land was to be used by the people and to be passed on to future generations for their use. Dessaline's policy of equitable land distribution not only drew on African cultural and political traditions of communalism, but his policies improved upon these traditions. Dessaline's policy of equitable land ownership was a revolutionary policy that was designed to see that in Haiti there would be no class of rich and poor Blacks. His policy of equitable land ownership was an improvement upon African communalism because it not only guaranteed land rights to the people, but this policy also guaranteed equitable land rights.

Dessaline demonstrated the mark of great leadership by voicing the people's vision for liberation and independence, while adding a new creative vision of his own that grew out of the people's vision. Dessaline's creative vision was similar to the vision of the great Black classical (so-called jazz) musicians. Just as Charlie Parker and John Coltrane drew on our people's culture, and learned from the great and not so great musicians that came before them, their patient practice enabled them to create a new music. So Dessaline's faithful service to African people enabled him to sharpen his military and political skills, and as Jacob Carruthers demonstrates in his book entitled *Race Vindication: The Spirit of the Haitian Revolution*, Dessaline built on the legacy of

Maroon resistance adding to it a creative revolutionary program that promised liberation to the Africans of Haiti.

Another example of the carry over of African leadership traditions to the Caribbean and the United States was provided by the great Marcus Garvey. The Garvey movement was a democratic movement. Great issues were debated in the annual conventions of the UNIA (Universal Negro Improvement Association). Officers of the UNIA were elected, often after heated discussion. The Garvey movement's success stemmed from Garvey's understanding of the aspirations of rural Blacks who migrated north in search of a better life. Garvey understood that when these new urban migrants faced the loss of jobs after World War I, and were victims of the bloody racial summers during the post-World War I period, that a movement for African liberation and independence were the order of the day.

Garvey's call for "Africa for the Africans, Those At Home and Those Abroad," built on the rural folk belief in Africa as the homeland for oppressed Africans abroad. Garvey's call for an independent Africa was the dream of many urban Blacks who had hardly got the southern mud off their feet. Most urban Blacks, recent migrants from the rural South, thought in rural agricultural terms. When jobs started to dry up, and racial violence began to explode, many former rural Blacks began to think about a future in Africa. Garvey understood this thinking, which was strong in the Caribbean. True to the democratic African leadership tradition, he was serving as a spokesperson for the group. His voice was strongest and most militant when he was close to the base of this movement in the United States. Once exiled from that base, Garvey began to lose touch with the sentiments of his people. Still, in his prime, Garvey left an organizational base that was more far-flung than any organizational structure created by Africans in the 20th century. In the spirit of Dessaline before him, Garvey creatively advanced the Pan African ideal to an organized international structure. This kind of international Pan African structure is needed today, when the West carries out global policies designed to keep Africa and Africans everywhere on the bottom, economically.

Martin Luther King acknowledged that he did not initiate the Montgomery Bus Boycott, that he simply responded to the people's call and served as a spokesperson for his people. King's central message was that segregation was immoral. This position reflected the attitudes of millions of Blacks throughout America. King added to his message opposing segregation, his commitment to non-violence that grew out of his understanding of Ghandism, along with Greek concepts of brotherly love, and his belief that Christianity should minister to the political and spiritual needs of its believers. What King didn't know was that Greek philosophy was a pale imitation of Egyptian philosophy. The philosophy of non-violence originated in the thoughts of the world's first non-violent teacher, Pharaoh Akhnaton of Kemet.

As many of the barriers of segregation were broken down, King began to identify with the problems of the Black poor. King's "Poor People's Campaign," and his solidarity with the garbage workers in Memphis, reflected his identification with the people's desires to end poverty. King's opposition to the Vietnam war demonstrated that he identified with the oppressed people throughout the world. King was a spokesperson for the desires and dreams of millions of Black people and other oppressed people, who wanted full freedom.

Ella Baker, the Mother of the national Civil Rights movement, former organizer for the NAACP, and Executive Director for the Southern Christian Leadership Conference, "commended the (student) inclination for group-centered leadership."[11] She observed that the student movement toward group centered leadership "was refreshing" for many who wore "the scars of battle, frustration and disillusionment that comes when the prophetic leader turns out to have heavy feet of clay."[12] Ella Baker understood that the people make their own leaders. She encouraged the desire of the students within the Student Non-Violent Coordinating

Committee (SNCC) to develop leadership
among Black people. Ella Baker wanted
Black people to have the confidence to
shape their own plans, to organize their own
groups, and to select their own leaders.
Baker encouraged Black people to draw
on their own democratic leadership
traditions, so that those who led the Black
movement would live among the people
and reflect their needs and desires.

Malcolm X's strength as a leader
stemmed from the fact that he had been a
drug addict, hustler, and criminal who had
the strength to rise out of the mud of
oppression. This hard experience gave
Malcolm a deep understanding of Black
people. The study of African and African-
American history, opened Malcolm's eyes to
the rich history of African people, while his
study enabled him to see whites as
oppressors of Black people. As Malcolm
often said, his study of history instilled in him a
sense of being alive.

In the tradition of Dessalines, Malcolm X
left a creative imprint on the Black Liberation
movement. He internationalized the Black
struggle for Human Rights. In doing so,
Malcolm built bridges between the Black
liberation movement in the United States,
and the African liberation movements in
Africa. Malcolm served as spokesperson for
millions of Africans throughout the world, and
he continued the work of Garvey and

Dubois, by again putting Pan Africanism on the political agenda for Africans in the West.

Malcolm's creativity did not end with his international policies. On the domestic scene, he attempted to carry out a consolidation of the Civil Rights and the emerging Black Power movement. Consolidation meant that Malcolm was trying to merge the best of a dying Civil Rights movement with the best elements of the emerging Black Power, or Black Nationalist movement. To accomplish this consolidation, Malcolm attempted to join the Civil Rights movement and raise it to a Human Rights movement.

In pursuing a consolidation of the Civil Rights and Black Power movements, Malcolm called for a balanced, broad-based movement. This new movement called for Black self-defense, a Black Cultural Revolution that stressed Black pride; a Black United Front of Black organizations; an electoral program that called for Black ballots to elect Black officials who represented the interests of Blacks. In addition, Malcolm called on Blacks to use their economic power to build a strong Black economy.

In his last year, Malcolm came to see that Blacks in the United States occupied a strategic position. In his speech "The Last message," Malcolm concluded that Blacks inside the United States and inside the nations of the West, represented a greater threat to Western power than did Africans on the continent of Africa. For Malcolm, this conclusion represented a significant change in his thought pattern. Prior to this insight, Malcolm viewed the African Liberation movement as the key movement of the African world. With this new insight, Malcolm was beginning to come to grips with the great power potential of Africans in the United States and Africans in the West.

Malcolm was truly the Coltrane of Black politics. In the spirit of John Coltrane, who improvised a new music, Malcolm improvised and improved upon the political vision of not only his generation, but of the generations that came before him. He not only served as the spokesperson for Africans throughout the world, and in the United States, but he served as a visionary spokesperson who inspired us to go inside of ourselves and create a new world-view and a new set of strategies and tactics for African liberation.

Amilcar Cabral, organizer, theoretician and leader of the revolution in Guinea Bissau, was the greatest leader of the 20th century. Cabral possessed the ability to balance the twin skills of original political thinker and creative political organizer. Cabral did not simply sense the desires of the people of Guinea Bissau, he systematically studied his people's culture and history, and then shaped a program that rested on clear understanding of the people's social structure.

Cabral's analysis of the Guinea Bissau social structure is the most creative political study in the 20th century. This study was based on insights gained by Cabral as he lived among the people of Guinea Bissau. Cabral used this study to develop organizing strategies for his party, the PAIGC (Party for the Independence of Guinea Bissau, and the Cape Verde Islands). Cabral's social structure study enabled him to identify which groupings in his population would be supportive to the revolution, which would oppose it, and which groupings could be neutralized.

Cabral applied the lessons learned from this painstaking study to develop a national plan for the liberation of Guinea Bissau and the Cape Verde Islands. A part of his plan involved training organizers who applied their lessons by building support for the armed struggle throughout Guinea Bissau. When the armed uprising was launched, it was carried out throughout Guinea Bissau. This was a considerable achievement, because most liberation movements are launched on the border areas, which are close to their support bases in neighboring countries.

Cabral is the best example of the kind of organizer we need today and tomorrow. Cabral demonstrates that leaders must live with the people, and learn everything possible about their culture, history, and social structure. These lessons provide the basis for developing a scientific organizing campaign that builds on the people's strengths. By balancing theory with practice, Cabral demonstrates that creative leaders can anticipate trends in the people's movement and plan ahead for them. Africans in America and throughout the world need this kind of visionary leadership, which builds on the strengths of African people, to shape an old/new world-view, and a society where every African will be able to realize their full creative potential.

To shape a new world order where African people take their place as sons and daughters of the First World, we must remember and apply the lessons taught to us by Africa's visionary leader, Kwame Nkrumah:

"Go To The People
Live Among Them
Learn From Them
Love Them
Plan With Them
Start With What They Know
Build On What They Have."

CHAPTER TWO

GUIDING PRINCIPLES AND

QUALITIES OF LEADERSHIP

Leaders who help shape creative new tomorrows that transform the material and spiritual condition of the people are dedicated to high principles. For them, high principles are like the earth, they give support to all of their ideas and programs. They provide a solid foundation for the political structures, and values of the nation. High ideals are like the heavens, they inspire people to the highest possible good. High principles continuously raise the vision of the leaders and people alike. They are the basis of good policies: programs and actions without which a new society, and new person could not come into being.

For the ancient Egyptians, the highest moral principle was the principle of Maat. Maat was "the rudder of heaven and the beam of earth." As the rudder of heaven, Maat provided direction for the universe; as the beam of earth, it was the foundation upon which everything rested. Maat was truth, justice, harmony, right action and right words. Maat dwelled in the heart of God and governed the direction of the universe. It was the basis of order. Organization could not be considered without Maat. Disorder arose when the laws of Maat were violated. Therefore the people and leaders of Egypt (Kemit) were taught to observe the moral law of Maat

> "Speak the truth and act out truth because it is important, it is great, and it lasts."[13]

Leaders were taught that

> "If you become a leader commanding plans of the many seek out every excellent occasion; let not your governance be wrong. Maat is great and enduring it has not been confounded since the time of Wosir. In the end Maat endures a man may say it is my father's property."[14]

To practice Maat, you must think the truth, speak the truth, and act the truth. Justice arises from truthful thoughts and truthful actions. As the Egyptian mystery system taught: when your thoughts are true, and your actions are good, your life is just.

A just life is eternal because it rests on eternal truth that cannot be confused or confounded. Maat is 'great, lasting, and enduring.' It springs from the heart of God, and is the beam of earth. Leadership that practices Maat follows a heavenly direction, and its policies will be recognized as true long after its death.

Just policies and plans are great and win the hearts of the people because they vibrate according to their innermost needs. The people respond with love toward leadership that thinks, speaks and lives the truth.

For leadership that desires to serve the people, the truth must be its motivation and guide. By seeking the truth, inexperienced leadership will correct its mistakes and continue to grow.

The Egyptian mystery system taught that justice, respect, honor, and love required must be given according to those who are nearest to us.[15] Our parents, brothers and sisters, grandparents, and other relatives devote much of their lives to us. The love they have given us is two way, it is to be returned.

Now, very often, organizers will spend more time meeting the needs of strangers while neglecting the needs of their spouse, parents, brothers and sisters and relatives. The demands of organizing make it difficult for the organizer to give the kind of attention to the family that is expected. Yet, while it is difficult to give attention to family members, it is necessary. The closer our relationships are to us the more deserving they are of 'courtesy, friendship, love, sympathy, enjoyment and respect.16

When we are able to show courtesy, friendship, love, sympathy, enjoyment, and respect for our parents and family members, we will be able to have respect for ourselves and our people.

A good organizer rests upon truth and justice the way the water rests upon the earth. Dedication to truth and justice is the basis for serving the people. By cultivating truth and justice every day we refine our characters while we are improving our organizing skills. In this way we embody the ideals of the new society that grow out of the new African. The new person understands that the people's interests are embodied through unwavering commitment to truth and justice. Freedom from hunger, illiteracy, racism, and economic oppression can only be achieved when we have the commitment and determination to struggle for liberation without compromising our principles.

While truth and justice must flow from our lips and be expressed in our work and in family relations, the highest expression of truth and justice is when it is practiced universally for the good of the people as a whole. To practice universal justice is to follow the way of nature that gives life freely to all without discrimination or favoritism. It is like the rain that does not select who it falls upon.

Universal justice is like mother earth that supports all life on earth, without making any distinctions. And most of all it is like the heavens, which includes all things, from the smallest to the largest.

The practice of Maat (justice) through words and actions, within the family and the organization are of central importance. But there are other qualities of leadership that are also of great importance.

LEADERSHIP QUALITIES

Organizing techniques are important, but the principles and values of the organizer are even more important. The principles of the organizer are like the foundation of a building. They determine the strength of the building and how long it will last. An organizer's principles determine the effect the organizer will have on the group. Where the organizer is just, the foundation of the organization will be strong. While good leadership cannot be expected to be perfect, the demands of the job require that leadership be able to embody most of these requirements. The job of an organizer demands a commitment to high principles.

HONESTY AND SINCERITY

Good leaders have honest and sincere motives. Their word can be counted on, because they adhere to truth. They can be trusted in the most sensitive situations because they have demonstrated honesty and sincerity in character.

CONSISTENCY

Organizing is like the wind. It is an occupation that requires consistency. The wind blows consistently; a good organizer has to learn to develop the consistency and staying power of the wind. Having the endurance of the wind is necessary because liberation is a long term process, with many twists and turns. Since this is true, our organizations, have to be able to go for the long haul. "Fly by night" organizations, will not meet the trying test of day-in and day-out struggle.

To develop consistency our organizers have to learn how to pace themselves, by recognizing what they can and cannot do within a specific period of time, and by developing balance in their lives. Balance enables us to combine relaxation with hard work, attention to family life and political activity, and participation in social activity as well as political work. Most of us also need a spiritual outlet that complements our political work.

Now, if we are honest, most of our dedicated organizers have viewed socializing, attention to the family, and spiritual development as things that serious revolutionaries don't have the time to tend to.

According to this kind of thinking, a serious revolutionary puts his full time into the struggle, leaving no time for parties, family and friends, or spiritual and physical development. Instead, the true revolutionary is viewed as one who doesn't waste time smiling or shaking his hips.

The problem with this outlook is that it isn't human. Human beings fight for liberation so that they can have a better life. A part of living better includes enjoying life. The people we claim to represent have no problem with this view. Whether it is in church or in a bar, at home or at a party, our people want to have some time when they can relax and have a good time. True, some of our people are dancing their lives away. But this truth doesn't justify the opposite view that to shake our hips will undermine our political trip. Shaking our hips every now and then can give some soul and life to our political work.

Whether we know it or not the view that work and pleasure cannot be mixed is a Western view. African people have traditionally combined music with work. Balance is necessary in life and it is necessary in political struggle as well. If we can't joke and smile, then to many of our people, we are going to seem inhuman. If we don't have social outlets that we enjoy, sooner or later, the struggle will become routine and boring. If we don't pay attention to our families then we run the risk of losing our wives and children. If we don't take time to exercise, we will find that our political ideas will not have a physical temple that is fit enough to exercise those ideas. If we treat all forms of spiritualism as mystical, we will find ourselves suppressing a yearning for insight into another side of existence.

Balance is the key ingredient for the organizer who wants to last the long race. When our families fall apart, we won't be able to maintain the same level of commitment; when we start dragging our feet we will not have the energy to work effectively, and our mental alertness will fall off; and of course when our hearts fail it is all over.

But when we strive to achieve balance in our lives, we will find happiness. We will find that it feels good to tap our full potential. Through a balanced approach to life, we will be able to expand to new horizons. A balanced life also make us more flexible.

FLEXIBLE AND NON-COMPROMISING

The organizer is constantly faced with unexpected situations that require innovative solutions. To be innovative the organizer has to be flexible through being receptive to new ideas.

Flexibility should be balanced with a non-compromising adherence to essential principles. A good leader does not allow himself or herself to be co-opted, bought off, or, otherwise, compromised. In this sense leadership is like a tree; it has to have the flexibility of a tree's branches and the firmness of the trunk.

WORK AND STUDY

Some leaders are more action oriented, others are more theory oriented. A good leader struggles with his weak side in order to achieve a balance between the two. When leadership sets the example for hard work, it inspires others to do the same. People who think that they can sit back and tell others what to do, while they do nothing, are poor leaders, and cannot expect others to commit themselves to work. Hard work is the school of experience, a school where organizing skills are sharpened and refined.

Although hard work is very important, it takes more than hard work to make a good leader Good leaders must be able to evaluate their own work, assess their strengths and shortcomings and learn from the experiences of others. Study is an extremely valuable tool for self-analysis and growth. Through study we learn how others have achieved success, or why they have failed. These lessons become integrated into our own experience. It is necessary for organizers to be in constant touch with the level of awareness of the membership, so that the organization keeps up with the times and meets new challenges. Study and work enable the organizer to see new trends in the struggle before they become evident on a general level. Anticipation of future trends in the struggle allows the leadership to prepare for future obstacles.

RECOGNIZING TALENT

Good leaders are not threatened when they see talent in their membership, but rather are skilled in recognizing talent in others and in encouraging them to develop their talent. This skill is important because members are often not conscious of their talents and are generally not confident about their abilities.

FIRING PEOPLE UP

Enthusiasm is contagious. Good leadership is enthusiastic about organizing, and about the struggle in general. An enthusiastic eader is able to fire other people up to dedicate their lives to the high principles of Black liberation.

SPEAKING

The spoken word is the main tool of the organizer. A good organizer or leader is able to use the spoken word effectively in public or in private. For Black people, soulful speech and conversation are vital. Leaders, who have potential as public speakers, can be trained to develop their talent. Training should be combined with a lot of public speaking experiences. The ability to engage in face to face conversation is also important. Often the organizer will feel embarrassed or nervous when facing an audience, or in a one-on-one situation. Nervousness and shyness are normal feelings that can be minimized by standing up before a group and expressing one's views, or through practice with face-to-face conversations.

LISTENING

While public speaking and one-on-one speaking are important, the heart of good organizing comes with listening. A good organizer finds out where people are coming from by listening to what they have to say. Listening is a discipline that is learned through practice. Listening involves more than just being quiet; it involves hearing what the other person is saying. Listening to the concerns of others shows them that their ideas are important. It is also the way to learn about new ideas and discover solutions to old trying problems.

PEOPLE

Native-American people have a saying: "Before you criticize me, walk a few miles in my moccasins." Good organizers like people, and they make people their most important subject of study. By getting to know the people they are working with, the organizer is able to see things from the people's standpoint. This kind of organizer is also able to fully utilize the people's talents. When the organizer knows the people he is working with, he is able to encourage them to do what they like doing. People who are doing what they like to do are more likely to stay in the organization.

HUMILITY

Arrogance is an American disease. Too often Blacks have been infected with this disease and   mistaken its symptoms for virtues. Arrogance is the death of an organizer. Black people make their own leadership. Consequently, when the leadership forgets where its authority comes from and starts acting like God's gift to Black people, the people will go to work and tear the leadership down. Humility is one of the most outstanding traits of good leaders. Humility comes from the realization that the people are the source of power and creativity. Leadership simply organizes and structures what the people want: therefore, leadership has to be responsive to the people. This means that good leadership lives with the people, and shares their joys and sorrows. This kind of leadership finds it easy to give credit to them for their accomplishments. Great leaders, such as Julius Nyerere, Malcolm X, and Ho Chi Minh were, or are, humble men who lived or live simple lives as servants of their people.

SELF-MOTIVATION

The struggle for Black liberation is not one where our commitment comes from the pay we receive. For good organizers are self-motivated and can keep themselves going even though they rarely receive praise or recognition. Only self-motivated leadership can be sent to some other city or country to organize. Self-motivation means that the organizer is seldom discouraged, and rarely considers leaving the struggle. Cynicism is a deadly disease that can immobilize an entire organization. While it will crop up occasionally, it cannot become a consistent part of the organizer's thought or behavior pattern.

FOLLOWING THE GROUP

As was stated earlier, leadership is a unity of opposites, or leading is following. Good leaders follow group decisions and the interests of their people. Leadership does not mean that we only follow those decisions that we agree with. It demands that we reflect what the group wants whether we agree or disagree. When leadership ceases to follow the decisions of the group, or fails to reflect it's interest, it ceases to lead. When this occurs, the people may throw the leadership out, or they may cease to follow.

SELF-TRANSFORMATION

Change is a constant in the Black liberation movement. We have gone through many changes: civil rights to Black nationalism, and non-violence to self-defense. Change, however, is not simply external, but is above all internal. The organizer has to change internally by turning weaknesses into strengths. As the organizer demonstrates the capacity for positive change, he sets an example and encourages the membership to undergo the same process. Internal transformation is the process whereby we create the new African.

IMPROVISATION

Organizing is an art, not a science. This means that it takes a considerable amount of creativity to carry it out. Each situation that organizers face is unique, even though it bears resemblance to something that happened before. So, good organizers have to improvise and make the best of each situation they face. When organizing a boycott, a good organizer takes full advantage of every opportunity offered in that particular campaign. When attending a national or local convention, good organizers get every thing they can out of the convention. When internationalizing the struggle, good organizers get everything they can from the host country or liberation movement. How much the organizer is able to get out of a particular situation depends upon the organizer's ability to improvise and create.

In this sense, organizing is like creating a New African music (so-called jazz). It is never played the same way twice. The musician may repeat certain notes and refrains, but each time it is played the overall piece is never exactly the same. A good organizer suits his or her tactics and strategies to the times, and the particular situation.

Improvisation in organizing is like music, it depends upon the mastery of the various elements of organization. Mastery of the elements requires practice and study.

PATIENCE

Revolution is not an instant process that heats up like instant coffee. Liberation movements mature over a long period of time, and only people with patience can "hang in." Often times impatience comes from our young people, or a lack of confidence in our ability to win in the long term. Through study and practice, good organizers learn that time is on their side. The enemy gets weaker over time, as its international power is eroded, and its economic and political crises increase. A good organizer has a short-term program that organizes around immediate needs, and a long-range program that stakes out an objective which, when achieved, will produce freedom for African people. Our main concern is over the problems that face us every day. The problems of hunger, unemployment, miseducation, police violence, drugs, expensive but run-down housing, the lack of recreation for our youth, and a host of other problems, these are the things that are our immediate concern. The short range program addresses these concerns by bringing about changes in these areas. Only through organizing our people around their problems can we get them to a point where they can see the need for more fundamental change in the society as a whole.

It is when the people take up the struggle for jobs that the organizer can begin to demonstrate that even when the job campaign is successful it will not be sufficient to provide jobs for all of our people in a particular city, let alone in the whole country. A job campaign deals with an immediate need, while also educating the people about the corrupt, exploitative nature of society. A good organizer takes the experiences that the people gain through specific struggles, and as Malcolm did, uses them as classroom lessons. When Malcolm said, "a chicken is not designed to produce a duck egg, and America is not structured to produce freedom for Black people," he was summarizing, through simple examples, lessons that we had learned through struggle. He was linking up the short term struggle for reforms to the long term struggle for revolution.

Put another way, we cannot expect to ever organize Black people if all we talk about is the need for a unified Africa, or a socialist America. The people have to be able to see, taste and feel what is being talked about. Otherwise, they will write you off as being impractical.

LOVE

A good mother or father places the welfare of their family above their own welfare. The love of a mother for her children, or a husband for his family, is the strength of the family. Good organizers are like good mothers or fathers: they have genuine love for their people.

The organizer knows that self-love comes from a collective source. It is the people, in their movements against oppression, that set the heroic examples that instill pride in us as individuals. The people collectively decided to embrace Blackness; no single individual made that decision. Our love of self comes from our people, so we have an obligation to return that love, through committed work for Black liberation.

High leadership qualities are necessary because the unexpected twists and turns of political struggle will present the organizer with temptations to sell out, give up, become cynical about the struggle, or arrogant toward the people. Starting off with good intentions is not enough, a good organizer has to be flexible and principled at the same time, in order to respond to the rapid changes of the movement while holding onto the principles of self-determination and truth.

Organizing demands that the organizer continues to grow. Growth must occur through study and work. Humility and self confidence and most importantly, growth occurs through self-love and an undying love of the people.

The organizer not only needs to cultivate high political qualities but the organizer also needs to understand that there are different levels of leadership.

CHAPTER THREE

LEVELS OF LEADERSHIP

There are three levels of leadership: local, national, and international. National and international leadership is first developed at the local level.

Unfortunately, our leadership often moves through these levels in a haphazard manner. At times charismatic leadership emerges on the national scene without any local organizing experience, and little political orientation. Before long, this type of inexperienced leadership is faced with challenges it cannot handle. Confusion caused by organizational and political inexperience can, and has, led to the disruption of promising Black movements.

Confusion and disruption occurred mainly because our movement had not developed a process for grooming promising leadership from the local to the national and the international level. Today we can choose to ignore these tragic lessons, or we can begin to develop systems for moving leadership from one stage to another.

The national liberation movement in Guinea Bissau was one of the most thoroughly organized, creative revolutions in the 20th century. It was led by Amilcar Cabral, an agronomist, creative theoretician, and organizer. Cabral, working as an agronomist, traveled throughout Guinea Bissau, and gained a deep insight into the culture and social structure in the rural areas. He wrote a monograph entitled "Taking Stock," which analyzed the cultural and social makeup of the people in the countryside of Guinea Bissau.

Cabral founded the PAIGC (Party for the Independence of Guinea Bissau and the Cape Verde Islands), and began to organize cells in the main town of Guinea Bissau. However, on August 3, 1959, a strike by workers organized by PAIGC was brutally suppressed and over 50 demonstrators were killed. PAIGC's cells were destroyed by the Portuguese police, and the party withdrew to Guinea, to examine the causes behind their failure, and to reorganize the struggle.

In Guinea, Cabral established the party's first school to train organizers. The theoretical and practical training gained by PAIGC members enabled them to go back to Guinea Bissau and organize one of the most scientific national liberation movements in the 20th century. To quote from Gerard Caliand, who wrote *Revolution in the Third World* :

The party in exile concluded that while there was no chance of carrying on an urban struggle in Guinea Bissau, the countryside offered ground in which it could hope to take root. A school was set up in Conakry to train young cadres for six to eight weeks at a time, to build a political support structure inside Guinea. This basic training, which later developed into more or less continuous training, aimed at the help of a simple and repetitive terminology at instilling a new way of approaching problems based essentially on the idea of a shared countrywide struggle against colonial domination. The cadres would go back to mobilization, seeking out sympathizers among the people, isolating the agents of Portuguese rule, preparing people's minds for the battle, making sure who could be trusted to help.[17]

Cadre training in Guinea Bissau developed out of the errors made in trying to organize a national liberation movement in the cities. For the Black liberation movement, organizing training is necessary to correct the mistakes we have made in our past movements. The Garvey movement failed for many reasons, one of which was the failure to train cadres who could organize the various aspects of the movement both during Garvey's period of leadership and afterwards. The Civil Rights movement and the Black nationalist movements that followed were mainly trial and error movements where activists had to learn from their own experiences. Today we need to sum up our experiences, and develop organizers who can build a planned movement on the local, national and international levels.

The systematic development of our leadership requires that the experience gained in local organizing be combined with comprehensive training, that moves step-by-step. Progressive experience in local organizing should be matched with organizing training to deepen the entire experience.

As our local organizers demonstrate their skills in various aspects of organizing, they should be progressively moved into certain national organizing functions. This work should progressively become more challenging, with training and work combined. Organizers should earn the right to move from one level to another, by demonstrating mastery of the lower level.

Mastery of national organizing techniques should be the condition for moving national organizers into the international sphere. Promising national organizers should be given opportunities to travel internationally so they can broaden their outlook. Travel and political activity at the international level is an essential part of training national leaders, because organizers are exposed to new ideas, programs, and models of organization. A seasoned national organizer has reached the point where he or she can assimilate the positive lessons of the international movement into their national identity.

National and international organizers should also understand that they will have to go almost anywhere in the country or the world when the circumstances call for it. As a consequence, it is not enough that organizers show skill on the local level. They must also be committed to traveling and working outside their local communities. The appendix outlines a sample organizing training program. It is important to remember that organizing training should be suited to the specific needs of the group, and that local, national, and international organizers should display a commitment to high principles.

Organizers are leaders with human strengths and weaknesses. The best organizers make mistakes. Mistakes serve as the mother of wisdom. Through our mistakes, we are able to gain insights and learn new lessons about our people and about the enemy. Both through mistakes, and through efforts to improve our organizing work, good organizers are able to develop specific leadership qualities. The qualities of leadership are a mixture of complementary and conflicting qualities.

Organizing is a lifelong occupation that requires that we be consistent. It also places us in new and challenging situations that require us to be flexible while being non-compromising on essential issues. To maintain a fresh and progressive outlook the organizer needs to gain a great deal of experience in organizing campaigns, but the organizer also needs to find the time to study. This is easier said than done, because action can take up a lot of time leaving little time for study. Conversely, study requires considerable time, which takes away from the time required for action. Achieving balance is no easy thing.

The main subject of organizing is people. The organizer must study people, look for talent among the organization's members and encourage members to believe in themselves. An organizer must be good at talking whether that involves public speaking or private conversation. However, the organizer must learn to listen, really listen. Organizers have to have a humility, confidence, and a sense of self-motivation. Other important qualities that an organizer must have are being able to follow the will of the group, being able to grow, having the ability to improvise, and to be patient, and above all else having a love for the people.

While these organizing principles are important, the successful organizer needs to master the state of the Black community and the state of the white power elite.

CHAPTER FOUR

ESTABLISHING A SENSE OF AFRICAN COMMUNITY

KNOW YOUR PEOPLE, KNOW YOUR ENEMY

As the organizer goes to the people, lives among them, learns from them, loves them and plans with them, it is essential that he or she works with the people to develop a strategy or approach to organizing. A successful organizing campaign depends upon a successful organizing strategy. A successful organizing strategy is based on mastering two realities, that of the enemy and that of the people you are organizing.

In joining with their people, effective organizers must gain a deep understanding of their people's enemy, while mastering the reality of the people themselves. As a great military strategist, Sun Zi, once observed: "If one knows the enemy and knows oneself, one may fight a hundred battles without defeat. If one does not know the enemy but knows oneself, one may have an equal chance to win or lose. But if one knows neither oneself nor the enemy, one will lose every battle.[18]

The political organizer needs to know the enemy and his or herself because politics is another form of warfare, albeit a less bloody form of warfare. The organizer needs to have a deep knowledge of the people's enemy because many of the problems that plague the Black community, such as high unemployment, run down housing, homelessness, and drug addiction can be traced back to decisions made in high places of power. So if we are going to be able to effectively fight the drug crisis that plagues the Black community, we need to understand the role that powerful figures have played in spreading drugs throughout the Black community.

In the same way, the organizer needs to understand how economic power is distributed among the Corporate Elite. Knowing the Corporate Elite is essential because the most powerful forces in the United States are those who control the largest corporations. This group makes decisions that determine whether Black people, and other people will have jobs, or be out of work. It pulls the strings that can send large numbers of Black and poor youth to war. Knowing this Corporate Elite is essential if the organizer is to have a chance of being successful in organizing a jobs campaign (or a campaign for low income housing), because the Corporate Elite controls the corporations that provide large numbers of jobs, and they have the power to influence hiring policies at the local, state and national levels.

As Sun Zi observed, knowing the enemy is only half of the problem. The good organizer must also have a deep understanding of the State of the Race. To shape effective organizing programs, the effective organizer needs to know the State of the Black family, the State of the Black Community, the State of the Black Economy and most importantly, the State of the Black Mind and Black Culture.

THE AMERICAN PRESIDENCY, DRUGS, AND ORGANIZED CRIME

Mastering these two worlds - the world of the enemy and the world of our people - is absolutely essential for successful short-term and long-term strategies and programs. Today, the drug crisis threatens, as Dr. Wade Nobles notes, to reverse African-American culture. The destructive drug world of nothingness and self-destruction threatens to destroy the Black family, the Black community, and the Black psyche. If we are to shape an effective strategy for dealing with the drug problem, we must understand the connection between organized crime and the exalted office of the Presidency of the United States.

For the drug crisis that plagues the African-American community, most communities of color, and growing sectors of the white community is an extension of President Roosevelt's alliance with organized crime in World War II. This alliance, known as Operation Underworld, arose initially from the threat of sabotage of the New York docks by the supporters of Mussolini.[19] By 1942 German U-2 boats had sunk American merchant ships right off the east coast. By 1942, the French luxury liner Normandie was burned just before it was to be turned into an American allied freighter. Roosevelt had good reason then to fear continued sabotage of the New York docks by Mussolini's and Hitler's supporters.

At this time Meyer Lanksy, a key leader of the Mafia, was trying to turn organized crime into a corporation along the lines of big business. Lanksy was a Jew, and though he was operating in behalf of Lucky Luciano, an Italian, other Italian organized crime families were finding it difficult to join a cooperate structure under the leadership of a Jew. When Lanksy promised Roosevelt that he could keep the East coast docks safe from sabotage in exchange for the release of Luciano at the end of the war, he was able to cement a relationship with the presidency while convincing organized crime's leading bosses that a corporate merger of crime paid off. It is not clear whether the deal struck by Lansky included a national governmental protection for organized crime. Whether it did or not, organized crime became a part of the American corporate network, with the help of the president of the United States. In 1943, when Patton's forces began sweeping through Italy, Roosevelt ordered Patton to fly Luciano's flag with the red, white, and blue. Patton was instructed by Roosevelt to use the Mafia, which operated under Luciano, as "guides and informants."[20]

In 1944, Roosevelt asked Lansky to talk to the Cuban dictator Batista, in order to encourage him to step down as president of Cuba. Lansky was in a good position to convey Roosevelt's instructions, because since 1934 Lansky had worked out an arrangement with Batista to turn Cuba into a gambling establishment for organized crime. Cuba also provided molasses from Cuban sugar cane for the thriving prohibition liquor distilleries operated by the Mafia in the United States.[21] Again, the United States government cooperated with organized crime around an area of common interest.

In the post-World War II period, the United States government supported the Corsican syndicate against the well-organized Communist Party of France. With United States support, the Corsican syndicate gained control of the Marseille's docks.[22] From that point on, Marseille became the chief producer of heroin in the West. Needless to say, the heroin produced in Marseille was destined for the Black and Brown communities of the United States.

Similarly, the Iran-Contra hearings have revealed the C.I.A.'s role in supporting drug dealers in Southeast Asia. According to the Christic Institute, some of the forces operating under the direction of Oliver North were the same forces that directed the drug traffic in Southeast Asia under the direction of the C.I.A. during the war in Vietnam. Recent revelations show that the United States has been a long time supporter of the Noriega government, which has allowed Panama to be used as a drug transit point and a laundering place for drug money. Clearly, the problem of drugs in the Black community is bigger than the drug pushers we see on the streets. It is even bigger than the corrupt police and local government officials that allow it to thrive in our communities.

Put another way, the drug traffic could not exist without the permission of the American Power Elite. American corporate rulers, who are the real controllers of the Presidency and the government, are the real controllers of the drug traffic in the United States and much of the rest of the world, because they allow the drug traffic to continue.

NORTHEASTERN AND SOUTHWESTERN CAPITALISM

The organizer will not be effective unless he or she knows the true enemy, the puppeteer, the one who controls the puppets on the string.

The Power Elite in America has two wings: the Northeast and the Southwest. The Northeast wing consists of major corporations based in the Northeast. The leaders of the Northeastern establishment, which covers a geographical area from Chicago to New York, and Boston to the region of Philadelphia, are the Mellons, Carnegies, Rockerfellers, Morgans, Fords, McCormicks, Vanderbilts, and others.[23] From the Civil War to 1963, the Eastern establishment exercised economic and political control over the United States.

As DuBois illustrates in his classic Black Reconstruction, the Civil War represented the consolidation of northeastern economic and political power over the entire United States. Northeastern economic interests defeated Southern slave agricultural interests through the Civil War. The great railroads, and the great oil syndicates were given huge tracks of American land by Lincoln. From the Civil War, until 1963, the eastern establishment dominated the economic and political life of the United States. The northeast's political dominance was so complete that "between 1869 and 1945 only two presidents were elected from outside of the northeast."[24] As Kirkpatrick Sales notes in his book *Power Shift*, it was the Northeast:

> "that controlled the houses of Congress, that determined American foreign policy, that set the economic priorities and directions, that more or less created the cultural and moral standards, that determined who were to be the powerful and the powerless. And such provincial areas as did manage to grow up at the time -- the San Francisco Bay Area, say, with its "upstart" A.P. Giannini, founder of the Bank of America, or New Orleans, prosperous through the Mississippi river traffic -- were largely contained in their remoter regions and allowed to exert very little economic or political influence on a national scale."[25]

Just as the Civil War was the basis for the consolidation of northeastern economic and political power, so World War II provided the basis for the rise of a new Power Elite. This Power Elite arose in the southwestern region of the United States, which covers California, through Texas, and south all the way down to Florida. The leaders of this southwestern power structure include the Hunt family, Texas oilmen. H.L. Hunt, the founder of the Hunt dynasty, was once the richest man in America.[26] Another member of this elite group is Patrick J. Frawley, whose father moved to California after the second World War and founded the PaperMate Pen Company. Patrick Frawley, Jr. inherited this business and extended the family empire into manufacturing electric shavers, safety razors and color film.[27] Still another southwestern Power Elite member is Joseph Coors, owner of Coors beer, based in Colorado. Clint Murchinson, and the late Howard Hughes, are only a few of the better known members of the southwestern rich.

Economic forces such as Howard Hughes developed their wealth out of the defense contracts gained during World War II. Other members of this group have profited as a result of the post-World War II technological advances. A transformation that has favored the southwestern rich has been the change from heavy manufacturing, concentrated in the northeastern industrial belt, to the new technology enterprises of the southwest. The areas of new technology are aerospace, defense, electronics and air transportation. Of all the areas in which the new wealth is concentrated, the most lucrative, and therefore the most important, is defense. This nas been the largest growth industry in the United States, thanks to the unlimited use of our tax dollars. The growth of the "military-industrial complex," is a product of the close cooperation of large corporations with the Pentagon. The defense industry has grown steadily ever since. What is especially important is the fact that there has been a steady shift of defense spending away from the northeast to the southwest. According to Kirkpatrick Sale:

> "...in the second decade -- the years of Vietnam and the moondoggle -- the effect was even greater. During those years the balance of Pentagon prime contracts shifted sharply to the Southern Rim, with the percentages mounting every year, until by 1970 its states accounted for 44.1 per cent of all the money going to the defense industry, the northeast only 38.9 per cent. Texas surpassed New York as the number two state behind California, and those two between them accounted for 28 per cent of the contracts, more than twice as much as the next states, New York and Illinois. By 1970, too, the Rim had five of the top ten states in terms of total Department of Defense spending (California, Texas, Georgia, Florida, and North Carolina), four of the top five states in aerospace funding (California, Texas, Florida, and Alabama) and four of the top five states in Atomic

Energy Commission grants (new
Mexico, California, Tennessee,
and Nevada)....."[28]

The data showing defense spending
shifts from the northeast to the southwest is
much longer and extensive than the above
list. What is particularly important about the
shift in defense spending is that it reflects a
serious political power struggle between the
two regions, a struggle that has now broken
the northeast's control of the Presidency and
its control of defense spending.

SOUTHWESTERN CAPITALISM'S STRUGGLE TO CONTROL THE PRESIDENCY

Since World War II, the new
southwestern rich have challenged the old
northeastern rich for control of the most
important American political prize, the
Presidency. The new southwestern rich have
financed a variety of Right Wing groups for
the purpose of challenging the northeast's
control of the federal government. The Right
Wing, with the new riches financing, has
attacked "federal economic and social
programs."[29] The Right Wing has also tried to
blame the eastern establishment for the loss
of China, the American defeat in Korea and
Vietnam, and the federal government's
concessions to the 1960's Civil Rights
movement. By blaming the eastern
establishment for these setbacks, the New
Right sought to prove that these eastern

establishment administrations were Communist controlled.

The Communist "witch-hunt" launched by Senator Joseph McCarthy, was financed by H.L. Hunt. This movement not only ruined the careers of many whites, but it had the effect of weakening the militant forces of Black national leadership. DuBois and Paul Robeson were both attacked as Communist by this Right Wing campaign. Many progressive and radical Blacks on the local level were also driven out of work by this new rich financed campaign.

By the 1960s, the Civil Rights movement had forced the federal government to shift a greater amount of money into social programs. The New Right at the local level in the form of White Citizens Councils, John Birch Societies, and Ku Klux Klan chapters, carried out an open campaign of violence against the Civil Rights movement. At the national level, the New Right with strong southwestern financial backing, succeeded in 1964 in capturing the presidential nominating machinery of the Republican party. Goldwater was the standard bearer of the new rich and the New Right. While Goldwater was defeated by Lyndon B. Johnson by 1968, another person supported and financed by the southwest and the New Right, Richard Nixon, was elected president. Ronald Reagan's capture of the presidency represented the southwestern rise to full national political power.

The Reagan administration has completed what Nixon started. Reagan has created the biggest defense buildup in peacetime history. A defense buildup that has transformed America into a second-rate industrial and technological power. The best technology is in defense and space areas, while the civilian technology is behind Japan and Germany. America, under the Reagan administration has moved from being a creditor nation to being a debtor nation.

SOUTHWESTERN CAPITALISM, REAGAN AND BLACKS

The shift to the greatest defense buildup in American peacetime history has occurred at the expense of social programs, many of which were put into place due to the pressure from the Black movement in the sixties. The federal government, under southwestern economic control, has ceased pretending to be the protector of the rights of Blacks and other people of color. Instead, the Reagan administration has gone about dismantling every progressive program it could get its hands on. It very nearly destroyed the Voting Rights bill. More important, this New Right southwest controlled administration has stripped the Roosevelt New Deal measures, leaving millions homeless.

The Reagan administration has pushed the most Right Wing foreign policy conceivable. Shortly after coming to office, in a nationally televised speech, Reagan announced his administration's support for the racist government of South Africa. It is to the credit of Blacks and other progressive forces, that many American corporations have been forced to divest from South Africa. The Reagan administration, representing the interest of this new wealth, has overthrown the government of Grenada, a progressive Black nation. These reactionary Right Wing forces continue to back Savimbi in Angola. In the Phillippines, at the last minute, the Reagan administration shifted its support from Marcos to Acquino. At this time, the United States both supports Acquino and opposes her. While Reagan voices his support for the Acquino government, the United States, through Right Wing generals such as General Sinclaub, supports Right Wing military forces in the Phillippines. In general, American foreign policy is a reflection of its domestic policy. Domestically people of color are repressed while America's foreign policy is represented by her attempt to repress people of color.

As organizers, we cannot separate what the power structure does abroad from what it does at home. The decision by Roosevelt to support organized crime abroad had a devastating impact on this country. The traffic of drugs in the Black, Brown and Red communities, can be directly tied to decisions made by the federal government during World War II.

Similarily, the struggle between the northeast and the southwest cannot be separated from our struggle to organize our people, because the Right Wing forces that now control the Presidency have carried out an unbridled attack on the Black community. More particularly, the economic transformation in the U.S., which has led to a shift in new technology, away from manufacturing, has placed hundreds of thousands of Blacks out of work. The jobs that have been created in place of the manufacturing jobs have either been in areas where few Blacks have skills, or they have been in lower paying service jobs. Even worse, the number of service jobs have not kept pace with the number of jobs lost in manufacturing.

JESSE JACKSON AND THE DEMOCRATIC PARTY

Politically, the Presidential candidacy of Jesse Jackson has introduced another element into the regional struggles just described. The base of Jesse's candidacy is in the South, where part of the southwestern base exists. Jesse has created a solid block of southern Blacks, along with Blacks in the North and a growing number of whites and people of color. This bloc is demanding that the Democratic party give up its effort to be more conservative than the Republican party. While Jesse did not succeed in being the Democratic party's presidential candidate, he has succeeded in building a progressive coalition inside the Democratic party. This is necessary because we need a progressive voice within the political parties that counters the reactionary trend in both parties. This progressive trend is needed to call for an end to U.S. support for the racist government of South Africa; this voice is needed to demand an end to U.S. support for Savimbi, the Contras and the Right Wing forces all over the world. Most important, this progressive coalition is needed to press for a progressive economic agenda in the United States. Such a force is needed to call for massive low and moderate income housing programs, so that the homeless will have homes. This force is needed to press for full employment for all who can work, and a guaranteed livable income for those who cannot work.

In understanding our enemy, it is important to understand that as organizers we are not only fighting against racist wealthy elites, but we are fighting against a Western world view. The Western world view is out of harmony with mother nature. In every area of thought Western man has separated the rational process from the spiritual source. In science, physics was separated from its spiritual side metaphysics, and reduced to a "linear mathematical equation."[30] In the area of politics, John Locke removed spirituality from politics, reducing it to a rational political theory. In economics, both Adam Smith and Karl Marx stripped economics of its spiritual side, and reduced it to a system of gain for the few, or economic benefit for the many. While the socialist system is more just, through guaranteeing work, social services, and education to the people, its exclusive reliance on materialism denies the spiritual side of humanity. Materialism, not the progressive growth of humanity, becomes the central goal under both systems.

Western science has waged a war on mother nature, breaking up her resources. Western science has too often been used as a destructive weapon. It has destroyed coal, iron, trees, and land; it has polluted the water and the air.

Because of the combustion of fossil fuels, the amount of carbon stored in the soil has decreased and the amount in the air and oceans has increased. Carbon dioxide released into the atmosphere is the major contributor to the current "greenhouse" effect, which is the warming of the earth's atmosphere by keeping radiation coming from the sun from escaping back into space. This destructive science has caused the opening of a hole in the ozone, which is exposing people, especially lighter skinned people, to the danger of skin cancer. Today the world stands on the brink of nuclear war.

RETURNING TO A OLD/NEW AFRO-CENTRIC WORLDVIEW

What all of this indicates is that the Euro-centric world-view that has reduced the world to a material equation is fundamentally bankrupt. It will not do to simply patch up this unbalanced system: it is instead necessary that we struggle to create a balanced old/new world view that is in harmony with mother nature. Our communities are in crisis not only because of economic, political, and racial attacks. Our communities are in crisis because we have become infected by the Western world view. For too many of us the central goal has become that of exclusive "material gain." Spiritually, religion has too often become a secular concept that operates outside the person. Instead of seeing God as being inside all of us, religion too often sells us solutions that offer salvation through some outside force. Jesus will save us, the Bible will save us, confession will save us, Jim Jones will save us -- too often salvation is pictured as being a force outside of us. What we need to understand is that God is in each of us. Salvation on the spiritual and the material plane is in our hands.

The spiritual life and the political life should not be separated. They are, in fact, one. People are part of the universe. We, each of us, are miniature universes. We have the power to bring about change in the universe, for good, or we can see ourselves through the eyes of our oppressors and continue to carve out a place at the bottom of this unbalanced corrupt society. We can choose to act in harmony with the universe, or we can worship our oppressors and silently consent to war being waged on the universe and our people.

The State of the Race is a state of fragmentation. Our families are fragmented, our economies (what little we have) are fragmented, our groups are fragmented; and most of all, our identities are fragmented. Our communities need unity, our communities need wholeness. We need to develop in our communities an old/new state of mind. We need to take the minds of our people home to their historical, spiritual, communal roots. As organizers we need to Africanize our reality, by taking the best out of our historical past and reworking it into this setting.

In our communities we need to form family study groups that carry on the serious study of our people's history. This is necessary because we gain a vision and sense of who we are from our history. Our parents need to be armed with truthful historical information to teach our young children who they are.

ORGANIZERS NEED TO BE ABLE TO ORGANIZE PEOPLE AND IDEAS

The need for our people to draw on our history, means that we need a qualitatively different kind of organizer. We not only need organizers who can organize institutions, and campaigns, we especially need organizers who can mobilize and organize ideas. The community organizer of the 20th and 21st century has to be able to transform Western attitudes, Western thoughts and Western behavior, into African-centric attitudes, thoughts and behavior. We need organizers who are internalizing African values, organizers who practice what they preach. Our communities need organizers who base their thoughts and actions on the truth.

DRAWING RELEVANT VALUES FROM OUR AFRICAN PAST

As we work to rebuild and create strong community organizations we have to dig into our great past to draw relevant values and lessons for our communities today. More than anything else, our people need a sense of our African and African-American past, to have a sense of "people-hood" and a sense of African "community-hood." As we draw from our past, we gain a sense of African identity, self-knowledge, self-respect, self-love and self-confidence. Our past shows us that our people have assumed responsibility for building great family systems, great communities and great nations. This in turn encourages us to have the sense of responsibility and discipline to build strong families and communities today. In drawing from our past, we need to also draw out African-centric thought systems that will be useful in our organizing efforts. Very often, we will find that some of the most important traditional African thought systems have been carried over into our African-American culture. The task for us as organizers is to link up the positive African carry-overs with their historical source. Then we must take these relevant ideas and struggle to internalize traditional African and African-American values. One very important concept that arises from the folk culture of African-Americans is the notion of complementary dualism. This is an idea that needs to be understood, and with great effort internalized into our thought and behavior patterns, because complementary dualism reflects a universal law of life. We can appreciate the idea of complementary dualism by drawing on our people's culture.

HARMONIOUS COMPLEMENTARY DUALISM

The people's culture defines special approaches to organization and group unity. The culture of Black people in America draws from strong African roots, which have been mixed into an American setting. African-American culture is rooted in rich African tradition of complementary dualism. Lerone Bennett, Jr. has described the complexity of this tradition in his book *The Negro Mood* :

> "The tradition, in the beginning, was not sharply separated into sacred and secular strains; and the tradition and the Blacks who bear that tradition cannot be understood without holding these two contradictory and yet complementary strains-sacred-secular-together in one's mind. This is, I think, the essential genius of

the Black tradition which did not and does not recognize the Platonic-Puritan dichotomies of good-bad, white-black, God-devil, body-mind. This has caused no end of misunderstanding, even among Black mythologists who elaborate a blues mystique as opposed, say to a spiritual mystique. The Black tradition, read right, recognizes no such dichotomy.

The blues are spirituals, good is bad, God is the devil and every day is Saturday. The essence of the tradition is the extraordinary tension between the poles of pain and joy, agony and ecstasy, good and bad, Sunday and Saturday. One can for convenience, separate the tradition into Saturdays (blues) and Sundays (spirituals). But it is necessary to remember that the blues and the spirituals are not two different things. They are two sides of the same coin, two banks, as it were defining the same stream."[31]

This rich complex tradition which Lerone Bennett so eloquently describes, goes back to the banks of the Nile, and to the mother of world civilization, Nubia. From this ancient root, the branches of this dualistic tradition flowed into North, West, East and South Africa.

Our ancestors also carried this tradition to Asia, the South Pacific, Europe, and the Americas.

DUALITY ARISES FROM UNITY

According to this tradition, all things, and all life in the universe, derives from the one great unity, God. When the universe was created, one divided into two. Duality sprang from unity, and everything had its complementary dual. In the ancient mystery systems, the first expressions of dualism was beings that were both maleand female. These dual sexed spirits symbolized the balance between complementary duals, who were the central duals in life. The fact that these spirits contained both sexes in one body symbolized ideal balance. Man and woman were taught to model themselves after these symbolic beings, to achieve a balance between males and females. Similarily, people were taught to achieve a balance between the physical and the spiritual. All of this encouraged people to regenerate themselves to new levels of consciousness.

COMPLEMENTARY DUALISM: THE KEY FOR AFRICAN SURVIVAL IN THE DIASPORA

This dualistic tradition, which Africans carried to the Americas, was the key reason that we were able to survive and resist oppression. Africans in the Caribbean and South America were able to use this complementary system to keep their culture alive. In the Caribbean and South America, Christianity was used as a mask to hide the traditional African religion. To the outside white world, Christian saints and the Christian trinity appeared to be the religious system. Actually, the Christian figures were a cover for the African Orishas, divine spiritual forces. African religion survived because it was flexible enough to tolerate Christianity, sometimes drawing parallels between the two religions, while continuing to practice Voudoun.

For Africans in the United States, African retentions were not as pure as those in the Caribbean and South America. The African in the U.S. mixed his Africanisms into Christianity. The Obeah man, or African Priest, was an important figure during the early period of slavery, and African religion is still practiced in some parts of the U.S. Many of these early Africanisms were mixed into early Black Christianity. In the United States, however, the Christian religion, and after reconstruction, the Black minister and the Black church became the dominant religious force.

DUALISM

The Nat Turners, however, did not make a sharp distinction between the sacred and the secular. Neither did the Denmark Vesseys. Nat Turner had visions from God, which told him that he would lead a war of liberation against the whites. Vessey interpreted the Bible along lines that supported slave rebellions. Both of these men came out of an African tradition that did not divide the world into sacred and secular (political) categories. For them, God dwelled within man and woman, while man and woman operated on the spiritual and political plane at the same time. The spirit within was an aid that told you 'to do it when the spirit said do it.'

Today Black institutions face a crisis of impotency. The Black church, the Black family, and Black community organizations lack the potency they once had.

AFRICAN SPIRITUAL TRADITIONS IN THE BLACK CHURCH

Historically, the central institution in the Black community was the Black church. Its appeal rested on the strong African spiritual and cultural foundation that was carried by Africans from Africa to America. As DuBois correctly noted, in the beginning Black religion was African religion, not Christianity. Gradually, African religious concepts were worked into Christianity, transforming Christianity into a mixed bag made up of European and African elements. The strength of the original African Christian church was that it rested on a set of African traditions and beliefs that accounted for its great appeal to the masses of our people.

Carried over into Christianity was this African idea that God was everywhere, and therefore the sacred and the secular (political) could not be separated. The early Black church, both the church of the Free Men of Color, and the hidden church that operated on the plantation after dark, was a church that preached a religion of salvation. The Nat Turners, and Denmark Vesseys, saw themselves as men of God who had the responsibility to act as God's agents of deliverance. The great strength of the original Black theology was that spiritual salvation and political liberation were one.

Early Black Christianity drew upon the traditional African belief in a distant high God that rested on justice, truth and righteousness. During the early period of slavery, the Obeah man or African priest, drew on ancient spiritual powers, as DuBois said, to "function as the interpreter of the supernatural, the comforter of the sorrowing, and as the one who .... expressed the longing and disappointment and resentment of a stolen people."[32]

Carrying on this early African tradition, the Black minister of the reconstruction and post-reconstruction period, adopted the idea that to minister to the people's needs the minister "must sit where they (congregation) sit."[33]   This was simply a carryover of the African tradition of leadership already noted, that a leader was the "servant and the shepherd of the people." These early Black ministers came from among the people, they were self-educated, and they built businesses, schools and publications.

THE POWER OF THE SPOKEN WORD

Part of the appeal of the Black church rested on the African power of the spoken word. The power of Nommo, or the word, was and for many Black ministers still is a spirit power. The word is life in motion, it is music and harmony, it is soul and reason. Most Black church-goers still prefer to have their sermons with some 'gravy' on it. The powerful soulful word of the Black minister carries the powers of ancient Africa, the power of the priest's words.

THE BLACK CHURCH STRAYS AWAY FROM SPIRITUAL POLITICAL ACTION

Yet, while the Black church has carried the strongest African survivals over into African-American life, today it is losing its potency as a vital institution. While most Black churches give most Black church-goers the spiritual lift to carry on through the next week, most are not tending to the political, educational, and economic needs of their members. Put another way, the central weakness of the African-American church today is that too many of our churches have strayed away from the source of the church's power. The power of the Nat Turners, Denmark Vesseys and Martin Luther Kings has been their commitment to a holistic sacred and political experience. To the degree that many Black churches confine their ministry to saving souls, without saving minds, filling empty stomachs, and building community political and economic power -- to that very extent does the Black church lose its potency and its vital meaning to African-Americans. The clearest proof that the Black church is losing it's potency is illustrated by the failure of most Black churches to attract young members.

THE BLACK CHURCH MUST RETURN TO ITS SACRED SECULAR ROOTS

To restore its integrity and potency, the Black church needs to fuse the spirituality of the church with the political power of the Black community organization. The Black church needs to become a spiritual, religious, righteous community organization. This is the kind of church that Martin Luther King , Jr. led. It is the kind of church that operates in the tradition of Denmark Vesey, Nat Turner, Henry Highland Garnett and Richard Allen. The desperate condition of the Black community calls for an old/new church that ministers to the whole person.

To renew itself, the Black church has to draw on its African roots. The African tradition of complementary dualism is the foundation of African and African-American spirituality. This power is the power of the Spirituals, Gospel, the Blues, Rhythm and Blues, and Black Classical music (Jazz).

As mentioned before, the successful mass movements led and supported by Blacks in this country, (The Garvey Movement, the Southern Civil Rights Movement and the Nation of Islam) did not separate the spiritual from the political. In fact, they saw religion as complementing politics, and politics complementing religion.

Just as politics and religion were viewed as complementary, so the tolerance of difference was the basis of the democratic tradition, which grew out of Africa. The small African political units were usually democratic, with the people having the power to send even the council of elders back to review their decision. Blacks in the rural south drew upon this democratic tradition to involve the community in decision making.

The system of complementary dualism was always a system that understood that life is a constant, continual change. No matter how bad your situation was there was always the possibility of change. Day would change to night, life to death, the bottom would sooner or later take the place of the top, and what goes around would come around. This was hardly a hopeless, pessimistic outlook. To the contrary, the understanding that life was change, created a powerful sense of hope. Those on top could fall with some help from God, and those on the bottom could rise to the top.

INFUSING THE EMOTION OF GOSPEL WITH THE REASONED CREATIVITY OF JAZZ INTO COMMUNITY ORGANIZATIONS

Underneath this complex complementary balance is the tension between the emotion of the spirituals and blues, along with the reason and improvisation of Jazz (Black classical music). No Black political movement in the U.S. has ever succeeded that has appealed to only one side of this complementary pair. Any movement that has been purely theoretical has not had the soul to reach the grass roots; and any movement which has relied exclusively on emotionalism has not been able to overcome the dual knife of reform and repression.

The combination of reason and emotion, Jazz, the Blues and Gospel, and Rhythm and Blues, combines the two sides of the Black creative coin. When reason and emotion are combined the mind and soul are able to improvise and create. Reason alone is only capable of categorizing ideas, and creating logical order to life. Emotion, like water, is a powerful force, but it needs shape and containment. When the two are combined, the mixture is like Aretha Franklin and John Coltrane, a powerful, soulful creative combination. This is the inspiration that blows to us from this complementary tradition. It inspires us to be heavy in balanced soulful ways. It contains the force that renews our spirit and minds.

Effective organizing requires that the organizer develop programs and organizational structures which reflect the peoples culture. Our complex African-American tradition is one that demands balance. Balance between the sacred and the secular; balance between discipline and democracy; balance between reason and emotion.

To paraphrase Duke Ellington 'our organizing won't mean a thing if it don't have that swing.' The swing we need is a swing that is similar to Jazz, the Blues, and Gospels. Our organizations must have the soul of Gospels and the reasoned creativity of Jazz. Reason alone will not move us, and soul without program is like emotion without reason. We need to fuse reason and emotion, spirituality and politics to create an old/new harmony with our people, with mother earth, and the universe.

Our return to our roots is the way we recreate a sense of African-American community-hood. This requires that we recreate a sense of potency in African-American institutions.

REBUILDING THE VOLUNTEER NO COMPROMISE COMMUNITY ORGANIZATIONS

In the past, the cutting edge of potent Black community institutions was the volunteer, committed, non-compromising, agitating community organization. the Universal Negro Improvement Association, the Student Non-Violent Coordinating Committee, the Southern Christian Leadership Council, the Congress of Racial Equality, the Nation of Islam, the Organization of Afro-American Unity, the Republic of New Africa, the Revolutionary Action Movement and the Black Panther Party, to name a few, were groups that agitated, educated, mobilized and organized our communities around economic development. They inspired race pride, Black Power, self-defense, community control and political independence. These organizations were independent, and they were the organizational fuse that spread a sense of identity and direction in the Black community. The most potent community organizations were those that blended the sacred with the political.

Today there is a near absence of this type of volunteer grassroots, issue organizing, institution building type of organization. The demise of this type of community organization has many causes. First, the militant forces of the sixties failed to consolidate their gains. This simply means that militant organizations such as SNCC and CORE did not pay sufficient attention to seeing that the people who waged the struggle benefitted from the movement. Also, economic victories in the North, and political victories in the South, were often not policed through follow-up organizations that were vigilant in seeing that the political and economic agreements were enforced.

Our failure to follow-up on our victories was directly tied to a failure on the national level to institutionalize our movement. Today, most of our youth know practically nothing about the struggles of the sixties, let alone earlier struggles, because the institutions that waged those struggles are virtually nonexistent. Institutions that are committed to raising consciousness and organizing around issues are essential if a sense of history and a sense of identity is to be maintained in the African-American community.

CIVIL RIGHTS REFORMISM, DEFICIENT THEORETICAL MODELS : BLACK NATIONALISM, AND MARXIST LENINISM

Partially, the demise of the committed volunteer community organization reflects the failure of the leadership of these organizations to master African and African-American history. The youth of the sixties inherited deficient theoretical models which arose from Civil Rights, Black nationalists, Pan Africanist, and the ideological nationalism (Marxist Leninist) camps.

THE DEFICIENT CIVIL RIGHTS MODEL

Youth who made up the rank and file as well as the leadership of the Civil Rights movement, entered the movement thinking that their adult leadership had correctly thought out the direction of the Civil Rights movement. Later these youths discovered that the Civil Rights model was deficient. For the Civil Rights leadership the ultimate political goal was integration and equality in every phase of life. This meant that Black communities and Black institutions were at best temporary places that would eventually be torn down when the era of integration arrived. This outlook led to the conclusion that group power, economically and politically was unimportant. The national Civil Rights leadership offered no direction for building cooperative economic power, and when a dissenting member of this group DuBois, did put forward an economic development model, he was kicked out of the NAACP.

THE LIMITS OF PROTEST

As a consequence of the failure of the National Civil Rights leadership to develop an economic and political plan for building economic and political institutions, these organizations had only one answer to every Black problem, protest. By the middle sixties, Black youth coming out of the Civil Rights movement concluded that protest alone was not sufficient. More than protest was needed to build Black power. Black people would have to pool their wealth to build economic institutions; and Black people would have to organize their vote along the lines of a political party if they were to have meaningful power, free from outside control.

DOGMATIC BLACK NATIONALISIM

The deficiencies of the Civil Rights model, and the failure of Black youth to balance the positive part of reform with the positive aspects of Black nationalism, account for the dogmatic shifts from Civil Rights to Black Nationalism among the militant wings of CORE and SNCC by the mid-1960s. Too often, the young militant wing of the Civil Rights movement turned its back on all aspects of the Civil Rights movement, including the powerful local movement bases in the south and the north. While this sincere youthful leadership was correct in rejecting the insulting position of assimilation, they were wrong in assuming that all aspects of the Civil Rights movement were negative. The southern Civil Rights movement, and some northern Civil Rights movements correctly proved that the local movements were the laboratories and examples that triggered national movements. SNCC demonstrated the importance of being flexible and learning from the local situation. The local movement was the primary creator of Black pride. Black people who saw other Blacks unite and fight for change, gained a new sense of power and self-respect.

MILITANT CIVIL RIGHTS GROUPS NEEDED AN INDEPENDENT ECONOMIC BASE

Still, the militant Civil Rights organizations discovered that when they took non-compromising stands that were critical of the

Democratic party, and United States foreign policy, their funds dried up. Militant protest wouldn't be financially supported by the liberal white power structure when their political interests were threatened. To sustain militant struggle, Civil Rights organizations needed an independent economic base that could finance the movement. So the youth were correct in calling for Black power. Still, just because the Civil Rights protest model was deficient, did not mean that it was totally bankrupt. The strength of the Civil Rights reformist model was that it organized Black people around the right to vote, the need to end segregation, and in some northern Black communities it organized for jobs. These issues were appealing because they spoke to the needs and desires of Black people. Where the reformist Civil Rights leadership was wrong was in treating these reformist objectives as ends, when they were simply means to an end. The right to vote or the end of segregation would not produce liberation for Black people, rather, they were a means to organize Black people for a movement for more fundamental change.

MILITANT CIVIL RIGHTS ACTIVISTS FAIL TO SYNTHESIZE THE BEST OF CIVIL RIGHTS REFORMISM AND BLACK NATIONALISM

The central failure of the militant wing of SNCC and CORE was their failure to understand the need to work out a synthesis between the best aspects of the Black nationalism and the positive aspects of reformism. Such a balanced synthesis, would have enabled SNCC and CORE militants to combine issue organizing around the vote or jobs, with institution building. The combination would have provided a nationalist theoretical direction for reformists struggles, and it would have kept the emerging nationalists centered in community struggles at the local and national level. Without a synthesis of reform and nationalism, it was inevitable that the new nationalist would divorce nationalism from the day to day local struggles for reforms.

When the militant wings of SNCC and CORE woke up to the deficiencies of Civil Rights reformism; many moved to a form of nationalism that was unable to cope with the positive aspects of the Civil Rights movement that produced them. The Black nationalist wing of SNCC adopted a form of Black nationalism which on the positive side rallied Black people around Black power, but on the negative side removed SNCC more and more from local grass roots organizing. As one wing of SNCC moved to embrace Pan Africanism, it made the mistake of subordinating the Black struggle in America to the African struggle for independence. The Pan Africanism of DuBois, and Padmore, which did not separate the worldwide struggle for Black liberation from the struggle for the liberation of the African continent, became transformed into Continental Pan Africanism. Continental Pan Africanism according to the SNCC nationalist wing, became the unification and liberation of Africa under scientific socialism. The problem with this formulation was that it provided no direction for Africans outside Africa. This was clearly an error, because in America, the struggle to liberate the African-American is a central struggle and cannot be made a shadow of any other struggle.

STRENGTHS AND WEAKNESSES OF THE GARVEY MODEL

Part of the reason that former Civil Rights advocates moved to this form of Pan Africanism was the nature of the popular nationalists model, the Garvey model. Garveyism represents the largest organizational model for Black people in the West. It is not suprising that this model had such a profound influence on Black youth coming out of the Civil Rights movement. On the positive side, the Garvey movement demonstrated the central importance of African identity. Garvey's movement instilled a deep sense of race pride among millions of Black people. Garveyism also proved that a program of economic development could only gain mass community support when that program was tied to a movement stressing Black pride. Garveyism offered an international model for organizing an international people. The Universal Negro Improvement Association was a worldwide movement, which cut across national boundaries, and demanded the liberation of Africans worldwide. The Garvey movement was democratic, it allowed sisters to assume leadership, and it stressed the spiritual and political needs of African people.

BLACKS IN THE TWENTIES, A RURAL PEOPLE IN TRANSITION

These are only some of the strengths of the Garvey movement. What the students of the sixties did not understand was that the social composition of Black people had changed in a fundamental way since the Garvey movement. As I explained earlier, Garveyites in the North were a people in transition from rural to urban life. Blacks who migrated from South to North were gaining their first experience with northern industrial urban living. When hard times hit this group, they fell back on their rural land instincts. A people who had a long connection to the land and agriculture did not find it difficult to consider a land solution. A movement calling for migration to Africa could be appealing to a people who knew the land, and saw the benefits of living in the land of their ancestors.

BLACKS SINCE THE SIXTIES, A PRIMARILY URBAN PEOPLE

For Blacks in the sixties, seventies, and eighties urban realities are the primary concern. The triggering movements of the sixties, (Montgomery; Durham, North Carolina; Birmingham; Washington, D.C.; Watts, Detroit; etc.), were all urban movements. Cities of the North were the base for the most disciplined nationalist organization in U.S. history, the Nation of Islam. Like it or not, the fundamental truths of the sixties arose primarily from the urban centers. Rural struggles in the South were important, but the central struggles were urban. The newly awakened nationalist's youth of the Sixties had the task of translating nationalism and Pan-Africanism to urban realities. If the youth had been more perceptive they would have seen that the urban Blacks of the South and North were much more concerned about jobs and economic development than they were concerned about land. Earning a living is the first concern of the urban dweller. Successful Black movements in the urban areas, such as the Nation of Islam during the Sixties, combined a nationalist sacred secular appeal with a program of economic self help. For those who draw on the Garvey movement call for "Africa for the Africans," they should not forget that Garvey too had a strong economic program for Africans in the urban areas. Garvey's Black Star Factories Corporation established a large number of Black owned cooperatives.

But the key point that separates the social make up of the Black communities of the eighties and on, from those of the twenties, is that Black people are not a rural people in transition. Blacks are not a people who have moved recently from rural to urban roots. The majority of Black people today are urban people, with basically urban problems; nationalists and Pan-Africanist movements today must understand that the aspect of Garveyism that says that Black liberation is solely and completely tied to the liberation of Africa fails to understand the realities of economic and racial oppression today.

Africans throughout the world are oppressed by western corporate tentacles that stretch to key urban areas located in New York, Atlanta, Dallas, Chicago, Philadelphia, San Francisco, Paris, London and Tokyo. Whether Africans live in the urban or rural areas of America, or the urban areas of Europe, or the Caribbean, Asia, or the Islands of the South Pacific, all are oppressed by a racial and economic system that is based in the urban areas of the West and Japan. Wherever Africans go in the world they will find themselves strangled racially, economically, culturally, and politically by this same system of corporate capitalism that makes the rich richer, the poor poorer and more and more of our people expendable. The Garveyite proposal of flight to Africa, will not solve the problem of Blacks, it will only shift the arena of the fight that African people will have to wage against the greedy system of corporate capitalism and corporate imperialism. Whether we like it or not, the principal enemy of African people and oppressed people throughout the world is a dual racial and corporate system of big business that respects no national borders. Today we need a Spiritual, Psychological,

Philosophical return to the best of our African past and present, which must be adapted into pour lives today.

STRENGTHS AND WEAKNESSES OF THE MARXIST MODEL

Another deficient model that contributed to the near demise of volunteer community organizations was the Marxist model. To date, the Marxist model has not been adopted by any large Black organization or Black mass movement. Still, the Marxist model has had an impact on the Black Liberation movement. The Black Panther Party, a wing of SNCC, the African Liberation Support Committee, and the Congress of African People were all at one stage in their history influenced by the Marxist model.

The Marxist model, while offering a more humane economic order by seeking to place control of the means of wealth (production) in the hands of the workers, has a number of deficiencies. First, while Marxism proclaims a belief in the dialectical model, a model that says that everything contains its opposite, it denies the spiritual and centers on the material realities. From a dialectical standpoint this makes no sense. Dialectically speaking, everything contains its opposite. If you have day you have night; if you have left you have right; if you have the material you must also have the non-material, or the spiritual. In denying the spiritual reality, Marxists contradict their own dialectical reasoning. More important, they run up against the spiritual reality of African and African-American life. One reason that Marxist movements have failed to gain a mass following among Black people is that they run against the spiritual grain of the Black community. An organization that rests its appeal on dry political logic without any soulful spiritual appeal, will not move the masses of Black people. This is one reason that Marxism has reached only a small sector of Black intellectuals who are inclined to engage in dry ideological debate.

The second deficiency of Marxism emerges out of its practice. In theory, Marxists advocate a "dictatorship of the proletariat." What Marx meant by this term was that the workers should rule and should dictate to the rich bourgeoisie. It would have been better if Marx had described this system as the democracy of the workers over the ruling class. Marxist government has not developed this workers democracy, instead, Marxist states have developed a dictatorship of the Communist party over the workers, peasants, and former members of the bourgeoisie. Party dictatorships in the Soviet Union and China have produced government bureaucracies. The Stalinist party dictatorship, which was really the dictatorship of Stalin over the party, destroyed most of the party's revolutionary intellectuals, and over a million peasants. The Soviet economy finds itself in a position where an economy such as Japan, which lacks natural resources, and has a much smaller population, can outproduce on a quality level, the Soviet economy. Gorbachev's Perestrokia is an attempt to correct the deficiencies of Stalinism, through a system of democracy that to date seeks to keep the party in the leading positions in the state and the economy.

The third deficiency of Marxism is its failure to perceive the profound significance of racism in the world. Simply put, a strict Marxist solution argues that racism is a by-product of capitalism. Therefore, racism will be destroyed when capitalism is destroyed. This simple formulation fails to take into account the fact that racism is a part of the culture, economy, and politics of capitalism. As a consequence, racism becomes an instinctive attitude that is acted on without thought. To paraphrase DuBois, 'racism is a reflex action among whites throughout the world.' Furthermore, racism precedes capitalism. The caste system of India is based on "varna" which means color. The lowest caste, the untouchables, are the darkest people in India today. They are also the original Dravidians that ruled India before the white Aryan conquest. All of this means that racism has not only found a home in capitalism, it has thrived under earlier systems. If racism existed under pre-capitalist systems, what should make us think that racism does not exist under Marxist or Socialist systems today and will not exist tomorrow.

The inability of Marxism to accurately take into account racism is part of the reason why Marxists have failed to note the racist reactionary character of the European working class. According to Marxist theory, the working class is supposed to be the leader of the western revolution. Actually, whenever the western colonial powers have suppressed the working people (farmers and workers) of Asia, or Africa, the western working class has lined up alongside their capitalist governments in support of colonial repression in Algeria and Vietnam. In the United States of America, and the Union of South Africa, the white worker has been in the front ranks of the oppressors of Black people. The Ku Klux Klan has received strong support from many white workers of America.

THE AFRICAN COMMUNAL TRADITION

On the positive side, Socialist systems have stressed the importance of collective ownership of the factories, land, and economic wealth of the nation.

If Africans in America are going to move to a position where we can free ourselves while contributing to the African and other worldwide movements for liberation, then we must free ourselves from the ghosts of our past, as well as the European past. We must draw from the strengths of the Civil Rights movement and the Black reformist tradition in general. Reformist movements teach us that we reach and move our people by addressing their needs. The great anti-slavery movement appealed to African-Americans because that movement embraced Black people's aspirations for freedom from slavery. Similarily, the great Civil Rights movement received the support of African-Americans because it sought to end segregation, as well as the denial of civil rights to Black people. These two great mass movements recognized that the people are not moved to action by ideology, they are moved to action when organizations, leaders and movements respond to the people's call for freedom from slavery, the abolition of segregation, and the achievement of the right to vote. The great strength of reformist movements is that they have recognized the importance of addressing the people's immediate needs.

While the reformist movement's strength has been their ability to address the short-term needs of Black people, particularly in the arena of protest, their great weakness has been their exclusive reliance on the philosophy, strategy and tactics of reform as the way to achieve freedom, justice and equality for African-Americans. This exclusive reliance on a reformist philosophy of integration, as well as reformist strategies and tactics, has placed the national reformist Civil Rights leadership in an ultimately bankrupt political position. Their long term, position is bankrupt because the philosophy of reformist integration is based on the historically incorrect position that America is a democratic melting pot. The melting pot thesis assumes that Blacks lost their African culture through the institution of American slavery. According to the melting pot thesis, full freedom will occur when America breaks down the racial, economic, educational and political barriers to Blacks achieving full freedom. The Black reformist leadership operating on the philosophy of reformist integration, assumes that their job is to use the ballot, legislative action, and occasionally the threat or the actual use of mass demonstrations to force full enforcement of the Constitution's promise of full citizenship.

The melting post thesis, that America is a melting pot which has absorbed all Americans into the American cultural, economic, political system is false. In fact America is a multi-national nation that consists of Irish-Americans, English-Americans, German-Americans, Chinese-Americans, Japanese-Americans, Native-Americans and African Americans, to name only a few. Each ethnic group in America has pursued an ethnic agenda, with the white Anglo-Saxon Protestant carving out the lions share of economic and political power. Each ethnic group, with the exception of the reformist integrationist Black Civil Rights leadership, has drawn from their past to shape a relevant political and economic agenda for their race.

Harold Cruse, in his book *The Crisis of the Negro Intellectual*, correctly describes the deficiencies of the Black Bourgeoisie's integrationist philosophy:

"Taken as a whole, the Black bourgeoisie in the United States is the most politically backward of the colored bourgeois classes in the non-Western world. It is a class that accepts the philosophy of whites whether radical, liberal, progressive or conservative, without alteration or dissent and calls it leadership. It is a class that absorbs very little from the few thinkers it has produced -- Martin R. Delaney, W.E.B. DuBois, Booker T. Washington, E. Franklin Frazier and Carter G. Woodson -- men who left something behind them. It is the one non-white bourgeois class in this world that fears to express its own legitimate nationalism, waiting on the benevolent nod from the power structure before it moves to achieve its limited social aims. Eschewing its own nationalistic birthright, the Negro bourgeoisie compromises itself and undercuts its own political potential in advance. Hence, its class is sold out by none other than itself, not by white industrialists in Civil Rights organizations. Because it refuses to be assertive about its African heritage, this class fails to be revolutionary on any social front in the United States, not even in Civil Rights. It is a class whose social politics are so inept it seeks civil rights without seeking group political power, and then demands economic equality in the integrated world without having striven to create any kind of ethnic base in the Black world."[34]

It is this flight from historical and political reality that led a wing of Black youth in SNCC and CORE to reject Civil Rights reformism in favor of Black nationalism, and in some cases socialism. In shifting from reformism to Black nationalism a sector of Black youth during the Civil Rights movement correctly attempted to draw from the African and African-American intellectual an historical tradition that Cruse talks about. In fact, the radical Black nationalists and socialist Black youth of the sixties went further than Cruse proposed and also drew heavily from the radical internationalists scholarly tradition of Frantz Fanon , Kwame Nkrumah, Patrice Lumumba. Where a number of other youth coming out of SNCC, CORE and other movement organizations often erred was in their failure to understand that while Civil Rights reformism needed to be rejected philosophically, as a long-term solution to

Black oppression, it still has value as a short-term tactical approach when it was tied to a long-term Black nationalist, Pan-Africanist philosophy.

What the radical nationalistic and socialistic Black youth of the sixties needed to do was to marry the philosophy of Black nationalism, which recognized Blacks in America as a nation, and Pan-Africanism which understood that Africans everywhere are one people facing a common oppressor. This synthesis allowed for short-term, reformist programs and tactics that organized Black people for jobs, encouraged economic development, and supported independent Black schools. This new combination also provided a basis for changing the curriculum in the public schools, organizing for self-defense, as well as electoral politics and independent Black political party formations. Our history as a nation (within a multi-national nation) demands that we synthesize Black nationalism Pan-Africanism, and Communalism on a long-term basis, with reformist tactics and programs on a short-term basis. This is necessary because Black nationalism infuses the kind of pride Blacks need to unite and to draw from the lessons of the African and African-American historical past. Pan-Africanism provides the international framework for linking up the national struggle for Black liberation with the struggle to liberate African people throughout the world. Communalism provides the ideal for the collective control of great wealth by the people, rather than a few controlling the great wealth of the country. Reformism as a short-term tactic is necessary because it enables us to reach our people around their real needs.

THE AFROCENTRIC EDUCATIONAL THRUST

The synthesis of Black nationalism, communalism, and Pan-Africanism on a long-term basis with Civil Rights reformism on a short-term basis allows us to provide a Black nationalist content to otherwise short-term reformist struggles. For example: when the philosophy of Black nationalism and Pan-Africanism is linked to educational struggles for reforms, the kind of reforms we talk about become different. Under the philosophy of integration, reforms such as integrated schools, which often involves busing, becomes the tactical orientation. However, when Black nationalism and Pan-Africanism become the philosophical basis for educational struggles, the goal changes to the philosophical content of public education, by shifting the orientation away from a Euro-centric orientation (with Greece as the center of the world,) to an Afro-centric focus (with African humanity and historical achievements as one of a number of multinational focuses). Very often reformist tactics such as school boycotts and electoral campaigns will be necessary to achieve the implementation of nationalist oriented programs. With a Black nationalist, Pan-

Africanist philosophical orientation, the goal shifts from integrated education to excellence in Black education.

This primary urban reality in America, and to a lesser extent the West, is one where Blacks are strategically located in key urban centers, which are the political and economic nerve centers of the U.S. and Western corporate capitalism. Africans in the West have demonstrated a capacity to influence the political motion of other ethnic groups, including white youth. Black political movements located at the strategic nerve center of racism and imperialism, have been able to disorient and weaken the presidency in the United States, and it has been able to weaken the American two-party system. Even more important, the economic costs of suppressing the Black liberation movement in the Sixties, demonstrates the capacity of Black political movements to weaken the American economy, especially when the political and corporate rulers are also trying to suppress people of color internationally (Vietnam).

So we need a new, up to date appraisal of Black nationalism and Pan-Africanism, one which recognizes the strengths of Africans in the United States, and the Western world, This re-orientation in no way alters the African-American, and the African in Europe's commitment to African liberation. It is still true that Africans in one part of the world will not be free, as long as

Africans in other parts of the world are oppressed.   However, a correct understanding of the strategic position of the African in the West means that we are avoiding our historical responsibility if we subordinate our struggle for liberation in the West, to the struggle for liberation in Africa. No African struggle anywhere in the world should be subordinated to any other struggle for African liberation. The blood of Africa that flows through the veins of Africa's sons and daughters, is no less precious because it flows in the veins of some Africans who happen to live in the United States, Europe, the Caribbean, South America or Asia.

Given the current political realities of Africans in the West and the rest of the diaspora, while Africans have the right to return home physically if they choose, what we need more than a physical return is a cultural, spiritual and philosophical return to the best in our past. This cultural, spiritual, and philosophical return to the best of the African past, will provide the values that are needed to create a sense of African community-hood, and African people-hood. This cultural revolution, will provide a foundation for carrying out a well organized balanced political struggle for liberation.

As African people we need to shape an economic vision based upon the ancient African communal tradition. One of the great strengths of traditional African societies was their communal democratic composition.

This great communal tradition was founded on a deep understanding of the unity of life. Our African elders understood that the land, the air and the water are God's gift to all living things. No individual could own the land, air and water because it does not belong to humanity, it is God's gift to all of God's creatures. God, and mother nature did not invent the idea that land, the airwaves and the water are private property. Put another way, the great African communal tradition teaches us that true liberation cannot exist under a system that allows a few to control the land, water, and airwaves.

Africans in America and throughout the world must draw from our communal tradition to shape a collective economic vision that will understand that human rights, and democratic freedoms include the right to housing, health care, a job and a relevant education. Put another way, while Marxism is a deficient model, which will not produce liberation for Africans in America and throughout the world, capitalism is an even more bankrupt economic system that will keep Africans on the bottom economically and politically. When capitalism is combined with racism, Blacks are guaranteed to be the poorest, and the most expendable. Africans throughout the world need to throw off the illusions of Marxism and capitalism, and in its place adopt a form of communal economics that is suited to African cultural, spiritual, and political realities.

More than anything, we must internalize this new political, spiritual, cultural and economic vision through creating committed non-compromising volunteer community organizations that are dedicated to drawing from our historical past to instill a sense of African community-hood, locally, nationally and internationally.

One way that we can begin to rebuild the committed volunteer community organization, and one way we can strengthen Black institutions in the Black community is to institutionalize a system for training organizers. In ancient Kemit, good was described as order, and bad was defined as disorder.

TRAINING AFRICAN AND AFRICAN-AMERICAN YOUTH FOR LEADERSHIP

African communities across the United States and around the world suffer from a state of disorganization. Our families, our churches, our schools, our businesses, and our social and community organizations need support. Our youth need to have a sense of our past in Africa, in America and throughout the world, if they are going to have a sense of their potential future greatness. One way we can strengthen our community institutions is to create a body of trained people in the Black community who have the responsibility to organize economic, political, cultural, educational, housing and social programs that will benefit our people. We need organizing training schools on the international, national, and local level. These schools need to tap the organizing talent of our people by bringing together African organizers from across the world to share their experiences in organizing. Our young should be cultivated to assume leadership of the race through a process of organizing training. Organizing training should prepare our young people to assume leadership through using struggles of educational and economical development to serve as leadership classrooms. This kind of system will prevent us from producing generations of Africans who have no sense of the history that precedes their generation. Organizing training schools would work to create organizers who have a mastery of our history and a mastery of our peoples' problems. Such a program of organizing training could develop a body of leaders who have vision and political organizing skills.

This organizing training book is designed to assist in the process of training organizers. Since the local struggle provides the classroom for testing out ideas that can later be applied on the national and international level, the Pan African Peoples Organization, based in the San Francisco Bay Area, has started an organizing training school. This school, which is known as the Ella Baker, Amilcar Cabral Organizing Training School, is now providing organizing training in the Black Community. Ella Baker, was selected as one of the names for this school because as the mother of the national Civil Rights movement, Ella Baker taught us that our people are the true leaders. Ella encouraged the students of SNCC to continue to rest their leadership on group leadership. Today, Black people need to understand the teachings of Ella Baker, and the organizational strengths of SNCC (Student Non-Violent Coordinating Committee). Today, more than ever, we need to develop layers and layers of leadership at the local, national and international level. We need a collective leadership, because the system has shown us time and time again that it will wipe out individual charismatic leadership.

AMILCAR CABRAL : A MODEL FOR AFRICAN LEADERSHIP

Amilcar Cabral was chosen as the other leadership model because he, more than any organizer in the twentieth century, shows the need to combine a mastery of our peoples history with the practical painstaking day to day organizing of our people. Africans in America are faced with a complex enemy. If we are to achieve liberation we will have to master this enemy, and we will have to have a deep understanding of our own people. As Nathan Hare said, "We need organizers who can organize ideas and people," as well as institutions and mass struggles. No Better model of this balanced organizer could be found, than Amilcar Cabral.

In creating a balance between understanding our history and applying our historical knowledge to a campaign for organizing our community, we need to draw from our elders' wisdom. Harold Cruse, in his book *The Crisis of the Negro Intellectual*, was correct when he observed that movements that are centered around charismatic leadership are doomed because singular leadership will not be able to respond correctly to economic, political, military, cultural, and social attacks coming from an enemy whose power is based in institutions, not charismatic individuals. Just as the exclusive reliance on singular individual charismatic leadership is doomed, so a race whose leaders fail to shape a plan for economic development is also doomed.

ECONOMIC DEVELOPMENT PLAN

Every intellectual group in the world has sought to develop a plan for economic and political development for their race, except the so-called Black intellectual. The failure of the Black intellectual group, in general, is nowhere more striking than in the area of economic development. There have been four efforts to develop an economic plan for African-Americans. Booker T. Washington, W.E.B. DuBois, Marcus Garvey, and the Honorable Elijah Muhammed have been the only ones who have. put forward a national plan for Black economic development, yet we have some Black economists who work for major U.S. corporations, teach in colleges or work for other institutions. At the same time the Black community continues to lack a national plan of economic development.

Clearly, Black people are going to continue to be under siege, with the drug traffic representing a greater part of the Black economy than any other part, until we develop and carry out a national plan of economic development. Similarily, our organizations are going to lack meaningful directions if we are not able to harness the skills of a wing of this group of Black intellectuals. Fortunately, the history of successful worldwide movements for liberation demonstrate that it is not necessary for a liberation movement to enlist the services of all, or even a majority of its intellectuals. It is sufficient if a movement is able to enlist the services of a minority of committed, conscious, nationalist-minded intellectuals.

A MARRIAGE BETWEEN CREATIVE BLACK INTELLECTUALS AND COMMUNITY ORGANIZERS

What our people need at this time is to tap the creativity of Black intellectuals who have vision. Black institutions and community organizations need input from Black thinkers because very often our institutions don't have the time or resources to devote to national planning. The other side is that usually the intellectuals are so involved in research, writing, and public speaking that they don't have the time to put their ideas into action. So a marriage between the intellectuals and the organizers is needed for the benefit of both, as well as for the development of the Black community locally, and nationally, and internationally.

THE BLACK STUDIES DEPARTMENT'S ROLE IN REBUILDING THE BLACK COMMUNITY

As organizers, we need to draw on the special skills of different institutions that should serve the Black community. Black Studies departments that have not lost their political and intellectual integrity should be called upon to develop "Black Studies Institutes," which use the skills of faculty, students, and community members to assess the State of the Race in all areas of Black life and shape programs for action. These institutes should draw on the skills of their departments and the Black community to determine the State of the Black economy, Black politics, Black education, Black health, Black crime, Black housing, and welfare, Black religious programs, relevant theologies, youth organizations, health programs, relevant political agendas and directions for the Black family. This type of Black Studies Institute would not be a purely exclusive research arm, it would also attempt to prod community institutions to take action around different areas of the Black Agenda.

The Black Studies department at San Francisco State University has started a research program that has the primary responsibility to aid in "community revitalization." Our goal is to work with creative committed members of the Black community, to shape an agenda that will have national and international implications. This research arm will be available to local and national and international African institutions. Currently, Black Studies Research Institute has designated the public school as our top priority. The Institute's public school focus is on Afro-centric curriculum development. Teacher training, defining criteria for excellent Black schools and retention of Black students in school, and encouraging more Black students to go into teaching.

Obviously, one Black Studies Department will not be able to solve the problem of harnessing a committed group of Black intellectuals to the service of the race. Neither should it be assumed, that there are no groups of Black intellectuals that aren't already doing some very important work in reclaiming our history and providing needed directions for our communities. Certainly, the Association for the Study of African Classical Civilizations is doing important work in recovering and writing the history of Ancient Africa, with primary focus on ancient Kemet (Egypt). Groups such as Wade Nobles Institute for the Study of Black Family Life and Culture, are also doing important work. Dr. Carter G. Woodson did pioneer research and writing through his Association for the Study of Negro Life and Culture. As important as each of these groups and individuals are, our people need research/action institutes that have the special responsibility for shaping national agendas of action.

Individual Black scholars such as J.A. Rogers, W.E.B. DuBois, Zora Neale Hurston, John Jackson, John Henrik Clarke, Chancellor Williams, Cheikh Anta Diop, Edward Wilmont Blyden, Martin R. Delany, C.L.R. James, Asa Hilliard, Nathan Hare, Maulana Karenga, Ivan Van Sertima, William Leo Hansberry, Jacob Carruthers, Muhammad Ahmed, and Askia Muhammad Toure- all of these great intellectual giants and many more have left us with a great historical legacy.

First, and foremost, such research/action bodies must shape an economic development agenda that provides a blueprint for a national economic development plan. This research/action body should be composed of conscientious Blacks with economic development skills, as well as Black business people who have developed some business models, along with Black organizations and others who have ideas on economic development. In shaping this kind of agenda, we should look for business development models that have been developed in different parts of the country. These positive models should be incorporated into a national plan of economic development. For example, the Omaha, Nebraska, economic development program should be studied and used as a partial basis for an economic development plan. In Omaha, Black economists have joined together and developed housing cooperatives and cooperative businesses. In Kansas City, Missouri, the Kansas City Black United Front has developed a system for acquiring buildings free of costs. Kansas City BUF has identified white businesses who own unused buildings that could be transfered to nonprofit corporations for tax write-offs.

In shaping a national plan of action, DuBois' economic development plan (which is discussed in the economic development section of this book) should be analyzed, and the Nation of Islam's plan of economic development should also be examined. The basis for business development cannot be the existing capitalist system because this model allows for only the few to profit from the efforts of the group. The communal ideal should be the theoretical basis for economic development. Business development, like every other area of Black life, needs to draw from our rich African world view. Communalism provides a better framework for economic development than capitalism, because communal economics requires that the businesses we develop in the Black community should be owned by those who contribute financially to the development of the business. Communal or cooperative economics allows the Black community to have a say in the operation of Black businesses. By involving the financiers of Black businesses in the decision-making of those businesses, we are drawing on another African cultural tradition African democracy. The democratic system gives the community the responsibility for maintaining the community's economy.

REBUILDING STRONG EXTENDED FAMILIES

The central economic unit, the base for local and national economic development, and the foundation of our community, organizations, churches, and social organizations is the Black family. The African-American family is not a rootless family. From Africa we carried to America an extended family system that slavery did not destroy. Dr. Wade Nobles has demonstrated through detailed research that the extended family is an African carryover that was also adapted to brutal American realities. Extended families include members of the immediate family, relatives, and adopted family members such as friends, parents, and play relatives.

While the extended family survived slavery and Blacks, during plantation slavery, held onto a value for the family unit, nevertheless, slavery did make the African-American woman prey to the slave master; it introduced sexual promiscuity, which was largely absent in African societies, and it often separated families. It is impossible to measure the damage done by slavery to the Black family unit and Black moral standards. Certainly, some negative family rearing patterns have slave roots. Slavery introduced an attitude of love/hate into many Black relationships. Sometimes, the hatred of the slavemaster was transferred by the slave to other Blacks. At times the slave masters brutal treatment of the slave was transferred by the Black man to the Black woman, or the Black parent to the Black child. Very often, our great grandparents were not aware that when a whipping turned into a beating some deep seated confused hatred mixed with love was surfacing. The negative side of this slave legacy should not be minimized, otherwise, we fail to realize that there is psychological and spiritual damage done to ourselves and our families that need to be repaired.

As painful as it may be, we must realize that the slavemaster worked to control the African-American slaves socialization system. As Dr. Asa Hilliard correctly points out, the system of slavery worked to "destroy the historical memory of our people; it worked to destroy our peoples sense of group identity; it sought to destroy our people's cultural base and it sought to control our socialization system."[35]

This whole systematic attack on our people's social system rested on inducing in the mind of the slave a state of historical amnesia. For when the descendants of this slave system are unaware of their history, they fail to realize they are living out a reality of psychological slavery, even today.

So the organizer must alert the Black man and Black woman to the legacy of Africa that has been carried over into the African-American family system. At the same time, the organizer must raise our people's consciousness through a return to our historical and cultural roots, so that we can repair the damage done by plantation slavery.

CAUSES BEHIND THE DECLINE OF THE BLACK FAMILY SINCE THE LATE SIXTIES

As important as this two-fold approach to strengthing the Black family is, it will not be complete if we do not take into account the damage done to the Black family since the late 1960s. Drs. Nathan and Julia Hare, in their book *The Endangered Black Family*, point out that the Black family is now suffering from a sustained attack led by the federal government. The federal government has moved to control the means of reproduction in the Black community. In 1970, the Nixon administration established the Commission on Population Growth and the American Future. This commission, made up of leading businessmen, congressmen, and labor leaders, noted that: (1) continued population growth would aggravate some of our most pressing social and economic problems; (2) an average two-child family may be achieved by "varying combinations of nonmarriage or childlessness." This non-marriage and childlessness would be "free choice." Abortion and birth control were made the means to prevent or terminate unwanted pregnancies on grounds that "a nation's growth should not depend on the ignorance or misfortune of its citizenry" (that is, social disadvantages accruing from class and/or race). Another means advocated by the Commission was increased employment and career-centeredness of women; (3) also increasing public conviction and concern (to be orchestrated of course) over the allegedly negative effects of population growth, at best a popular value judgment but not at all a proven scientific fact; (4) discouraging youthful marriage while encouraging youthful preferences for smaller families and increased access to abortion and contraception, especially among the Black and the poor. In addition, mass media are to be encouraged to downplay traditional sex roles (unisexualization).[36] Drs. Nathan and Julia Hare, go on to show that this same commission noted that unwanted fertility was heavily concentrated in populations of people of color, where the main emphasis of this program was aimed.

Drs. Nathan and Julia Hare also stress that in this effort the Commission proposes not only the allotment of billions of dollars (at least 1 1/2 billion annually!) but also the transformation and denigration of motherhood, childbearing, social values, and the very nature of male and female, including the very nature of the females' physical body, now to be embellished with the muscles attainable from barbells, (and) transexual surgery for willing males.[37]

What all of this information tells us is that the government has been carrying out a program of social engineering designed to discourage marriage and reduce family size, mainly among people of color. In fact, this same government has developed programs to increase family size among whites.

Drs. Nathan and Julia Hare also note in this same book that the 1974 Census Bureau reports that the decline in fertility in the United States is most pronounced among Blacks, Native Americans and Mexican-Americans. There is also more family decay, more broken marriages, and more single mothers. Among Black females and males in their 20s the suicide rate will skyrocket.[38]

In addition to the government policies designed to reduce, weaken, and destroy Black families, and families of color, the U.S. economy has worked to further erode the Black family. The American economy has shifted away from an industrial economy to a service economy. This shift has had a very negative impact on Black families, because a large number of Blacks (especially Black males) were concentrated in the manufacturing sector of the economy. With these jobs drying up, many Black males find themselves in the position where either no jobs are available for people of their skill level, or only lower paying service jobs provide opportunities for employment. Black males find it harder and harder to find work that will support a family. This is a major contributor to the decline in two parent households.

Urban living has also eroded the Black extended family pattern. More often than not, Black elders are living alone or away from their children and grandchildren. The economy of capitalism has encouraged many of our people to act on the individualistic level. On the one hand, large numbers of our people are putting their parents in old folks homes. The reverse side of this reality of individualism is that many Black seniors believe that they will impose a burden on their children if they live with them. Individualistic values have broken down the idea that every elder in the Black community was responsible for enforcing respectful Black behavior. Now any elder that attempts to discipline a child has to be prepared to deal with an angry parent that doesn't want another Black person disciplining their child, as well as having a disrespectful Black child.

RAISING AFRICAN-AMERICAN POLITICAL AND CULTURAL CONSCIOUSNESS

For the organizer, a top priority has to be given to strengthening the Black family. While there are many steps that organizers can take to provide support to our families, it is important to realize that our families and communities will remain fragmented as long as our peoples consciousness is low. Our central responsibility as organizers is to encourage our people to study African and African-American past so that we will gain a sense of "communityhood, family hood and nationhood." It is a serious mistake to think that the Black family and the Black community can be made whole by quick-fix solutions. We have to make the development of strong Black men and strong Black women a high organizing priority. We need to realize that the Black family is strengthened when our people begin to gain a sense of pride in our African heritage. This heritage, both ancient and modern, provides models of wholistic equal relationships between African men and women. We need family study groups all over the Black community that struggle to internalize African and African-American family and community values. We also need to organize family support groups that offer organized extended family strategies for childraising and the development of positive Black male/female relationships.

With the rise of drugs, and the increasing war that is being waged against Black youth, especially Black male youth, we need to organize African brotherhoods that teach and practice Black manhood values of self-respect, self-love, and self-discipline. We also need African womanhood groups that teach African values of African womanhood. Older African-Americans must take up the responsibility of building strong African-American men and women.

Rites of passage rituals that are being used in some Black communities should be institutionalized in the Black community. This is important because the institutionalization of rites of passage will enable the conscious adults in our community to regain control of the socialization process by defining African manhood and African womanhood.

So the art of organizing requires that we master the state of our race and the state of the enemy. We have to understand the impact that corporate decisions have on the Black community, and we need to have an understanding of the strengths and weaknesses of the African and African-American community.

Once we understand where our community stands we are in a position to apply specific organizing skills to restore a sense of African communityhood. Organizing is an art because the job of organizing people is too complex to be programmed into simple formulas. Therefore, the specific skills described in starting a group, and other aspects of group dynamics require a great deal of creativity. Although organizing is an art, there are some basic fundamentals to organizing that are only violated at the expense of the group.

CHAPTER FIVE

STARTING A GROUP

Starting a group is like building the foundation of a house. The foundation of the house is the first building block. The foundation's strength will determine whether the house has a chance of withstanding the shocks of nature; the foundation also provides the stability for all the rooms in the house. Starting a group is the foundation stage, the first stage of organization. Just as concrete is the material of a house's foundation, people are the building material of organizations. The qualities of the people that you recruit to form the foundation of the organization , will determine the stability of the organization. Of all the qualities you will look for in your members, the most difficult to find is the quality of consistency. The consistency of the core group is the cement that provides the stable foundation for the organization. The consistent members are few in numbers, but their consistent dedication to Black liberation gives them the strength to keep the group going. When starting a group be careful in selecting people who have the potential to serve as the foundation of the group. Once you have identified the people you want to recruit, then your organizational approach becomes extremely important.

In initiating a group you can use one or a number of different approaches. You may choose to call a public meeting, you may go door-to-door distributing flyers in the community, or you may decide to meet with people on an individual basis.

While you may choose to call a public meeting or leave flyers in the community,in the beginning it is better to meet with people on a one-to-one basis at first, because this type of meeting provides the kind of intimacy that encourages people to ask questions, voice their concerns, and most importantly, get to know and understand each other.

Very often people will make commitments in one-to-one settings that they would not make in group meetings. People respond better to personal meetings, because they feel that the organizer is paying special attention to them as unique people with important ideas.

Individual meetings allow the organizer to explain in detail the objectives of the organization. The organizer should listen closely to the ideas voiced by potential recruits. As much as possible your explanations to questions should be geared to the personality and outlook of the person you are talking to.

When these meetings are completed the organizer should set aside time for assessing the qualities of potential recruits. If possible other organizers who are working with you to build the group should get together and compare notes on the people each of you have met. In reaching your decision you should consider everything you know about the person. You should also consider carefully the ideas the person expressed. Ultimately, you want to know if the person is reliable, honest and has the kind of personality that can fit into the group. Finally, your decisions will be subjective, and there is no way of guaranteeing that you have made the right choice. Only time will tell whether the person you recruited is a stable, honest hardworking person that can work well in a group setting.

Another consideration when organizing a group is the size of the Black community. If you are organizing in a small Black community you will have certain advantages over organizing in a large Black community. You will also have some disadvantages. A small Black community has the advantage of intimacy almost everyone knows everyone else. This makes it a lot easier to check out potential members. Smaller communities have closer friendships and family ties that make many people feel that they are a part of a close-knit community.

Smaller Black communities have their organizations, cliques, militant and moderate leaders, and depending on the group or individual leader varying relationships with the downtown power structure. If you are not careful, you can find yourself isolated in a small Black community. Therefore, its very important that you assess the groups, leaders, and potential supporters when you are shaping your organizing strategy. If your organizers come from within the community they should have good relationships with most of the established groups and leaders in the Black community. When the organizer comes from outside the community, she or he will have to devote an extensive period of time establishing relationships with community leaders, community groups, and potential recruits.

Larger metropolitan areas pose different problems and possibilities. Larger Black communities may have pockets (neighborhoods, friends, organizational associates) of intimacy, however, as a general rule people in large cities are strangers to each other. Often next door neighbors don't know each other. In this kind of impersonal environment it is harder for the organizer to know a lot about prospective members. This difficulty requires that you make careful background checks to determine a person's job history, associates, and personal as well as political characteristics. Sometimes, just going to a persons home can tell you a lot about the person. Whatever approaches you use, you should not take anything for granted. Sometimes things are not the way they seem.

Large Black communities have a number of advantages for organizing. One is that a large Black community provides a larger pool of potential recruits. Another advantage is that a large Black community has a lot of potential political and economic power. You have to be creative enough to help develop that potential power. Your chances of organizing some strong community power will largely depend upon the foundation, or core members.

The experience of Denmark Vesey is useful here. Vesey organized the most elaborate slave revolt in the history of the United States. He was a good judge of Black people, and he used the one-on-one method of organizing to build up his core group.

"One by one he began recruitment to the cause. Divulging the plot to others was a hazardous pursuit. If the whites got wind of it, every Black involved could expect to lose his life by hanging. The men he brought initially into the inner circle of the plot proved to be deserving of his confidence. Proud, fearless, mostly literate skilled craftsmen, every single one of them was fiercely dedicated to the cause of Black liberation. There were only six of them at first, including Vesey. The others were Peter Poyas, Ned and Rolla Bennett, Monday Gell, and Jack Pritchard, the latter known as Gullah Jack. He was a native of Angola in Africa, a physician and conjurer.

Gullah Jack was a legendary figure in the Charlestown area. It was said of him that he possessed supernatural powers and could not be killed by mortal man, and that he could and would endow such powers on other co-conspirators. They went quietly about their work from day to day, some laughing in the faces of white folks, all of them happy and contented niggers, and each night they plotted revolution under the cover of darkness, in an atmosphere sometimes thick with great distrust, especially as they went about recruiting others."[39]

The leaders of a slave revolt had to be secretive, brave, intelligent, and able to act independently. Vesey picked men who met these requirements. The core members of your group should also be carefully selected.

The initial one-to-one contact phase may take a few weeks, months, or a year or more. This will depend on the specific features of your community.

THE FIRST COLLECTIVE MEETING

Now that you have obtained commitments in the one-to-one meetings, it is time to call a collective meeting of all the individuals you have been working with.

Combine the positive ideas expressed by people in one-to-one meetings with your own, and develop a meeting agenda.

Establish a time limit for the meeting and remember that people lose interest if the meeting drags out, so set time limits for each agenda item.

Select a site that will accommodate the number of people that will attend the meeting. If the meeting is small you may want to meet in a home and take advantage of the personal atmosphere. For a larger meeting you can use a community facility, such as a church, community center, newspaper conference room, night club (before it opens for business), or bookstore, etc. It's also a good idea to have refreshments.

MATCHING GROUP SKILLS WITH ORGANIZATIONAL ENVIRONMENT

Prior to the first meeting you should assess the skills of the group members, for it is their skills that will determine the type of programs the group can carry out.

As an organizer, you should be familiar with the community in which you operate. You should know the other group's key personalities, and the stands that different groups have taken on key issues.

Knowing your community is not enough. You should also know your enemy. It is important to know his economic, political, and social structure. More will be said about this later when the enemy power structure and the Black social structure are analyzed.

Your group operates within a community environment, which has its own personality, political make-up and social interaction. For the group to be successful it must be like the deer in the forest; it must fit into its organizational environment. To fit into its environment, the group should match its skills with the environment it is working in. This is done by making a survey of your group's skills, an assessment of community needs, and an assessment of the programs of other community groups. When this assessment is completed, you should develop programs that draw on group skills that meet community needs. Your program should not duplicate existing community programs.

For example, if a large number of your memers have economic skills and your community is lacking a program of cooperative economic development, you may decide to develop a cooperative economic business. On the other hand, if your group is made up of people with mass organizing skills you may decide to help another group get off the ground. Whatever program you choose, it should have a high likelihood of being successful.

HAVE A RETREAT

A week-end retreat is a good time for a newly-formed group to establish organizational programs that their environment. A free flow of ideas should be encouraged through brainstorming.

Consider these basic rules:

"Criticism is out. Everyone should suspend judgment until evaluation time.

Freewheeling is welcome. The wilder the ideas the better. Everyone should let his imagination soar.

Hitchiking is invited. Each person is encouraged to ride on, improve on, add to, divide from,and combine with everyone else's ideas.

Quantity is wanted. The more ideas the better. Piling up ideas produces an atmosphere that encourages people to be spontaneous."[40]

The ideas coming out of this type of session should be written down and evaluated by the entire group, at a later date. When the evaluation is completed a program should be developed.

DECIDING ON TASKS AND DEVELOPING STRUCTURE

Now that you have a program, you can begin to assign tasks and make plans for carrying them out. This is where structure comes in. Organizational structure defines how tasks will be performed. The structure should reflect the jobs that need to be done; in this way you will be able to carry out your programs.

The organizational structure should spell out the duties and responsibilities for the committees and officers. Your organization is only as strong as your organizational structures. Strong organizations have clearly defined lines of authority and responsibility. Weak organizations are fuzzy about the duties and responsibilities of its members. There is much that we can learn from the Vietnamese revolution on the question of organizational structure. In the words of Le Duan, a Vietnamese leader:

> "A strong party branch and a strong party executive committee give rise to strong party members and cadres. Wherever the party branch and committee are rickety, the party members and cadres find their fighting strength reduced and are prone to degeneration and backsliding. Of course the reverse in this case is

completely true, because in their relations with the organization, party cadres and members are at the same time the effect and the cause. However, even if this or that individual is the cause of the shakiness of the organization, the question still remains essentially a question of organization. Because those individuals who are members of the organization, but have thought and acted contrary to its requirements have done so because the organization either lacks the necessary guarantees in criteria or the necessary rules for activity and behavior or is not strong enough to compel the individuals concerned to comply with the norm, rules and decisions of the organization. That is why, in any case we must proceed from organization to examine and resolve the question. We must realize that the question of individuals here is essentially a question of organization and must base our criticism of the ideology of these individuals on the organization; we must base ourselves on the requirements of the organization, on the criteria and principles of the organization when we have to determine the responsibility of individuals. That is the principled method of work."[41]

Disorganized individuals reflect group disorganization. If members are not paying their dues consistently, this is not simply a reflection of stinginess or individualism (which may be the case), but it is especially an indication that the organization has not developed an ideological commitment to self reliance, and that it either lacks the rules (or means) to enforce dues requirements. Similarly, if only one part of the organization turns out to work on organizational projects, this is an indication that there is a breakdown in organizational structure.

The strength or weakness of organizational structures also depends upon whether the membership believes in itself. The propaganda systems of the West have conditioned most Blacks to follow whites, and distrust Blacks. The inferiority complex has done more to disorganize our race than anything else. Marcus Garvey had some important observations to make on this subject:

> "The Negro in Western civilization, because of his environment that forces upon him an inferiority complex, is the most stubborn

individual to discipline. He has but little, if any, respect for internal racial authority. he cannot be depended upon to carry out an order given by a superior of his own race. If the superior attempts, in his presence, to enforce the order he is undermined and accused of 'putting on airs.' If the order is entrusted to a lieutenant he in turn, changes the order to suit himself and endeavors to constitute himself the superior individual.

In my experience, as head of the largest serious Negro organization in the world, I have found that to every hundred orders given to be executed for the absolute good of the organization and race, not two percent of them have been carried out in their entirety. This lack of obedience to orders and discipline checkmates the real worthwhile progress of the race. This accounts for the Negro's lack of racial nationalistic ideal. the only cure for him is his removal to an atmosphere entirely his own, where he would be forced under

> rigid civil and other discipline to
> respect himself and his own racial
> authority."42

The experience that we have gained
since Garvey's death indicates that more
than a national environment will be needed
to instill a sense of self-respect in Black
people. The Euro-centric mentality will only
be transformed when a new society, and a
new world view takes the place of the
bankrupt view and social system of the West.
Until this happens Blacks will find themselves
reproducing bankrupt Western systems in
separate geographical environments,
where Europe is viewed as the motherland,
white women are seen as the ideal of
beauty, and a white mind is believed to be
the only mind capable of thinking.

This places a double task on the
shoulders of Black organizations. Black
organizations have to transform thought in an
alien environment, while developing
liberation strategies and programs. For us this
means that program and nationalism can
never be separate. We have to develop
race pride to provide the spirit for racial unity
and collective action, to change the
oppressive conditions that we live under.

So a strong organization needs to put
forward a new world view, and it needs to

have clearly defined lines of authority and responsibility.

In summary, its important to hold individual face-to-face meetings before calling a group meeting. The organization's programs should be developed through matching the skills of the group with the unmet needs of the community. Organizational programs determine the type of structure that will be needed to carryout the group's programs. Clear organizational structure is necessary for unity and discipline.

Ultimately, your success in building an organization that serves the needs of the people over a long period, will depend upon your ability to transform thought and behavior patterns that will inspire each member to struggle to build a new society and a new person. Long term vision is the basis for long term action.

Maintaining a strong organization requires that the organizer also understands how people in a group interact. This interaction is called group dynamics.

CHAPTER SIX
GROUP DYNAMICS

Organizations have two structures, the formal structure and the informal structure. The formal structure conforms to the organizational flow chart, the organizations constitution, and job descriptions. The informal structure is made up of various cliques that shape attitudes, affect group morale, and either help or hinder the group in carrying out its objectives. The challenge for the organizer is to understand the make-up and operation of the informal organization so that strategies can be devised to keep the informal group in line with the formal organization. This is necessary because organizational cliques have their own leaders who may not be the same as the formal leadership. Clique leaders can shape sentiment and behavior in positive or negative ways. Different cliques will interact through conversations, social gatherings, and through the attitudes they project towards each other. All of this has a profound effect on group morale. If the organizer is not conscious of the makeup and interaction of these informal groups he may find himself out of step with the movement of the organization. Clique leaders and members can subvert the programs of the

organization, or they can make a positive contribution. A lot will depend upon how the organizer handles the cliques in his organization. To manage cliques the organizer has to identify them, keep on top of them and develop positive relationships with them. This is the heart of group dynamics. It requires a sharp eye, an open ear, and a creative mind, to see what is often hidden to hear what is often uttered within closed circles, and to develop a creative strategy that joins the informal group to the formal one, the way land is joined to water.

INFORMAL GROUPS

"People join people, not groups," said Reverend Herbert Daughtry. Usually people join a group because a friend recruited them into it. Even in the exceptional case where a person joins a group for nonpersonal reasons, their relationship to people will largely determine whether they stay or leave. Most Black people leave volunteer groups because of personal conflicts. So the relationship of people in any Black organization should be the primary concern of any organizer.

Since people usually join people when they join a group, they become members of friendship circles, or cliques. Organizations consist of a number of cliques, or informal groups. Members of informal group's cliques usually have something in common.

FRIENDSHIP GROUPS

People who were friends before joining the organization, or who make friends after joining the group, form a friendship circle within the group. People who are part of a friendship circle are members of an intimate group where reinforcement is given, confidences are shared, informal social activities take place and attitudes about the overall group are formed. Friendship circles are very strong informal groups that can work in either a positive or negative way in the formal organization. As a rule, members of a friendship group tend to support each other on issues considered crucial to the friendship group. The decision by one member of a friendship circle to leave the formal organization can, and often does, lead to the departure of everyone within the friendship circle. Also, a friendship circle may take hostile action against the formal group if they feel that one of their own members has been treated unjustly by the formal group. Needless to say, friendship circles are very influential in any group.

INTEREST GROUPS

Interest groups are informal groups or cliques, where the members are tied together by common interests, or common problems. In an organization where there are a lot of family members and only a few single members, single members may band together to give each other reinforcement.

Single sisters' circles, or single brothers' circles will come into being. In other cases, members who are into self-defense, dance, or athletic activities, may take part in the same activities, and in doing so, develop a relationship.

Informal interest groups can also be formed because a number of people share similar problems. These problems could arise from similar experiences with the opposite sex, or they could relate to the leadership, or specific people whom members within the group believe to be causing problems.

Interest groupings are a natural development that give people with similar interests a social outlet. Groups formed around problems can give their members support in solving these specific problems.

Interest groups and groups formed around specific problems can influence their members in positive or negative ways.

FAMILY GROUPINGS

In volunteer organizations, family members represent the most stable and consistent group in the formal organization. This is because the family unit is usually more stable and predictable than the individual. Stable family units may consist of two-parent households, or single-parent households. Both types are stable forces within an organization. Single men and women who are young are usually going through changes in their lives, and may make up their minds to leave the city, or channel their energies somewhere else. Some will become consistent members; however, they generally lack the stability of family units.

Each family unit is an informal clique within itself. Some family members may discuss issues before meetings. Others may respond to issues as they develop in meetings or informal settings. In either case, they will give great weight to what other family members think. This is not to say that wives will support their husbands on all issues or vice versa. In fact, family relationships consist of some of the most independent relationships that can be found in a clique. However, family cliques do serve as self-reinforcing units, that shape opinions on various issues. Rarely will members of a family unit go against each other on important issues.

Not only do individual families make up cliques, but groups of families that have common interests, friendships, or problems also make up cliques. Family circles or cliques socialize together, talk to each other, and can either reinforce the family unit or weaken it.

Since family circles are the most stable groups in volunteer Black organizations, they usually represent the largest body of members. As a result, family circles can have

a profound impact on the direction, for good
or bad, of the group.

COMMON PERSONALITY GROUPINGS

Some informal groups are made up of
people who have similar personalities.
People who have similar traits are often
drawn to each other. Introverts may at times
be attracted to each other, as will people
with managerial or other business skills,
undisciplined types, or persons with other
common personality characteristics. If you
observe people closely, you can often
predict which types of new members will be
likely to relate to other members in the
organization.

Commom personality groups can also
consist of people with opposite personalities.
Where these types of cliques form, they
usually form because each person realize
that each person has certain interests and
characteristics in common while their
differences complement each other.

OPINION GROUPS

Opinion groups consist of people who
share similar opinions on specific questions.
Usually, opinion groups change depending
on the issue. People who unite on one issue
may differ on another. Of all the groupings,
opinion groupings are the most healthy

because they are formed around agreement on organizational issues.

NEGATIVE PERSONALITY GROUPS

Negative personality groupings or factions, are factions which are organized against a particular person or persons. Often these break down into rival factions. Negative personality factions are the most dangerous type of clique formation that can develop in an organization because they bog the group down in infighting that has nothing to do with the direction of the organization. Negative personality factions arise for many reasons, including personal dislikes, power struggles, etc.

An example of negative personality groupings in our organizations is the Coard faction that existed inside of the New Jewel Movement in Grenada. The leaders of the NJM who have survived the internal power struggle and the invasion, agree that there were no serious political differences between Maurice Bishop and Bernard Coard. Both agreed on the need for a mixed economy in Grenada. Both worked hard in the Grenadian revolution. The differences between the two were not political, but personal. Coard placed members of his clique into key positions within the NJM political bureau. When they had obtained a majority, they moved to grab political power. Their arrest and assassination of Bishop, and other key leaders of the NJM, provided the justification for an American invasion.[43]

To this date we cannot conclusively prove CIA involvement in the Coard led coup. Certainly it cannot be ruled out. However, if the CIA played a role in the coup, it was able to play on the petty personal differences that motivated the Coard faction. These petty differences had to do with who should control Grenada. The Bishop grouping failed to realize the dangerous threat that the Coard faction posed to the revolution until it was too late. Of course we realize that this was an extremely young revolution, and the leaders were inexperienced. But for us today, the Grenada experience should drive home the fact that personal differences can be more deadly than political differences. In our organizations we have to monitor the various cliques. And we have to pay special attention to negative personality cliques, for in the end they can be very deadly.

Good organizers use their knowledge of group dynamics to do everything they can to prevent negative personality factions from forming. Their existence endangers the survival of the group.

FORMAL STRUCTURE GROUPS

Formal structure groupings, or cliques are cliques which form out of the formal structure of the group. People who are members of organization committees, or who hold formal offices within an organization, may form friendships, share common opinions, have similar personalities, and they may meet informally to share their ideas. Often within a formal organization there will be cliques within the committee. Over time, as membership in formal committees and formal officers change, the cliques will also change. Cliques that form out of the formal organizational structure can be either positive or negative depending upon the particular circumstances.

SINGLE MALE AND SINGLE FEMALE GROUPS

With the rise of single-parent households in the Black community we can expect to find a large number of single women and single men in our organizations. Often the existence of an active single women's clique will depend how active the single men are. Similarly, it takes enough single women to activate a single men's clique. If either the number of single men, or single women, declines drastically then this can lead to a reduction in clique activity. Sometimes these activities can be used to raise money for the organization. Single men and single women interact with members of their own sex because they share common interests. Single and married women will often keep an eye either formally or informally on sexism within the organization. Single women can be expected to speak out against organizational sexism that may include confining women to housekeeping roles and giving the brothers credit while sisters are kept in the background. Leaders who disrespect Black women will generate considerable opposition from Black women who expect to be treated on an equal footing with brothers. On the other hand, sometimes single sisters will provide a base of support for charismatic Black male leadership even when that leadership disrespects Black women. Where this attitude exists among single sisters, conscious sisters and brothers will have to work to educate and discipline the leadership while getting sisters to understand that supporting leadership that disrespects them makes them partners in their own oppression. Single men may form brotherhoods to share concerns that males are interested in. Single men and single women's cliques can be either positive or negative depending upon the specific circumstances.

OLD TIMERS GROUPS

Old timers, groupings or cliques are made up of people who have been in the organization over a long period of time. Some old timers may be founding members of the group. Old timers cliques will usually have cliques within cliques that may be based on agreement on issues, friendships, common personalities, etc. Old timers cliques contain people who have an overall view of the organization. Some old timers are the true historians of the group because they have a mind for keeping things in order, and they are able to inject history into organizational discussions.

GEOGRAPHICAL GROUPS

Geographical groups or cliques are made up of members who come from a geographical area that is isolated from the area that most members come from. Geographical cliques will often consist of sub-cliques. Because members in a geographical clique are geographically isolated from most of the members it is very likely that this kind of clique will develop activities independent from the group if there are sufficient numbers of people to initiate activities. If the leadership of the organization does not anticipate the behavior of this kind of clique and channel it into positive directions the geographical clique can come to be seen as a threat to the leadership and direction of the organization. Needless to say, geographical cliques can be either positive or negative.

NON-INFLUENTIAL GROUPS

Non-influential groups or cliques consist of people who interact with each other and find that they have very little influence on the decisions of the group. Some members of non-influential cliques are members of minority factions within particular organizational cliques. Others are not popular because of how they interact with members or they have less education than many other members, or because of their social background. In some cases lack of a certain amount of education may reduce one person's influence while it has no effect on another person's status in the group. Whatever the situation, people deserve to be heard based on the merit of their ideas, and the consistency of their work, not on whether they do or do not possess a college degree. Similarily, the possession of a degree should not be used to put down a person's idea or contribution to the group. Again, non-influential groups can be positive or negative depending on the situation. If they are negative their negative status often derives from their powerless state.

THE LEADING GROUPS

The leading group or leading clique is made up of a group of people who either meet regularly and discuss the direction of the organization or operate without meeting and consistently work and provide leadership for the group. The leading clique may or may not conform to the formal leadership positions in an organization. The chair, vice chair, treasurer and secretary may or may not be a part of the leading group or leading clique. Members of the leading clique will have members who have strong personalities and a following within the formal and informal organization. This clique is the leading clique because its members are consistent workers, they have the respect of a significant body of members and they initiate ideas and programs that provide direction for the group. When a leadership crisis arises this group can be expected to provide direction for the organization. When conflict occurs between members, the leading clique will usually develop measures to solve the problem. Some informal leading cliques are skillful at joining formal committees to execute their decisions. When the leading cliques do not consist of the formal officers of the organization it can pose problems for organization. Where possible, the formal leadership should attempt to recruit them onto leading committees without allowing the informal leadership to overwhelm the formal leadership. When the informal leadership is trying to provide positive leadership for the group by filling organizational vacuums, every effort should be made to enlist their support by the formal leadership of the organization. In many ways the existence of a leading informal clique within the organization reflects the failure of the formal leadership to provide direction for the group. Needless to say, it will take a great deal of skill to direct the activities of leading informal cliques that have a following in the organization.

Informal groups or cliques are not limited to those mentioned above. Members of a clique could be friends, married, have common ideas, interests, and similar personalities. Or they could have only one or a few of the above traits.

HOW INFORMAL GROUPS INTERACT

Your knowledge of how informal groups work is absolutely necessary so that you can identify the various informal groups in your organization, and monitor their activity as well as work to keep them in harmony with the formal organization.

Informal groups or cliques are monitored by determining who talks to whom, when they talk, what they talk about, and how often they talk. This is the nuts and bolts of managing informal groups. By keeping track of their communication patterns, you are able to know how members will react to formal group decisions; how they relate to each other; and what problems are likely to arise.

All of the strategies that you use to handle informal groups are designed to see that the informal groups operate in harmony with the formal group, that they don't run counter to formal structures and decisions. Given what has been said about informal groups, this will often be an extremely difficult task to accomplish.

ACTIVITY

A good way to measure the influence of informal groups is to keep track of their member's work and activity patterns. One way that people influence each other in an organization is through the level and quality of their work.

Work patterns can be either positive or negative. Positive work patterns are those in which the worker is motivated to carry out the groups objectives through particular work activities. Positive workers communicate positive attitudes to those they work with. When problems arise, the positive worker puts forward solutions that are designed to bring about improvements, not more serious conflicts.

Negative workers may work just as hard as positive workers, but their work attitudes are often abrupt or insensitive towards those they work with. Very often they are extremely critical of fellow workers, while seeing very little that is wrong with their own work or in the way they relate to others. People who bring negative attitudes to a group project create negative feelings among other members of the group. Often a fall-off in group participation in work projects will result from negative work attitudes. Negative work can also consist of a person doing very little work. Little work suggests to others that are working hard, that too much of the work load is falling on them. Workers who do little can either encourage others to lighten up on their work, or, in some cases, they can cause others to give up working altogether.

Negative activity patterns also include situations where members who may make financial contributions do very little work in the organization. The lack of work suggests that the member is having some kind of problem. You need to find out what the problem is where work is negative or non-existent. You need to keep a careful eye on informal group activity patterns. If a member is rude to another member, you can almost be sure that those negative actions are going to lead to negative relations between people.

SENTIMENT

Members are not only influenced by the activities of other members, but they are also influenced by individual sentiments and by group sentiments.[44]   Sentiments consist of "emotional and mental processes that are inside of individuals."[45]   However, organizations also have sentiments that individuals share in common. The emotional and mental processes of the group, shape norms, "which are shared ideas and beliefs about what conduct is good or bad."[46] Informal group sentiments have a tremendous influence on formal sentiments.

Within informal groups there are sentiment shapers that shape the sentiments of the informal group in ways that promote or detract from formal group activity. Informal groups, through the interaction of their members, in conversations, and activities, also shape sentiment for the formal group.

There are a number of examples of how informal group sentiment is shaped. One is when a member of one informal group dislikes a member of another informal group. This personal dislike expressed by one member can quickly become the shared sentiment of all or most members of the informal group.

In another situation, one member of an informal group may be in competition for leadership and recognition with a member of another informal group. If the person who is competing with this other member can convince their group to support their competition, then a factional struggle for power can develop between two informal groups. This kind of struggle will have far-reaching influence on the organization as a whole.

Another example, which illustrates how informal group sentiment is shaped, could involve one member of a group encouraging others to join a spiritual circle that is operated by another religious group. The effect of this action on the formal group will depend on a lot of factors that you will have to monitor very closely. Some factors include whether the particular philosophy is in conflict with the formal group; whether the religious group discourages political participation from its members; whether the members can afford to pay dues to two groups, and if they cannot, how will the members know which group to contribute to? Of course, if your group has rules that prohibit your members from belonging to other groups, then this question will in some ways be easier to answer, but in other ways harder to resolve.

Some informal groups may have sentiments that run counter to the rules of the formal organization. An informal group that favors smoking weed, which is prohibited by the formal organization, would be running counter to the formal group. Or an informal group which has a thing against holding regular committee meetings to carry out group programs, could decide to make their decisions by telephone. Both group sentiments present real problems for the formal organization that will have to be dealt with.

CONNECTION BETWEEN ACTIVITY
AND SENTIMENT

Actions and sentiments have been discussed separately so we can understand how they work and what they consist of. However, it would be incorrect to think that these two categories operate exclusive of each other. Actions and sentiment are tied together and are causes or consequences of each other. At times behavior causes sentiment; at other times, sentiments shape and influence behavior patterns.[47]

A leadership struggle, for example, between two individuals may arise from the competitiveness of one or both parties, or it could arise from conflicts between the two people over program ideologies or personalities. Sentiment can shape behavior, and behavior can shape sentiment.

GROUPS ARE NETWORKS OF INTERRELATED GROUPS

Since organizations have a formal structure as well as an informal structure, they are in fact a network of what should be interrelated groups. Your job as an organizer is to use organizing strategies to get the informal group to conform with the formal group, and to develop a smooth pattern of interrelationship between informal groups.

ORGANIZING STRATEGIES

Structuring decisions should be made so that members of various factions participate on the same formal organizational committees. The interaction between members of different factions around group programs help to create a group sentiment and behavior.

It is extremely important that you maintain good relations with members of all of the factions in your organization. This means that you should develop friendships with as many members as possible. You should also avoid favoritism, which aligns you with one faction and against the other. Your strength as an organizer depends upon the direction that you offer for the whole group. By maintaining a friendly, open, and fair attitude, members will feel that they can discuss their problems with you. An open relationship enables you to monitor sentiments and behavior in your organization without violating the confidence of people who confide in you.

In your role as a friendly, fair person, you should take time to break down negative attitudes that exist in various informal groups. If some members of an informal group are slacking off on their work, talk to some of their friends to determine why this is happening. Once you determine the underlying problems, develop strategies for reactivating these members. As a general rule, a good way to activate inactive members is through friends who are active. So you should use the informal group members to bring about positive changes in the informal group.

If members of one informal group have inaccurate impressions about a member or members of another informal group, try to organize situations where they can have positive interactions, maybe at a party or some other informal social gathering.

A clear definition of duties and responsibilities spelled out in writing and enforced does a great deal to reduce the likelihood that an informal group will run into conflict with the formal group. Wherever the lines of authority are fuzzy, or poorly enforced, all kinds of opportunities for informal group subversion will arise.

The handling of informal groups is an art that requires that you stay on top of your organization, know your members intimately, practice a friendly open-door policy, and always remember the interests of the group. In order to successfully manage informal groups you will find it necessary to improvise. Each situation will have a new twist to it that will require you to turn it around carefully in your head, and in the heads of the other leaders in the group before you decide on an appropriate course of action.

The truth of group dynamics is that cliques are a permanent feature of organizations. Cliques simply reflect the human characteristics of the members. Cliques fulfill a human need to belong, to be recognized, to find friends and shared interests. To treat members as though they fit neatly into the prescribed structure is to view the organization as a mechanical process that operates as though it were the moving parts of a car. Organizations are made up of human beings who have human needs. These needs cannot be treated in a cold mechanical way. They have to be viewed as needs that spring from people who seek fulfillment, respect, love, and a sense that their contribution is important to the group.

The ultimate challenge for the organizer is to understand the special motivations of each individual. This is the heart and soul of group dynamics.

Group members also have the need to see concrete evidence of their work. Institutions that have visible programs and headquarters provide evidence that the group's efforts have produced meaningful results for the community.

CHAPTER SEVEN

INDEPENDENT BLACK SCHOOLS

Past history demonstrates that the best approach for building Black institutions involves developing a political organization that provides a solid base. A membership that develops a base for financial support, gives any institution a pool of committed workers, access to facilities, and a wide variety of skills. The alternative to an institutional membership is an individual base. An individual base has a few committed individuals who come together to form an independent institution. While this approach works for some, in too many cases the individual route suffers from ideological inconsistencies within the individuals starting the institutions, over reliance on one or a few people, and a tendency for the institution to deteriorate or collapse when the key individuals leave. Needless to say, developing any type of full-time institution requires committed workers, money, planning, a building, and constant attention. Your group should carefully assess its capabilities to determine whether it has the strength to operate a full-time institution.

Since institutions are full-time organizations, they require daily attention. A volunteer organization that develops a full-time institution should recognize from the onset that problems can develop because of the differences between them. The volunteer organization is made up of people who give up part of their time for the organization; the full-time institution requires a consistent hourly commitment from its workers. If the volunteer organization isn't careful, the full-time institution will outrun it and become a warring and independent entity. There are a number of measures that can be taken to reduce this possibility. First, when the parent organization has members who have administrative skills, some of them should manage and staff the institution. This minimizes the chances of conflict between the full-time institution and the parent-volunteer organization, enabling the volunteer organization to infuse its ideology throughout the institution.

If the parent group either lacks or runs out of people with the necessary administrative skills, then it should either postpone starting the institution or it should recruit people with a similar ideological outlook. When this option is taken, the parent organization has to be very clear in defining job responsibility and accountability of the staff, especially the administrator to the parent organization. And it has to carefully monitor the training and evaluation processes.

In either case, whether we have a member administrator, and/or non-member administrator, the volunteer organization should spell out the kind of support that its members can provide to the full-time institution. If some members have fundraising, publicity, or other skills, then a work schedule should be developed so these skills can be used.

Institutional structures vary, often reflecting the outlook of the parent organization. There are institutions where there is equal sharing of power between the parent organization and those who make up the full-time institution. In some situations the parent group may want to see the institution become independent, or the parent group may choose to run the institution either directly, through one of its own members, or through a paid employee, who operates under the direction of the parent organization.

Finances are vital to the success of any full-time institution. As a rule, the income of the institution must exceed the expenses, if the institution is going to last. Your goal should be that the institution achieves financial self-sufficiency, and that it provides funds to the parent organization.

More important than anything else is the impact the institution has on the community. The institution can have either a limited or mass impact on the community. Generally, the limited constituency institution is one that serves only a small part of the community, i.e. nationalists, Marxists, etc. While the limited constituency institution is one approach, it is more desirable to build a mass institution.

Mass institutions serve a broad cross-section of the Black community, meet vital community needs, and involve the community in shaping the direction of the institution. Mass institutions may develop out of mass struggles, such as the freedom schools that developed out of the Mississippi Summer Project in 1964, or the independent businesses that arose out of the Garvey Movement. Mass institutions can also be planned so that they incorporate a cross section of the Black community in their own operation and services.

THE MASS BLACK EDUCATIONAL INSTITUTION

The Civil Rights Movement and the Black Power movement of the sixties ushered in the movement for independent Black schools. This movement was the programmatic reflection of the cultural revolt of the sixties, which stressed Black identity, Black power, and a relevant Black education. The movements of the sixties taught Black people that a relevant Black education could only be achieved when Blacks gained control of their education through the development of Black Studies programs on college campuses; through community control of the public schools in Black communities, and through the organization of independent Black schools, which were controlled by the Black community.

BLACK STUDIES MOVEMENT

The San Francisco State strike started the Black Studies movement. It was a product of the political activities of that period, including the San Francisco Civil Rights movement and the Southern Civil Rights movement. The latter demonstrated the effectiveness of the direct action tactics of the Civil Rights movement, with the self-defense approach of Malcolm X, Frantz Fanon, and the Black Panther Party.[48] The nationalist outlook which came out of the Black Power movement, Malcolm X, and the Nation of Islam, also influenced the Black student leadership at State to take a no-compromise position.

The cultural revolt of the sixties, and the intense racism on a white college campus, created the conditions where Black students demanded a curriculum that taught their true history. Black students made this demand for Black Studies to preserve their sense of identity in an educational environment that taught about the Greeks and Romans, while teaching nothing about the historical contributions of ancient African civilizations, and Black historical achievements in the United States.

For the Black community, the most important consequence of a white-oriented curriculum was the development of Black graduates who were useless to the Black community. A European-centered educational system produced Black Europeans who escaped from the Black community to serve as lower level flunkies in white institutions. Even worse, many Black students who wanted to use their skills to benefit the Black community found that their Euro-centric orientation made it impossible for them to communicate with Black people. Their language and values were foreign to the Black community.

Therefore, Black Studies became a way to transmit an Afro-centric outlook that would make Black students useful to the Black community. Many of the founders of the Independent Black School Movement came out of the Black studies movement. The Center for Black Education, which was organized in Washington, D.C., was inspired by Jimmy Garrett, a central organizer of the San Francisco State Strike. In other cases, Black students coming out of Black studies programs upon graduation established independent Black schools in their communities.

In still other situations independent Black schools were the outgrowth of struggles for the control of the public schools. In 1966 Black parents from the Ocean Hill community in Brooklyn declared themselves a rump school board in District 17. In response to the pressure from Black parents, demanding community control of the schools, the New York Board of Education adopted a weak decentralized plan, which created a number of demonstration districts including, Ocean Hill Brownville in Brooklyn, New York.

Of 4,000 eligible parents 1,049 voted for seven representatives to a local governing board. The elected representatives selected five community representatives, two supervisors, and four teachers who were selected by their colleagues -- this group made up the local governing board.[49]

The United Federation of Teachers (UFT) conducted a series of strikes that opposed community control of the public schools. Black parent control of the public schools would overturn the colonial relationship that existed between white teachers, the board of education, and the Black community.

The UFT and the courts opposed community control, invalidating the power of decentralized boards. The state legislature failed to appropriate funds to enact legislation favoring decentralization of the public schools. The Ford Foundation, which had provided initial funding for the demonstration project, backed off. National Negro leaders were manipulated against the local governing board and a determined community struggle was crushed. But out of this defeat came an important victory. An independent Black school was formed, with massive support from the Black community.

UHURU SASA

The formation of the Uhuru Sasa school by teachers and parents who had taken part in the community control struggle enabled the Black community to control the educational process. Under the leadership of Jitu Weusi, Uhuru Sasa launched a national movement for independent Black schools under the framework of CIBI (Council for Independent Black Institutions).

What this experience shows is that mass educational institutions gain mass support because they embody the desires of the people. Mass struggles for community control of the public schools are interrelated to struggles for independent Black education. Not only can one lead the other, but both may embody the desire for Black control of our youth's education.

The way in which Uhuru Sasa school was organized illustrates one workable method that can be used to organize independent Black schools.

PAN AFRICAN EDUCATIONAL THRUST

Independent Black schools also developed out of the Pan African thrust in the late sixties and seventies. The Student Non-Violent Coordinating Committee popularized the call for Black Power, and its popular spokesman, Stokely Carmichael (Kwame Toure), later defined Pan Africanism as the highest expression of Black Power. Pan Africanism was defined as "the unification of the African continent under scientific socialism."

The Malcolm X Liberation University in Durham, North Carolina operated under this definition of Pan Africanism, as did the Center for Black Education in Washington, D.C. Both schools defined their primary educational mission to be that of supplying skilled technicians to the African continent. This was an important mission, however, both of these efforts failed to properly understand the central nature of the Black liberation movement in the United States. A political direction mainly focused on the unification and liberation of Africa would flounder, because no realistic direction was defined for the struggle of Black people in the United States. Pan Africanism needed to be tied to nationalism so that a primary emphasis could be given to the Black liberation movement in the U.S., while important material and political support was provided to African liberation movements and progressive as well as revolutionary African governments.

The educational thrust coming out of some other Pan African Nationalist institutions reflected a balance between nationalism and Pan Africanism. A school like the Center for Black Education in Portland, and the Pan African Center for Progressive education in San Francisco (an arm of the Pan African People's Organization), represented a balance between Pan Africanism and Black nationalism.

In striking this balance, P.A.P.O. (Pan African People's Organization) combined political and material support for African liberation movements, with food programs, struggles against police violence, and the organization of a mass educational institution.

The approach used by the Pan African People's Organization to organize an independent Black school shows another way that a mass educational institution can be organized. P.A.P.O. pulled together a cross section of the Black community to develop the plans for an independent Black school. A series of community meetings were held in San Francisco in 1972, where Black parents, teachers, youth, and community people came together to shape a curriculum. Workshops were held in the areas of math, reading, health, African history, science and administration. These workshops provided a forum where our people could shape the curriculum and structure of the school. Community involvement in planning the school was designed to make the school a community school, not a school that belonged to a few individuals in the Black community.

When the curriculum and structure had been shaped, a mass educational movement was launched with a march and rally of 4,500 brothers and sisters, chanting "educate to liberate," "free your minds from white institutions," and "build independent Black schools now." This mass march and rally demonstrated that there was broad support in the Black community for independent Black schools.

The School (Pan African Center for Progressive Education), and the Pre-School, (Njiani Nyumbani), were formed in the fall of 1973. This simply illustrates that there are a number of ways of starting an independent Black school. The important thing is a mass educational institution is built that our people, as a whole, will support. Our people will support such schools, because they will see such institutions as theirs.

The independent Black school was not formed solely because many of our youth could not read and write. It was also organized so that community people could control the curriculum taught to their children. Many of the organizers of the independent Black school movement realized that the curriculum taught in the public school system was based on a Euro-centric model. The Euro-centric educational model is centered around the philosophy, history, religion, economy, and political orientation of Greece, Rome , Europe, and Euro-America. The Euro-centric curriculum teaches Black students to worship Greeks, Romans, British, and European- Americans.

Black students are taught that their Motherland is a place of savagery and darkness. The great civilizations of Africa (Egypt, for example) are portrayed as white. African-American history is pictured as slave history. The negative portrayal of our history and the positive portrayal of white history teaches Black students to hate themselves and to love white people.

Fed a Euro-centric educational diet, the Black student becomes conditioned, to paraphrase DuBois, to see themselves through the eyes of others. Without a historical, cultural, philosophical, artistic, political, and scientific standard that is African-centric our definition of ourselves becomes their definition of us. If whites say that Black is ugly, then Blacks lacking their own standard of beauty will think and say that Black is ugly. When Blacks are ignorant of their great scientific achievements they are prone to believe that whites have the brains and the only way that Blacks can gain knowledge is from white people.

Not knowing that African people have built great civilizations, many Blacks think that white people are supposed to lead, and Blacks are supposed to follow. Minus an African-centric standard that grows out of the African and African-American past, Blacks are conditioned to carve out subservient positions as people who work for others without any idea of organizing an economy of our own. We end up dribbling basketballs, catching footballs, hitting baseballs, and playing the subservient roles in society. Stuffed full of worthless European ideas we turn ourselves on automatic pilot defending our crumbs, our so-called nation, and our white folks, without being told to. We become so brainwashed that we are quick to say that we don't want anything to do with any Black stuff, whether its Black history, Black politics, Black literature or Black philosophy. We have been so well-programmed that we believe African people have not accomplished anything worthwhile.

The independent Black school movement sees the need to construct an educational system that is based on an African-centric model, so that Black students will see themselves through the eyes of others. The African-centric view is centered around Mother Africa, which is the mother of human life and human civilization. By portraying a correct picture of the "Mother" (motherland), African-Americans are able to gain a sense of self-knowledge and self-respect. Through knowing the mother, the children of Africa can come to gain a deep understanding of themselves. Through gaining a respect for the "Mother," the race gains a sense of respect for itself.

An African-centric view of history shows that human life began in Africa over 3 1/2 million years ago. The first people, known as Twa people, migrated from the Mountain of the Moon (Mount Kilimanjaro) along the great waterway, the Nile. Early man and woman established the world's first civilization as they migrated along the Nile waterway. These early Black ancestors of humanity established the civilization of Nubia in North Africa. Nubia provided the basis for the Pharaohnic civilization of ancient Kemet (Egypt). Kemet was the name that the people commonly known in the west as Egyptians gave themselves. Kemet meant land of the Blacks. The Black people of Kemet raised civilization to the highest levels known in human history. The people of Kemet, building on the legacy of Nubia and Africa as a whole, constructed a great civilization where great architectural, medical , mathematical, scientific, astronomical, religious, and educational systems were constructed. These great systems were taught through a mystery system of education, that provided the basis for western education, distorted though it became. The people of Kemet constructed great pyramids, fathered medicine, invented geometry, gained a deep understanding of the heavens, established a high ethical order through their religious teachings, and developed the best educational system known to humanity.

But the historical achievements of African people was not restricted to one or two civilizations, or just to civilizations established in Africa. The African-centric viewpoint recognizes that African history is world history. Black humanity, who started human life, also migrated to Asia, Europe, America and the Pacific Islands. The first civilization founded in India was a Black African civilization called the Dravidian civilization. The Dravidian civilization was ruled by priests who, like the priest of Egypt (Kemet), were extremely wise.

Africans migrating throughout Asia founded the earliest civilization in China under the Shang dynasty. As Clyde Ahmad Winters demonstrates, these original Chinese were a Black people descended from African Kushites and African Mandingoes. Winters shows historical and linguistic evidence to prove the African origin of these original Chinese.

Between 800 and 700 B.C., Blacks founded the earliest civilization in America known as the Olmec civilization. The Olmecs introduced the pyramid, a mathematical system, and a theocratical system of government. The Olmec system provided the model for national organization, which the Mayans, Aztecs, Toltecs, and Incas followed.

In addition to these civilizations, Africans (known as the Moors) ruled Spain from 711 A.D. through the 15th century A.D. Spain, under the Black Moors, achieved its Golden Age of science and technology when the rest of Europe was in the dark ages of ignorance. In Western Africa, Blacks developed the great civilizations of Ghana, Mali, Songhai, Kanem Bornu, and the little known kingdom of Segu, to name a few.

Our history does not end with these or other great African civilizations, but it continues with the transplantation of Black people, and Black culture to the Americas. The slave trade not only brought on oppression, but it bred resistance. Some of the bravest warriors that have ever strolled onto the pages of history, arose during these great struggles for African liberation from slavery and colonialism. In Haiti, Africans drew on their great spiritual tradition to launch the Haitian revolution. Men like Touissant, Dessalines, and Christophe displayed great military ability defeating the combined armies of Britain, Spain, and above all France.

In Surinam, Africans escaped to the rain forests and organized guerilla resistance. Surinam African-Americans proudly proclaim today that they never submitted to slavery.

In Cuba, where wars were fought to free Cuba from Spanish colonialism, and slavery produced one of the bravest, most brilliant military strategists in history, Antonio Maceo. Maceo, an African, came from a family of fighters, he was a master of the machete, and he was an expert horseman. Maceo rose to the rank of General and he always fought in the front ranks of his armies. Maceo, like the great warriors of Africa, was totally fearless. In all the battles he fought he was always victorious. Maceo's two greatest characteristics were his bravery and his total commitment to principles. Maceo was such a great military strategist that he often won against enemies who outnumbered and outarmed him. Never did he compromise on the principles of national independence and freedom from slavery.

Great freedom fighters also rose up in America in Denmark Vesey, Nat Turner, Harriet

Tubman, Sojourner Truth, Gabriel Prosser and David Walker to name only a few.

The historical legacy of ancient Africa and of Africans in America is one of originating life, civilization, scientific, and spiritual knowledge, and a spirit of resistance against oppression. The curriculum in the Independent Black school when it puts forward this kind of perspective encourages our youth to have pride, respect, love, and confidence in themselves. With an African-centric view our youth understand that they have a responsibility to use their minds to create a position of independence and power for their people.

WRITTEN CURRICULUM

A written curriculum should be developed that stresses the academics, and Black political and historical theory. Curriculum content should include a course description, a syllabus, methods of instruction and evaluation, examination dates, required readings, and a bibliography. Lesson plan forms should be developed for the teacher's use. In the appendix you will find a sample course outline and lesson plan.

Very often, independent Black schools make the error of starting their schools without a written curriculum. When this happens, each teacher develops his or her own curriculum, and when new teachers take their place they don't have the slightest idea of what was being taught before they came. In developing the curriculum, you should draw on the expertise of your community to shape technical courses.

Above all, the African-centric curriculum is the basis for a truly independent Black school. Without an African-centric perspective our schools will be "oreo" schools: Black on the outside, white on the inside. We have to struggle to develop a meaningful curriculum that accurately describes our historical contributions to the world. To date, the Portland public school's African-American Baseline Curriculum represents the best African-centric curriculum in the United States. This curriculum was written as a result of the struggles of the Portland Black United Front. Dr. Asa Hilliard was selected by the Portland Black United Front as the chief consultant who was responsible for bringing together experts to write the African-American Baseline Curriculum.

The depth of your curriculum will depend upon how many grades you plan to have when you first open. This is where a lot of organizers make a mistake by overextending themselves. Very often the decision is made to try to open the school to all grades, or most of them. After opening, the organizers usually find that their resources aren't strong enough to support a first to twelfth grade school; often the enrollment falls, sometimes because of student strain on teaching and administrative resources. All of this shows that it is very important to correctly estimate what your institution can handle. As a general rule it is best to start with a few grades, and then gradually add more as you are able to handle them.

CONSTITUTION AND BYLAWS

A constitution and bylaws should be developed for the school in a way that clearly defines the school's philosophy, its governing board, officers, committees, and the duties and responsibilities of the parents. The constitution is both an organizational and political document.

The bottom line for any independent Black school is that it be consistent in following its philosophy. Too often independent Black institutions will start off in one direction, and with each change in staff and parents, undergo shifts in philosophy. The volunteer political organization has to struggle to see that the political line of the school does not shift. Without a clear consistent ideology the independent Black school, or any other institution, becomes an institution that is Black on the outside and white on the inside. The ideological base of the school is not something that is only summarized in the constitution and curriculum, but it must be internalized by the staff, students, and as much as possible by the parents.

JOB DESCRIPTION

Right alongside the constitution should be the development of a job description for the teaching staff and the administrator. Job descriptions should clearly define lines of authority and responsibility by clearly stating the duties of each job category. In the appendix is a sample job description and set of school bylaws.

WORK CONTRACT

It is also a good idea to devise a contract for your staff that spells out a minimum term of work, perhaps from one to three years. These work contracts are designed to get people to spell out their work commitment.

A key factor in determining the number of years your staff will be able to commit to the institution is the amount of pay they will receive. Some independent schools have a policy of paying survival wages, and they either encourage their teachers to supplement their income through welfare, or provide basic benefits such as free housing, etc. Other institutions try to provide a liveable wage that is not as high as the public school's but offer enough for a family person to live on. Ideally, the independent Black school should provide a wage sufficient to support the needs of a single or married staff member, because an adequate wage means that the staff is more likely to make a long term commitment to the institution.

Which salary approach you choose will largely depend upon the fundraising program you organize to launch the school, and the level of financial self-sufficiency of the school. The amount of money you need to raise depends upon your operating expenses: rent, or the down payment for a building, supplies, start up salaries, equipment (desks and blackboards etc.), advertisements, etc.

Even after you have raised your start up monies, you have to face a couple of facts. To begin with, a first-to-twelfth grade school does not generate the kind of monies from tuition (unless it is extremely high) to support a school. You will either have to develop some large annual fundraisers, or you may choose to set up a pre-school alongside your grade school. Pre-schools generate a larger tuition base than do grade schools, and they can provide the additional monies necessary to meet the expenses of the grade school. Ideally, the combination of large annual fundraisers and a pre-school operation would be the best combination for generating funds for the overall operation. Opening a pre-school gives you the opportunity to reach youth at a young age, and it provides a recruiting avenue for the grade school.

RECRUITMENT AND THE INTERVIEW

The hiring process for school staff should be treated seriously. It is best to choose your staff from the widest field possible. This means that in addition to personal contacts you should advertise widely for applicants. Candidates should be asked to supply resumes with personal references that can be verified. Since people tend to put forward their best appearance in job interviews, this method of recruitment can be deceptive. Candidates can come across as being very skilled and dedicated, when the contrary might be the case. At best it is good to have contacts with people who know the candidate and who are willing to give a fair evaluation.

The policy-making body of the school should clearly spell out the hiring criteria. Of course, candidates are expected to meet the requirements listed under the job description; however, in addition to technical requirements there are personal qualities that the school will want to look for. For the administrative position, the school may be looking for candidates who are mature, politically conscious, able to work with others, including coordinating their work, and taking initiative. Whatever the criteria is, it should reflect the particular needs of the school.

A great deal of attention should be paid to on-the-job training. Too often, new staff is hired and thrown into a new job with only the briefest explanation of the job responsibilities. This disorganized, unsupervised approach leads to new candidates shaping the job to their own whims, which can cause morale problems. A good way to get to know your prospective staff is to have a probationary period, so that you can evaluate the staff's performance. Immediately upon hiring, the new staff should be trained by a skilled person who can familiarize them with their job responsibilities.

Personal contact with the staff and parents is the key to the smooth operation of the school. The administrator should make friends with the staff and parents and take a personal interest in their lives. Staff meetings and parent meetings should be scheduled regularly so that complaints can be aired and solutions developed that will improve the school's operation.

The school administrator should work to develop an open atmosphere that encourages teachers and parents to express their views and take initiative to make improvements in the school. A crucial test for school effectiveness is the ability of the administrator to delegate authority. Administrative burnout occurs when the administrator takes on too many responsibilities and attempts to do too many jobs, personally. If the administrator gets trapped into teaching, then some other administrative area will go unattended. The administrative job is to oversee (not necessarily do) the planning, organizational staffing, recruiting, training, fundraising, and coordinating of the process. A good school has all of these processes operating simultaneously. As much as possible, the administrator should encourage others to assume responsibility for implementing each of the above processes.

Recruitment is one part of this continuous administrative process. The school should regularly advertise its program through leaflets, radio, and television. As important as these recruitment vehicles are, experience shows that the most effective recruitment technique is parent referrals. The school should develop a program to encourage parents to have get-togethers in their homes with friends, where recruiting can take place. Slides of the school can be shown, and parents and teachers can discuss the benefits of the school. Community programs where students display their talents are another good way to recruit new students into the school.

While there are a variety of methods that can be used in recruiting new parents, it is extremely important that the recruitment program be continuous. Without a recruitment program, student turnover will bring down enrollment. A low enrollment means a low income. A school that cannot keep its income higher than its expenses will soon go out of business.

PARENT INVOLVEMENT

Parent involvement in the operation of the school should be made a requirement for admission and continued enrollment in the school. Communications between the parents and staff can be developed through a school newsletter, and regular parent meetings. Parent meetings should be alternated between business and political meetings. At business meetings, the operations of the school should be discussed. A review of parent committee work should take place and decisions made. Political meetings should be devoted to bringing the parents up-to-date on the school's philosophy. Schools that are mass based will have parents with a variety of political outlooks. Political meetings with parents are designed to even out the political consciousness of parents, and promote greater consistency between what the parents teach in the home and what is being taught in the school.

Mass based educational institutions show our people the concrete results of political struggle. Because they serve the future of our people, they are seen as important by Black people. It is the job of a good organizer to see that the educational institution, and any other institutions, are committed to excellence and to provide a service superior to that of the system.

The task of educating our youth is a serious one that requires a life long commitment. The schools that we organize have to last over the long haul. This requires that we strike a balance between providing technical skills and an African-centric perspective that encourages our youth to serve their people. A strong curriculum is not enough, we must also have a solid administrative system that generates funds, recruits staff and students along with supervision of staff.

Fundraising is not only needed for independent schools it is also needed in order to provide a financial base for the Black movement as a whole.

CHAPTER EIGHT

ECONOMIC DEVELOPMENT

FUNDRAISING

A common characteristic of organizations in the Black Liberation Movement is a woeful lack of finances. Most Black organizations (not including the Black church) have empty treasuries, and little, if any idea of how their broke situation can be reversed.

Why do we find ourselves in such a poverty stricken state? Is it as so many of us say -- that we are just a poor people and cannot afford to pay the price for Black liberation? Is organizational poverty a virtue that proves that we are dedicated, because we don't have a large bank account? Is it true that the poor and humble are the blessed of the earth?

Certainly there has to be a rational answer to the above questions, because most of us are affected by this state of organizational poverty. To answer the first question, it is not difficult to see that as Black people, we have enough money to buy what we want. We are able to buy clothes, new cars, liquor, records, and a lot of things that we don't need. So for most of us it's simply not true that we don't have the money to pay to keep our organizations going. The Black church is the best proof of our people's abilities to finance their own institutions. The Garvey movement and the Nation of Islam both have proven that Black people will finance their own organizations.

Similarily, we know through experience that it takes money to organize a liberation struggle. Sooner or later our volunteer organizations have to cough up the money to pay a staff of organizers, fund raisers, and newspaper journalists, printers, and publishers. Being broke may prove that the system has not bought us off financially, but it certainly does not prove that we are effective. Neither does organizational poverty prove that we are virtuous. An African proverb says, "poverty is misery." If an empty stomach is not virtuous, how can an empty treasury be more so?

If we are honest about it, many of us are affected by the Christian mentality that makes poverty a blessing. Many of us deliberately structure our organizations so they cannot obtain a financial base. Some of us operate independent Black schools without charging sufficient tuition to keep the school going; or often we will let parents get by without paying, on the premise that they are poor and can't afford the tuition. Some of us even act like we are proud when we have to beg money for a plane ticket or gasoline to get to an important organizational meeting. For some, the poverty syndrome goes so far that our health suffers because we don't have the funds to pay for some of the basic necessities for our dedicated workers. Groups like SNCC and CORE showed a great deal of dedication by having organizers who were willing to work in the deep South for subsistence wages. But the subsistence wages meant that workers usually couldn't afford nutritious meals, or health care. As a result, many movement workers ended up with ulcers, bad teeth, and high blood pressure that could have been avoided if we had paid more attention to the basic needs of our organizers. This is not to put down simple living, but it is to put down organizational thinking that assumes that dedicated people who are putting all of their time into the struggle can afford to operate without meeting their basic financial needs. Maybe dedicated students can do it for a while, but sooner or later they will have to earn enough money to raise a family.

The poverty mentality that infects most of our organizations extends to the point that most of them don't have a budget and lack a fundraising program. This forces many local and national organizations to depend on out-of-pocket money from members to take care of airplane tickets and other financial expenses. Organizational poverty becomes such a constant state of affairs, that most of us treat it as a normal thing and adjust to it. We get used to running an organization with little, or no money, and lose sight of how much more we could accomplish with a sufficient amount of money.

If we are going to get out of the rut of organizational poverty, then we have to change our attitudes toward making money. We have to start treating finances seriously in the Black liberation movement.

ECONOMIC DEVELOPMENT STRATEGY

If we are going to take finances seriously then we have to develop a strategy for economic development. Fundraising programs alone will not be sufficient, because to finance a movement we need more than the small amount of money that we can raise through the small fundraiser approach. Instead we need to develop an overall strategy and program for overall economic development. Such a strategy and program will place our organizations on a sound economic footing, enabling us to hire full-time organizers, and carry out a long-term struggle.

CAPITAL DEVELOPMENT

A sound economic development program rests on a program of capital development. Capital is the income base that we have to possess if we are to build an economic development program. The goal of a capital generating program is to develop a continual flow of capital that will grow through wise investments, part of which is used to develop capital. A business development program that is organized to build a capital base has one great problem: small businesses have such a high failure rate, that we are more likely to find ourselves feeding a failing business that's not developing capital.

THE ECONOMIC ENVIRONMENT

Capital development requires that we understand the economic environment we operate in so that we can invest seed money into commodities or services that will produce a capital supply. A capital development program should be one that fits into the tax structure of this country in such a way that the tax structure also produces capital for our movement. This is certainly much better than being in the position of having a sizeable part of our profits going into the coffers of the IRS.

An effective program of capital development should also meet some basic needs of our people. Since Black people are economic consumers, a strong capital development program should fulfill some basic consumer needs, while it builds a capital supply for the movement at the same time.

REAL ESTATE

There are a wide variety of consumer areas that a capital development program could focus on, such as real estate. a basic capital generating mechanism. It is a commodity that is controlled by absentee landlords who charge high rents for run down housing. Today, the cost of housing is the largest single commodity cost for Black people. More of our money goes for rent, or mortgages, than for any other commodity, and the cost of housing is constantly going up. Many people find themselves on the streets without any place to live.

Our people's need for affordable housing is matched by our movement's need for building space to operate programs and housing for our organizers. These needs can be met by investing in housing. Housing is perhaps the best source of capital development, because a sizeable amount of money can be made by buying property that is being sold under value either because some repairs need to be made on the property, or the owner has to sell fast, and to do so they are willing to sell cheap; or the bank has repossessed the property, and wants to cut its losses by selling the property below market value. Property can also be purchased at a cheap price through probate sales and other distress sales.

EQUITY

The key rule in property investment is to purchase property that has equity of 30% or more. This means that a property purchased for $35,000 should have at least $45,000 market value, which enables the organization to make a $10,000 profit. Equity is the difference between the value of the property, and the purchase price. Good equity means buying at least 30% under the property value.

Property value is determined by what similar property in the adjoining areas sell for. Value is also determined by the demand for housing at a particular time, and the available financing. There are times when the price of housing is high, with demand being low, and property is harder to sell. This is usually called a buyers market, because buyers have the opportunity to make lower offers, and come up with creative financing.

While markets change from a buyer's to seller's market, housing investments will generate capital for our organizations, and housing for the Black community, so long as the buyer chooses housing in the right location, with sufficient equity and available financing.

REFINANCING, RENTING, OR SELLING

A profit can be made through wise investments, either through selling the property after it's repaired (if necessary), or by refinancing; and/or through renting the property. Selling property is what most people think of when they think of making a profit through real estate. At times this should be done. The problems with selling property is that it often takes time to sell, and when you sell you have to pay taxes on the profit. A better way to make a profit is to refinance the property.

To refinance property the property has to be in saleable condition. An estimation is needed to assess the value of the property. Applications for financing are then made to savings and loans or banks for either 80% or 90% financing. This means that the financial institution will either refinance the property for 80%, or 90% of its value. So if a house is valued at $100,000 and 80% refinancing, the loan would be $80,000, and 90% financing would be $90,000. If the organization paid $20,000 for the property, they would make anywhere from $56,000 to $57,000 profit on an 80% loan after closing costs and other financing fees were subtracted. At 90% refinancing, a profit of $67,000 (more or less) could be made.

It is advisable for the organization to take out an 80% loan, because this leaves sufficient equity for the next buyer, and will make it easier for you to sell the property when you choose to.

Refinancing should only be entered into when the income generated from rents either equals the refinanced note, or actually generates a profit. If this is the case, then refinancing is a better way to generate capital than selling property because you get your money quicker and you don't pay taxes, since you are not taxed on borrowed money. Moreover, the property is a tax write-off for two pieces of property, and will recoup most of the money that you put into it.

CAPITAL GENERATION

The reason that real estate is a capital-generating source is that this method can be continually repeated to raise more capital. Once a sufficient capital base is developed which may be $100,000 or $500,000, then the wise thing to do is to invest this money in a safe, high-interest drawing security, such as a money market account, or certificates of deposit. Your rate of return should be at least ten percent. The organization should then operate off the interests coming from capital investment, never the capital base. This kind of income should be supplemented by rental income and from additional income generated from other real estate investments. With this kind of program, the revolutionary nationalists could develop an economic base that is more secure and more independent than the base of the moderate reformist forces.

Such a financial base would enable you to hire full time organizers, on the national and local level, and it would give you the kind of resources you need to implement other needed programs in your community.

A self-generating capital base should not be confused with capitalism. A Black capitalist is one who owns and controls the means of production. A capital base founded on real estate does not constitute the ownership and control of housing production. Actually, it's probably too bad that it doesn't. But we should not allow this fear of being labeled Black capitalists to prevent us from getting out of the economic poor house, which condemns our organizations to death and render them impotent.

CONSUMER COOPERATIVES

A sound capital base not only allows us to hire full-time organizers; it also gives us a capital flow to establish cooperatives that will service other needs of our communities. W.E.B. DuBois, in *Dusk of Dawn*, put forward a proposal for consumer cooperatives that can be applied today. To quote DuBois:

> Already in the (Black) social group the consumer interest is dominant....His social institutions therefore are almost entirely institutions of consumers and it is precisely along the development of these institutions that he can move in general accordance with the economic development of his time and of the larger white group, and also in this way evolve unified organization for his own economic salvation. The fact is, as the Census of 1930 shows, there is almost no need that a modern group has which Negro workers already trained and at work are not able

to satisfy. Already Negroes can raise their own food, build their own homes, fashion their own clothes, mend their own shoes, do much of their repair work, and raise some raw materials like tobacco and cotton. A simple transfer of Negro workers, with only such additional skills as can be easily learned in a few months, would enable them to weave their own cloth, make their own shoes, slaughter their own meat, prepare furniture for their homes, install electrical appliances, make their own cigars and cigarettes."[50]

DuBois, like Carter G. Woodson, proposed that we build an economy on what we have. Black workers are skilled in most of the areas in which Blacks are consumers. DuBois proposed that some of the skills that are used for white businesses be transferred to a Black owned consumer economy. This would provide work for our people, and it would provide a significant measure of economic independence.

ECONOMIC EXPERTS

Even more important, DuBois' proposal was not a proposal for setting up a business, he was putting forward a model for developing a Black economy. What we need to do today, under a system of collective leadership, is to bring together Blacks who have economic skills, to ask them to assess the Black economy in America and project a national program for economic development. The National Black United Front would be the logical organization to pull such a task force together. A national economic development plan would be the basis for organizing a program of economic self-reliance.

While developing a plan for economic development is vital for the Black movement, it is also important to pay attention to organizing successful fundraisers, both small and large.

ESTABLISHING AN ORGANIZATIONAL
BUDGET

The first step in developing an imaginative fundraising program is to establish an organizational budget. Your budget specifies the cost of organizational programs and expenses.

In establishing a budget, prepare a list of the previous year's expenses (if you are a new organization, estimate these costs). Listing past year's expenses enables you to predict expenses for the coming year. Some of the expenses that you will want to list are utilities, phone, rent, or house note, travel, salaries, maintenance, insurance, office supplies, office equipment (copy machines, typewriters, computers, etc.) and program expenses. After you have listed your expenses, list your income. Income sources such as dues, donations, regular fundraisers, income from any programs, and any other sources of income should be listed.

Once you have assessed your expenses, you are ready to prepare a minimum, and a maximum budget. A minimum budget keeps your operating expenses as they were in the previous year. The value of a minimum budget is that it tells you what the basic necessities will cost for the coming year. By having a bare bones budget before you, it is possible to develop a fundraising plan.

The maximum budget goes beyond your last year's budget, but at a realistic pace. A maximum budget aims for the growth and expansion that is possible. Avoid making maximum budgets that are unrealistic, and are therefore unattainable.

When the budgets are prepared, they should be presented to the executive committee and membership for approval. The membership will be involved in budget projections by offering ideas for programs for the coming year. The price tag for programs will determine the cost of a large part of the organizational budget. Because money is one of the most sensitive issues in an organization, it is essential that money matters be openly discussed with the membership.

FINANCIAL RECORD KEEPING

Budgets give you an understanding of how much money you need to operate.

Even before you start raising money, you should establish a financial recordkeeping system. A financial recordkeeping system is an accountability system. It lets your members know how the money is being spent. At the same time a good bookkeeping system protects you from Internal Revenue vamps, and charges of misuse of funds, which arise from a shabby bookkeeping system. Often poor financial recordkeeping systems are products of a mentality that thinks that since fundraising is unimportant, then recordkeeping is also unimportant. This kind of thinking can be politically deadly. You can find yourselves in jail because you treated record keeping as a middle class question that revolutionaries shouldn't have to deal with. If you are a serious revolutionary, then you don't want to help the enemy put you in jail. When you keep good financial records you are able to file a legal tax form, which will give you the maximum amount of deductions.

A good way to start a professional bookkeeping system is to have an accountant set it up. Once the system is set up, your treasurer can make regular entries, and the accountant can check up on the books periodically. The accountant should also have a knowledge of the tax laws, so that he can get you the maximum number of legal deductions.

Your organization should establish a policy on reporting the proceeds from fundraising programs. The membership should receive detailed financial reports at regular periods.   Once a good financial record keeping system is in place and a budget is established, you can begin to develop a fundraising program.

ESTABLISH A FUND RAISING PROGRAM

The fundraising committee should be organized as the arm that plans fundraising programs for the organization.   The best people to recruit for the fundraising committee are those who like to raise money.   Whether people are new to fundraising or experienced, they should have an interest in raising money.   Fundraising projects call for work and creativity.

The first creative task for your fundraising committee is the development of a correct marketing strategy.   Marketing strategies are ideas about the overall direction of your fundraising program.   More than anything else, strategy decisions are the key to the overall success of your fundraising.

In developing a marketing strategy, there are some simple steps that you should take.   Look at your membership to see what unique resources they possess.   Maybe you have some people who have promotional skills, or selling talents, or other skills.   The unique skills of a group will point you in the direction of a unique strategy.   Most organizations don't make an inventory of their skills.   They just decide to organize a fundraiser.   Sometimes the fundraising projects complement the organization's skills, sometimes they don't. You have a better chance of organizing successful events when you use your unique skills to develop a unique strategy.

A part of developing a unique strategy involves identifying community needs that aren't being met by other groups. When listing these unmet needs, narrow your list to those that your organization has the skills and resources to meet.

When unmet needs are identified you can develop fundraising objectives. The first criteria for fundraising objectives is that the fundraising program is socially and economically useful. The second criteria is that you have a fundraising organization to carry out your objectives. The third and most important criterion is that the fundraising programs will generate profit.

In developing any fundraising program, you should identify your market the people who will support your fundraising event. Sometimes you will have a built-in market when, for example, you have a large youth membership that is supportive of dances. In other cases the event you organize will determine the type of market you will attract. In any case, you have to have a market for your fundraising program.

The market you are appealing to has an income range. If your market is high school youth, then their income will be low, and you will have to price your fundraising event accordingly. If your market is churchgoing Black people, then you will have to suit your prices to the income level of that type of audience. Whatever your market happens to be, gear your prices to your market.

One of the biggest mistakes that is made in planning fundraising events is not checking to see what kind of competing fundraising events are going on in the same area, and at the same time. At all costs, avoid competing with major entertainment events, or major sporting events that occur during the same time and in the same area. Similarily, do not compete with a fundraising event that will draw on your market, especially if that market is limited. When planning your event, your specific market will determine whether the politics of the organization sponsoring the event will be emphasized or played down. If your audience is conservative, or extremely broad-based, you may not want to emphasize politics. You can do this by creating a fundraising project that does not carry the name of the organization. Where your market is made up of those that support your political program, the fundraiser will be seen as a way for them to support your organization. Fundraisers of this type are openly political. In political fundraising events, it is a good idea to set aside a part of the event to discuss the programs of the group.

Of course, you need money to make money. How much money you intend to make will have a lot to do with how much you have available up front. Seed money can be obtained in a number of ways. Your membership can make loans. They can make outright donations, or you can organize small inexpensive fundraising events to raise the seed money for large fundraisers.

SMALL FUNDRAISERS

One reason that organizations remain broke is that almost all of the fundraising activity is concentrated on small events. The problem with small fundraisers is that they require a lot of work, and generate little income. While they may not violate the last fundraising principle that they be profitable they come very close. In the beginning small fundraisers are necessary, but they should not be seen as the sole avenue for raising money. Small fundraisers should be organized to develop seed money for large fundraising projects.

Your market survey and your organization's unique skills will determine the types of small fundraisers you will be able to handle best. The bake sale or food sale is a popular small fundraiser. Most Black churches use this type of fundraiser as a mainstay because the market (church and community members), and the unique skills of many of the members (mainly women who can cook), makes this an ideal fundraising project.   If you decide to organize bake sales, or combination bake and food sales, cut your operating costs to nearly zero by getting food donated. Where possible have a few of your members donate the plates, plastic knives, spoons and forks, and   aluminum foil.   Obviously your good cooks should prepare the menu and do the cooking.   But be sure the menu is geared to your market. It is true that most Black people like soul food, but some have reservations about serving it because a lot of it   is   unhealthy.   This   objection   is understandable   and   praiseworthy. However, remember the rule in successful fundraising: gear your product to your market.   It will do no good to prepare a vegetarian menu if the people won't buy it.

As usual, your market and the times will dictate the prices. Gear your prices to your market, and make sure that they are reasonable.

Allow yourself enough time for promoting the bake sale. The amount of time you will need to promote the fund raiser depends upon a number of factors. If you have a large membership you can probably count on most of the sales being made to your membership. In this situation you will need a very short time period to promote the sale. If, however, you are depending upon a broader market, you will need more time to get the word out.

In either case advance advertising can also be used to get advanced orders. Each food sale should be used as a buildup for the next food sale, so keep a list of the names, addresses, and phone numbers of your customers.

DANCES

Dances are another way to raise money with minimal expenditure. Before organizing a dance, check to see if you can draw the kind of market that will support this type of event.

If your organization can draw people who will come out and dance, then select a suitable site that is large enough, and has a low rental price. Disco dances are cheaper than hiring a band, provided that your own members or supporters play the role of disc jockey, which means that they provide their own music and bring their own stereo equipment. If you have to pay a person to use their equipment and play records, then negotiate a reasonable price.

In cases where you decide to use live entertainment, check to see that the music is popular with your market. Also make sure that the terms of the agreement are spelled out clearly in writing. Remember, in cases of disagreement, verbal contracts are hard to prove and enforce.

When advertising a dance, make sure your advertisement is aimed at your market.

If you expect high school students to attend your dance, then leaflet the high schools, appear before student groups, and schedule public service announcements on radio stations that young people listen to. If your market is middle-aged, then target the social clubs, fraternities, sororities, and other social organizations in the Black community. Above all, allow yourself sufficient time to promote the event. The size of the dance and whether your market is internal or external to your group will tell you how much time you will need. As a general rule, don't try to organize a dance with any less than a month's advance time. If it is a large dance, you may need more than a month.

RAFFLES

Raffles are a good way of raising money and small raffles require very little operating capital.

Like any other fundraising event, the determination of whether or not you will conduct a raffle depends on your organizational capacity and your ability to identify a market that will support a raffle. Often many of your members will show reluctance to sell raffle tickets because they are shy and inexperienced in the techniques of selling. If this is the case, it may be a good idea to have someone who is good at organizing a raffle and selling raffle tickets give a workshop on ticket-selling techniques.

When organizing the raffle, select a prize that is appealing to your market. Nothing is worse than having an unappealing prize. For a small raffle the safest prize is money. Use your creativity to come up with other prizes.

The number of tickets you print depends on the number of tickets that each member and supporter can be expected to sell. To guarantee a specific income from the raffle, set a sales quota for each member. Require that if the members don't sell the tickets they will have to pay for them. This gives members an incentive to sell, and it guarantees the organization a minimum income.

Allow yourself enough lead time to sell the tickets. During the sales period, appoint a few responsible people to phone members and see how their ticket sales are going. Many times, people receive tickets, but allow them to collect dust. Timely reminders and encouragement will do a lot to improve ticket sales. If people have become discouraged because of rebuffs, then give them a pep talk and some tips on selling techniques. The most important thing in selling is mental attitude. If your sellers are confident of their abilities, they will communicate this to the public. If they are doubtful, they will also transmit those attitudes.

As the time of the raffle draws near, remind people of the final date when the tickets have to be turned in. Don't allow people to turn their money in late. The longer the money is out, the less likely it is that you will get it.

Be consistent and fair in executing the raffle. Make sure that the prizes are given to the winners right away. Also, exclude members from receiving the prizes. This prevents people from having a basis for saying that the raffle was fixed. Upon the conclusion of the raffle give a public report on the amount of money that was raised and how it will be spent.

These are only a few examples of small fundraisers. There are many others that you may choose to organize. If you observe the basic principles of marketing, timing, and efficient organization, you should be able to make a profit. Still, there will be times when your fundraiser is a flop. Failures are discouraging, yet they are also building-blocks for success. Carefully analyze what went wrong and take measures to correct your mistakes. Whether the fundraiser is large or small, always have a follow-up meeting to evaluate the event. Draw from the experience of each fundraising event when you are organizing the next event. The experience and capital you gain from small fundraisers gives you the platform to launch larger events.

LARGE FUNDRAISERS

In planning for a large fundraising project, the fundraising committee should prepare a budget for the cost of the event. There are many different types of large fundraising projects. One popular type is a major concert. Obviously there is a strong supportive market for Black concerts of a soulful type.

One of the most difficult things to do is to make contact with major Black entertainers, because we underestimate their willingness to perform for benefits. In many cases our perception is correct. Black performers are usually controlled by recording contracts and agents that make it difficult to get them to perform for free. Still, there are a number of leading Black entertainers who have a history of doing benefits for progressive causes. Therefore, your organization should build up a file of these progressive Black entertainers.

Once you identify these entertainers, put them on your mailing list so they will be informed about your organization. When they perform in your area try to get an appointment to meet with them. If a member of your organization is not able to make direct contact with some of these leading entertainers, see if you can find someone in the community who has those kind of contacts.

Once you make contact with an entertainer you wish to work with, try to develop a relationship with him or her. When the time is right, approach him or her for a benefit concert, spell out the history and program of your organization, as well as what the money will be used for. Also, assure him or her of your ability to organize the benefit.

All of the preceding assumes that your small fundraisers, or membership loans, or donations, or a combination of the above, have generated the capital to finance the event you are planning.

Major fundraising events require a lot of lead time. Give yourself all the time you need to organize and promote the event. Some major events require a year to promote and organize; others can be put together in six months. Some can even be organized within three months. Your particular situation will dictate the lead time required.

One of the factors that will determine the amount of lead time you will need is the amount of time it takes for you to secure a concert site. The site you select should be large enough to handle the drawing capacity of your performer. The site should also have good acoustics. If you plan to have booths in the auditorium, then the site should have an area where booths can conveniently be set up without detracting from the entertainment.

For major performances, many auditoriums require that they handle the soft drink and food concession. Others allow you to set up your own concessions. Wherever it is possible to set up your own concessions, do so, because this is a very profitable enterprise.

When you find a site that meets all of your needs, and is financially feasible, you will be required to sign a contract. Make sure that the contract specifies all of the details, including opening and closing times, management's responsibility for cleaning the premises; lighting, sound, if it is provided, security, etc. The contract should specify when you can begin to set up.

A number of committees should be organized at the very beginning of the project. These committees should include a program committee, a program workforce, security crew if you are going to provide the security; a lobby and ticket area crew; a restaurant committee; a technical assistance committee; a booth coordination committee, a set up crew, and a public relations committee.

The program committee has to start its work early. This committee establishes the program and the time for the performances. It appoints a master of ceremonies, and has a group of people who assist the master of ceremonies with back up work. Back-up work consists of seeing that the performers are ready to perform on time. This is an area that the master of ceremonies cannot handle because he is involved in introducing acts, making comments, etc.

The security committee is responsible for providing security for the benefit. This committee will need to obtain floor plans of the building or will have to map its own floor plans. A security plan that is suited to the layout of the building will have to be developed. Entrances and exits will have to be secured; security will also have to be provided for the ticket salesperson; a roving security squad should be established for the auditorium itself. Other security systems will have to be developed to suit the specific needs of the building.

The lobby and ticket area crew consist of the people who sell tickets at the event and take tickets in the lobby. People who do this type of work should be able to create a good impression for the organization.

The restaurant committee establishes a menu, estimates the amount of food that has to be cooked, and handles the selling of food at the event. The head of the restaurant committee should be someone who understands how to organize mass cooking; knows how to purchase food at the cheapest price; and gets as much donated as humanly possible.

The technical assistance committee handles the coordination of any technical areas, including lighting, or other areas where support services are needed from the building management.

The booth coordination crew establishes booth policies, including the types of booths allowed, prices, etc. On the day of the event, the booth committee checks to see that booth operators conform to their agreements. The booth committee also establishes written booth contracts.

The setup crew has to be at the event early to set up the sound equipment, musical instruments, booth angles, etc.

Another very important committee is the publicity committee. An effective event has to be professionally promoted. The publicity committee develops the public relations campaign. This campaign consists of developing leaflets and posters of a professional quality; radio and television public service announcements; paid radio ads; newspaper releases; in-depth radio news interviews; advance ticket sales distribution; organizational endorsements and support; and media follow-up.

Planning meetings have to be held on a regular basis with committee heads. Regular meetings give you a chance to work on collective ideas or organizational strategies. They also help you to overcome problems.

When the project is complete, a follow-up evaluation should be organized. A written report of the entire project should be prepared. In the appendix you will find a written report on a musical concert done by Ajili Hodari.

Each of your respective organizations should pay special attention to fundraising, record keeping, marketing, and assessing the unique skills of your group. Through practice you can turn organizational poverty into budgetary prosperity. A prosperity that will allow you to staff organizations, and develop more effective programs to serve the people.

History teaches us that when people support the programs of the organizations, they are open to provide financial support to these organizations. The Garvey movement and the Nation of Islam put forward economic development programs instilling race pride and programs for political power, and the masses of Black people responded in large numbers by supporting those programs. Our organizations today need to learn from the success of yesterday and link far reaching programs of economic development with the admirable political, educational and cultural programs that are usually under financed. Without the finances to fund our programs most of them will remain dreams that will never see the light of day.

To win the people over to a program of economic, political, or cultural development, broad-based mobilizing has to occur.

CHAPTER NINE

MASS MOBILIZATION

THE MASS MOVEMENT

The mass movement is an important organizing strategy that enables the people to assume power over their lives through marching, boycotting, rallying, picketing, voting, and other forms of mass activities. The great Civil Rights movement of the fifties and sixties did not come into being instantly it was the product of little known movements that inspired, taught, and preceded it. The Civil Rights movement was a people's movement that created popular mass leaders. Martin Luther King, Jr. was the maximum spokesperson for the National Civil Rights movement, while Malcolm X, was the maximum spokesperson for the Black Nationalists forces. King and Malcolm illustrate another important feature of the mass movement. The mass movement contains within it dualistic forces that push it forward. In the sixties, the dualistic forces of the mass movement were best represented by Martin Luther King, and Malcolm X. King represented the stream of African-American history that promoted Black freedom through reformist struggles (such as mass movements

and picketing), struggles to secure the right to vote, and full citizenship for Blacks without overturning the political and economic system.   Malcolm represented the revolutionary Black Nationalist, Pan Africanists stream of African-American history. This stream of struggle, drew on African and African-American history to teach our people the importance of Black pride, the need for African unity, the importance of building Black institutions, and the need to transform the economic and political system, which Malcolm defined as "not being structured to provide freedom for Black people." The struggle between the forces of reform and Black Nationalism would push the national Civil Rights movement into new stages of struggle.   In the same way, African movements in one part of the world would have a way of influencing African movements in another part of the world. This was the Pan Africanist dimension of mass movements, which reared up in Africa, Europe, and the United States.

The flames of the Black Revolt of the 1960s burned across the United States in the form of the student Sit-Ins, the Freedom Rides, and the mass movements of Albany, Georgia, and Birmingham, Alabama. However, the great mass movements of the sixties did not occur overnight. These great mass movements were nourished and brought to birth by earlier, relatively unknown Civil Rights movements that occurred in Baton Rouge, Louisiana; Tallahasse, Florida;

Birmingham, Alabama; and Montgomery, Alabama.

Aldon Morris notes in his book, *The Origins of the Civil Rights Movement*, that Black communities which had been previously divided, were united behind the arrest of two college students in Tallahassee, the outlawing of the NAACP in Alabama, and the arrest of Rosa Parks in Montgomery, Alabama. Forty-eight organizations that, prior to these events could not work together began to form organizations of organizations that mobilized and organized the people into action.

In Baton Rouge, the united organization was the United Defense League; in Tallahassee, the Black community united behind the Inter Civic Council. In Birmingham, the Black community rallied around the Alabama Christian Movement for Human Rights, while in Montgomery, Black people from all walks of life created the Montgomery Improvement Association. Each of these local movements reflected a broad-based unity across different sectors of the Black community.[51]

Organizations of organizations, or Black united fronts, were not only responses to racist oppression, but they were also cultural expressions of southern Black life. The culture of the southern mass movements of the fifties and sixties was a progressive African-American church culture, which stressed the need to minister to the spiritual and political need of Black people. This progressive spiritual/political orientation was the key to the dynamism of the southern mass movements. As noted earlier, the successful mass movements among Black people, whether they were the Black Nationalist Garvey movement of the twenties, the Nation of Islam of the fifties and sixties or the Civil Rights movements of the fifties and sixties -- all of the successful Black mass movements have combined a deep spirituality with a program to provide businesses, jobs, education, the right to vote, and to end segregation. The combination of the spiritual and the political gave the southern mass movements of the fifties and sixties a soulful swing. The mixture of the spiritual and political streams led to movement songs, that are out of the Gospel tradition. Songs such as, "I'm Not Going to Let Nobody Turn Me Around," or "Before I'd Be a Slave I'd Be Buried in My Grave," -- these and many other soulful songs, expressed a movement spirit that enabled Blacks to face death and violence with determination.

The leadership of the mass movements of the fifties and sixties varied from the charismatic leadership of a Martin Luther King, or a Fred Shuttlesworth, to the carefully detailed, painstaking, self-sacrificing leadership of an E.D. Nixon and Ella Baker. E.D. Nixon laid the groundwork for the Montgomery Bus Boycott. Nixon also promoted the charismatic leadership of a new Montgomery minister, Martin Luther King, Jr. Ella Baker, on the other hand, encouraged the development of a group-centered leadership within the student movement. So the leadership styles of the southern mass movements varied from charismatic to collective leadership styles.

Whatever the style of leadership, the great quality of the mass movements of the fifties and sixties was that they were the avenue for Black people making history, with marching feet, voter registration ballots, and economic boycotts. These mass movements drew on another cultural trait of Black people, the art of improvisation. Similar to creative Black musicians, Black people improvised local mass movements using marches, boycotts, rallies, sit-ins, and voter registration campaigns to crush segregation in the south. E.D. Nixon described this creative, courageous quality of the southern mass movement in an improvised speech delivered in Madison Square Garden:

> "I don't know how, it just came to me all at once. I said, I'm E. D. Nixon, I'm from Montgomery, Alabama, a city that's known as the Cradle of the Confederacy, that had stood still for more than ninety-three years until Rosa Parks was arrested and thrown in jail like a common criminal." I said, "Fifty thousand people rose up and caught hold to the Cradle of the

> Confederacy and began to rock
> it till the Jim Crow rockers began to
> fall out." I said, "I'm from that city."
> And man, people just fell out. I
> could a sat down then, Right
> then."[52]

The Montgomery mass movement, other southern mass movements, the northern Civil Rights movement, and northern Black Nationalist organizations instilled pride into Black people. The southern mass movements created pride by Black people standing up and 'grabbing a hold of Jim Crow.' As Black people took part in movements to overturn segregation, these movements began to shape an attitude of pride and self-respect. The southern Civil Rights movement nourished the seed of Black pride, which would later emerge in the form of Black Power.

The Black nationalists' wing of the movement, in the fifties and sixties, was a northern product. Malcolm X, the central spokesperson of the Black nationalist forces, challenged Blacks to have pride in their history, and to abandon the policy of non-violence. This creative dualistic tension between the fiery Malcolm X who called for armed self-defense, and Martin Luther King, who advocated non-violence, gave Blacks political choices. Malcolm X offered a sharp, clear, Black nationalist analysis for Civil Rights activists in the south, and urban Blacks in the north.   But as important as Malcolm's message was, the seeds for Black pride started when people stood up and slapped Jim Crow in the face.

The pride and growing maturity of both the southern and northern Civil Rights movements was also the result of many movement activists beginning to realize that the federal government was in league with the local segregationists.   Serious members of SNCC and CORE learned through trial and error struggle that the federal government and big business, as well as the racist segregationists, were the enemies of Black people.   Knowledge of the enemy was gained through participation in mass movements.   In the case of SNCC, many organizers (and many of the people they organized) realized that the local segregationists in Birmingham were part of a bigger power structure with headquarters in Washington, D.C., and New York City.

The Birmingham movement not only was the first mass rejection of non-violence by Black people, but it demonstrated that many Blacks had gained an understanding of the true enemy. It was everyday community people from Birmingham, Alabama who decided to organize a "March on Washington," against the real national white political power structure. The term "White Power Structure" was popularized by grassroots Blacks in Birmingham, who had gained their political understanding of the enemy, not only from Bull Connor, but also from John Kennedy. Blacks in Birmingham witnessed the murder and beating of their children. When King called on Kennedy to intervene in Birmingham to protect Black lives, Kennedy said he lacked the constitutional authority to do so. However, when Blacks started whipping white heads after the bombing deaths inflicted on Black children, Kennedy finally found the authority to nationalize the Alabama National Guard. These and many other racist acts by the Kennedy administration taught many grassroots Blacks across the south and north that the real enemy of Black rights was in the White House and on Wall Street.

As the mass movement forced the Federal government to adopt voter registration legislation, and other civil rights legislation, the movement began to change, from a Civil Rights movement to a Black Power Movement. As Malcolm predicted, Black nationalism began to rise up inside the major Civil Rights organizations, SNCC and CORE. Contrary to popular opinion, the first Civil Rights organization to move toward a Black nationalist position was CORE under my leadership. In 1965, Black nationalist forces at the National CORE convention adopted 32 resolutions unanimously, calling for the restructuring of CORE along Black Nationalists lines. As chair of the resolutions committee, I had the pleasure of presenting these 32 resolutions to the convention. These resolutions called for financial self-reliance, and a grassroots organizational structure for local CORE chapters. The fact that these resolutions were adopted without dissent, reflected a Black nationalist shift among the southern and northern regions of the organization.

Unfortunately, James Farmer convinced a narrow majority within CORE's National Executive Committee (the National Action Council) to overturn the decisions of the National Convention. The failure of CORE to move to the Black nationalists stage of struggle guaranteed CORE's death. SNCC, a year later, would adopt the Black Power slogan, and in doing so SNCC ushered in the the Black nationalists phase of struggle.

The mass movements of the fifties and sixties not only arose out of racist American conditions, but they were also influenced and inspired by African independence movements. As Malcolm X noted, 'African freedom movements in one part of the world created a chain reaction among Africans in other parts of the world.' The Ghana independence movement, and other African independence movements, encouraged Black civil rights activists to step up their pace of struggle. Many expressed the belief that Africans on the continent would gain their independence before Africans in America could eat a hot dog at a desegregated restaurant. Interestingly enough, the African independence movement of the fifties and sixties followed the same peaceful phase that the U.S. Civil Rights movement followed. In Ghana, as well as, West, East and South Africa, the independence movements, with a few exceptions, followed the peaceful phase. Algeria, Kenya, the Portuguese colonies, South West Africa (Namibia) and Zimbabwe followed the non-violent path, and when this course failed to produce independence, they adopted the strategy of the armed struggle.

While the Montgomery mass movement of the fifties rocked old Jim Crow, the people of Ghana, under the leadership of Kwame Nkrumah made the British empire reel under the Ghana people's movement for independence. Kwame Nkrumah, studied in the United States and Britain during the late thirties through the mid-forties. As a student in the United States, Nkrumah studied the different methods used by Blacks to organize themselves. Nkrumah was influenced by the great events of his time. C.L.R. James, the noted writer, introduced Nkrumah to George Padmore, the organizer of the 5th Pan African Congress. Nkrumah learned a great deal about Pan Africanism, and the fine points of organizing from George Padmore. In addition, Nkrumah was influenced by the Indian independence movement led by Ghandi.

All of these influences contributed to Nkrumah's strategy of "Positive Action." Positive Action was a mass movement using leaflets, the press, public rallies, strikes, and boycotts, rallies and other strategies. Mass movements have a way of raising the level of the people's creativity through the collective inspiration of the movement.

While the spark that ignites the mass movement is usually unplanned, mass movements don't just emerge overnight. They stand on the foundation of earlier struggles. The mass movements of Tallahassee and Baton Rouge, although generally unknown outside of the South, influenced the better known movements of Montgomery and Birmingham. The leaders of these three bus boycotts were ministers and they met in church assemblies and exchanged information on their experiences. As organizers its important to remember that a lot of groundwork has to be laid before you can launch a mass movement.

The Civil Rights movement demonstrated that youth play a key role. Sometimes, as in the Sit-in movement, youth have the capacity to launch the mass movement. In other cases, they may serve as the shock troops for the mass movement. However, youth cannot carry the mass movement to its final conclusion without the support of other sectors of the Black community. This is because youth lack the financial resources and the maturity to build the long-term solid resources needed to sustain the movement. Also, where movements are protracted, youth will sooner or later have to get a job, build a family, and over time become adults. While youth do not have the capacity to carry the movement successfully through to the end, they bring vision, idealism and a no-compromise attitude.

Mass movements are gigantic classrooms that teach participants some of life's most important lessons including who they are, and who their enemy is. Knowing who you are, and who your enemy is, are the two golden keys to liberation. With self-knowledge you gain a deep understanding of your history and culture as well as your personal and historical strengths and weaknesses. For serious activists, the lessons learned from the mass movement become the inspiration for deeper study.

This is not a small point. The majority of Black people learn through doing. This is a cultural trait of African people. Most Black people learn the art of cooking through seeing others cook. The same with most of the things we learn. The mass movement teaches self-knowledge, self-respect, and self-love through action. Confrontations with the White Power structure, and the lessons learned from movement activists provide the stimulation for a lot of Black people to hit the books and learn even deeper lessons about themselves and the enemy.

Mass movements move in a dualistic way. People enter the movement with one set of assumptions and at a certain point the most important assumptions change. This is both the attraction and frustration of mass movements. The mass movement is the place where assumptions are tested. If they prove to be correct that's one thing: however, when the lessons of the movement teach you that your assumption about American democracy is wrong, then you will be put in the unpleasant position of having to alter your views, or accomodʌte yourself to oppressive conditions.

In the sixties, many Blacks, and a significant number of white youth, as well as many people of color, entered the movement with rosy American ideals. The students who launched the Sit-in movement had democratic ideals. They just wanted the system to deliver on the freedom it promised. By the mid-sixties many of the more serious youth questioned whether the system was capable of producing freedom, when racism, greed, and war were understood to be structured into the fabric of the society.

Many Blacks entered the movement with negro identities. Hatred of our Blackness was a common feature of the negro psychology. The mass movement helped to create a new measure of Black pride among Black people. The mass movement, along with the teachings of Malcolm X, the Nation of Islam, and other Black nationalists helped to transform negro identities to Black identities. Again the dualistic path was the path of many of our people's growth. Negro identities were transformed in the heat of struggle to Black identities. Non-violence, pushed to its limit revealed the unwillingness of Black people to continually turn the other cheek. Non-violence pushed to its extreme led to self-defense. Local movements were transformed into regionwide and national movements. National movements in one part of the world inspired national movements in other parts of the world. The mass movement became a global classroom. The participants found themselves being transformed from spectators to actors.

While we can say the mass movement is a useful mobilizing strategy, we should also understand that mass movements have their limitations. Mass movements not only take a long time to build, they have a life span of their own. The people cannot stay in the streets forever. The mass movement for Civil Rights was transformed by the victories it achieved and the defeats it suffered. King's failure to stay in jail in Albany long enough to force the power structure to meet the movement's demands, created a degree of disillusionment with his leadership, that encouraged the development of local leadership across the United States. Conversely, the very success of the Civil Rights movement, marked by the passage of the voting rights bill and other civil rights legislation, meant that the strategy of the mass movement struggle had to give way to strategies that could build economic and political power among Black people.

Unfortunately, many of those who gained their political birth through the mass movement lacked the skill to build organizational structures. King admitted this when he observed that his training in the southern mass movements did not equip him to build institutional power in the Black community. As organizers, it is important to understand that the mass movement is a way to arouse and mobilize the people into action. But the mass movement is not an end in itself; the mass movement is one means of laying the groundwork for organizing Black people.

As organizers you need to be skilled in mobilizing and organizing. You need to master the art of the mass movement, and the art of building mass-based institutions. Mass mobilizing should be seen as a precondition for mass organizing. This requires mastering the fine points of planning and organizing a public meeting. Similarily, organizing boycotts, outdoor rallies, marches, and other creative forms of mass movement requires special skills. These skills are gained through paying attention to the fine points of mobilizing.

MASS MOBILIZATION:
PUBLIC MEETINGS

One important technique we can use to influence the thinking of our people and in recruiting new members, is the public meeting. The public meeting or rally, whether large or small, is a mobilizing technique that can be used to create the atmosphere for subsequent organizing. The Black Liberation movement has a rich set of mobilizing experiences to draw from. Every Sunday, Black people in large numbers are mobilized for church services; the Garvey movement, in its prime, held mass rallies of over 20,000 Black folks; tremendous mass mobilizations took place during the Civil Rights movement, and during the Black Power and Pan Africanist stage of struggle. Yet with this rich body of experience, too many of us ignore the fundamentals of mobilizing when holding a large or small public rally. When the fundamentals are ignored, we end up with a poor turn out, a late meeting, and little or no follow up. Mobilizing, like every other part of organizing, is an art, and like every art, mastery of the techniques makes the difference between success or failure.

POLITICAL ATMOSPHERE

While technique is important, the phase of struggle also has a lot to do with the type of turnout you can expect. During times when there is a great deal of motion and political activity, the people's interest in political questions is high and the turnout for political rallies is higher than periods when mass struggle is at a low level. For example, during the mid-sixties, average attendance for Sunday Pan African People's Organization mobilizations was between 150 and 200 people. By the early seventies, 100 to 150, and by the late seventies between 50 and 75 attended. Now these were not major mobilizations, they were regular public rallies. What we called a good turnout in 1960 was different from what we called a good turnout in early or late 1970. The particular period during which you are mobilizing has to be understood because it has a great deal to do with your potential to mobilize and organize. In the 1960's there was a great deal of optimism among Black people based on the great movements we had pushed forward. By the late sixties and early seventies the internal errors of these movements were becoming apparent to the people, and fear was being driven into the hearts of many Black people by the COINTELPRO state terror. But state-sponsored terrorism wasn't the movement's sole enemy. An even greater enemy to the movement was the reformist war on poverty, model-city type programs, which conditioned our people to struggle for pay. This mercenary attitude began to replace the committed attitude in the sixties, when the people's liberation was placed before money. The people were not paid to organize the Montgomery Bus Boycott, the student sit-ins, or the self-defense struggles of the Black Panther Party. This decline in commitment to struggle was also related to the government's destruction of the militant national Black leadership (through assassination, imprisonment, and exile) and the creation of a new moderate group of Black leaders who held political office, including mayors, city councilmen, state representatives, and national legislators. With the rise of this new moderate Black leadership, many Blacks concluded that there was no longer any need to struggle in the streets. Many Blacks began to look to this new moderate Black leadership to struggle for them. Also by the seventies, many more Black people were hit by hard economic conditions, which led more and more of our people to adopt a "go for yourself" outlook.

Today, the conditions are even harder, driving larger numbers to drugs, hustling, armed robberies, ripping each other off, and other types of negative behavior. As an organizer, it is your job to see that drugs, and crime are only symptoms of oppression. The challenge is to organize this frustration and anger into a well organized movement that can struggle for short and long range changes. Mobilization is an instrument for transforming our people from helpless victims into conscious agents of social change. The candidacy of Jesse Jackson brought thousands of Blacks into the arena of political struggle. This is the kind of motion we can use to mobilize and organize our people.

This type of mobilization raises consciousness and prepares the people for future organizing campaigns. Public rallies may be organized to provide support for an existing community struggle or they may be called for other purposes including recruiting, or raising money, launching an organization, or carrying out a specific campaign. Whatever the purpose of a particular public meeting you must pay special attention to planning.

PLANNING

The planning process may be time consuming and painstaking but without it the best ideas can end up without an audience. In planning, the most important task is to select the issue, or program that you want to center your public meeting or conference around. At times you may want to use the brainstorming method to generate ideas. At other times, the theme may be so obvious that you will want to spend your time structuring the program into workshops, keynote speeches, and resolutions. If the mobilization is a major one, which is held occasionally, then a theme will have to be selected to dramatize the issue. Whatever issue you choose, it should be topical or current. Try to offer solutions to specific topics. If your mobilization is informational, then you can put forward ideas for action. If the mobilization is designed to launch a campaign, then be very specific about the course of action that you are proposing.

The type of speaker you choose has a lot to do with the type of meeting you are organizing. For a large meeting, you may want to choose a "name speaker" who will draw a large number of people, or you may want to mix a major speaker with a local speaker. Regardless of your decision, you should confirm the date and time that they will speak. Early confirmation is necessary to have enough advertising time. Speakers should know the topic you want them to speak on, and the length of their address. Even after a letter is sent, it is a good idea to call and discuss the event prior to the meeting. When your speakers are coming from out-of-town, get a verbal confirmation, then send them a letter spelling out the details of the engagement. You will usually have to provide transportation, and in some cases an honorarium. Decide in advance what you will be able to pay the speaker. Try to use existing community resources to generate money to cover the cost of the honorarium and transportation. Schedule paid appearances at local colleges. Ask some of the groups that you are allied with in the community to contribute to your expenses, and/or take up a collection among your membership. For out-of-town speakers, determine if community housing is acceptable.

The selection of the program or issue has a lot to do with the historical period and the pressing issues facing people at that time. The most important Black political conference of the 20th century, the Fifth Pan African Congress, grew out of the post-World War II break-up of western colonialism. As C.L.R. James observed, "African people and people of color saw that you could mobilize people of color in China, and Vietnam against imperialism and win."[53]   The Fifth Pan African Congress was able to draw a grass roots representation because the theme, the independence of the African continent, was the most burning issue facing African people. This is a good example of creative planning. If you want to reach the masses, then offer programs that deal with a pressing issue. If your conference or public meeting is action-oriented, use the forum to rally people around the issue or program. This was the key to the success of the Fifth Pan African Congress - the planners put forward a program for African independence that planted seeds of a truly all-African movement for liberation. The Congress endorsed the demands for self-government for the Sudan, Tunisia, Algeria, Morocco, and Libya. It also defended the only independent Black republics at the time: Ethiopia, Libya, and Haiti. A few of those in attendance at this historic congress would later link the struggle for national independence to the movement for African unity.

But the success of this historic conference not only was due to its historic theme, it was also due to the people who were invited as speakers and participants. These people were representatives of a broad cross-section of African life, and many of them were political activists who were committed to ending colonialism. Dr. W.E.B. DuBois, who served as Chair of the Congress, was recognized as the father of the Pan African movement since he had convened most of the earlier congresses and had played a leading role in shaping the ideological thrust of the Pan African movement.

Many of those who spoke became future leaders of African independence movements. Kwame Nkrumah, who would later become president of Ghana, presented the political report on West Africa. This report condemned imperialism and demanded "complete and absolute independence for the people of West Africa." Nkrumah became the first African leaderin the 20th century to successfully mobilize and organize African people for independence from colonialism. He incorporated many ideas of the Congress into his new government. Jomo Kenyatta, later to be president of Kenya, presented the East African report, which called for reforms in the East African colonial system.

The key organizer of the Fifth Pan African Congress, Malcolm Nurse (known as George Padmore), understood that Africa must be free, and the only way was through the mobilization of the African population. To achieve this, Padmore wanted to appeal to a grassroots base that would be representative of the desires of African people for political independence. He succeeded in drawing the attention of political leaders, trade union representatives, farmers, and student activists. This made the Fifth Pan African Congress different from the previous Congresses, which involved the Black elite instead of representatives of the African masses.

So this Congress shows us how important the careful selection of speakers is to the success of a conference. For a mobilization like this, it was absolutely essential that activists play a leading role. With this kind of participation, it was not suprising that many of the leading figures at the Congress went back to Africa to mobilize the masses for liberation.

All of this was the product of a well-planned conference that felt the heartbeat of the African people who wanted to rid themselves of white rule. Careful planning produced a historic theme and program, and attracted important participants who would later make history by breaking up western colonialism. The principles used in organizing the Fifth Pan African Congress should apply to the organization of all public meetings.

SITE SELECTION

In organizing a conference or public meeting, the choice of an appropriate site is very important. When choosing a site, there are obvious considerations such as the size of the meeting place, and its location. Not always so obvious are other considerations such as the capacity of the group to organize the conference or public meeting, and to influence public officials, or community groups to provide a site. Other considerations are the ability of the sponsoring group to provide housing, transportation, and food. Just as important is the atmosphere in the community. If you are planning a conference on education, is there an active interest in the conference program? A lot has to do with how much work the sponsoring organization is doing to mobilize and organize around that issue on a day-to-day basis.

The Fifth Pan African Congress illustrates how important these considerations are in organizing a successful public meeting or congress. Ras Makonnen, a leader of the Pan African movement during this period, selected Manchester as the site of the conference because he had access to Manchester politicians, and he had a financial base there. Manchester also provided strong support for African independence. Makonnen's political contacts made it possible for him to secure a meeting place for the conference. It was not all that easy to secure a meeting place in Britain where Africans could demand an end to British colonialism in Africa. Since Makonnen had a restaurant in Manchester, he could feed the conference participants, as well as contribute money to the conference, and the Pan African movement in general.

The site you choose should be large enough to handle the turnout you expect. For small meetings try to get a meeting place donated. If this is not possible, keep your rental expenses as low as possible. For larger events you will usually have to sign a contract. Be sure that the contract spells out the responsibilities of the owner and your group. Compare locations and prices so that you get the best location at a price you can afford. For community meetings that occur on a regular basis (weekly, bi-weekly or monthly) it is easier for people to find a consistent location.

Thorough planning, the selection of relevant speakers, and a good site are important not only for earthshaking conferences, like the Fifth Pan African Congress, but the same organizational process is also required for successful community meetings. Well-planned community meetings provide a forum for education and mobilization of the community around important issues. Public meetings prepare the community for campaigns to come. They are also good for raising funds and soliciting ideas from the community; they can contribute to a winning spirit. Regularly held public meetings can be used to recruit new members, because they give community people a forum where they can discuss their problems and get support for solving them.

PUBLIC RELATIONS

Getting the word out to the community, through an organized public relations campaign, is the difference between a successful and unsuccessful meeting. Leaflets, press releases, radio and television interviews, and door to door canvassing are some of the ways to promote a meeting. The amount of time you will need for a public relations campaign will depend on the projected size of the meeting or event.

Press releases for newspaper stories are a good way to reach a large segment of the community. Often though, good press releases never reach the columns of the paper because you have not developed relationships with key members of the press. It's very important to cultivate these relationships. Take time to get acquainted with them, and familiarize them with your organization. Once you have personal contacts with members of the press, it is much more likely that your releases will get coverage and not end up in the trash.

In most Black communities there are a few brothers and sisters who have their own radio or TV programs. Establish good relations with them and keep them informed about what is happening in the Black community. When you have an issue that you want pushed, give them enough time to fit your activity into their schedule. Follow up with a thank you letter to let them know you appreciate their support.

In the course of your work there are times when you have to mail materials to supporters. Today the costs of mailings are astronomical, and promise to go higher. Secure a bulk rate mailing permit to cut your mailing costs. Check the post office's rules for sorting mail according to zip code. These rules seem to be designed to discourage customers from using this cost effective method. As ridiculous as the rules seem, following them is the only way the postal workers will approve your mail, and it pays off.

When you use leaflets, newspaper articles, and other methods of advertisement, the response is about five percent, therefore, the more people you reach the more will turn up for the particular event. Be sure the leaflets are professionally designed.

A very important resource for reaching interested people is the mailing list. Work to build up a large mailing list with other organizations. Lists have to be regularly updated because Black people move frequently. Lists should also be separated into categories such as political, religious, business, media, supporter, contributors, demonstrators, etc.

Today the computer is the most effective method for storing information. When your treasury allows, secure a good computer, and use it to keep track of mailing lists and other organizational records. Because mailing lists are very sensitive, you should develop a method for making it difficult for opposition forces to get their hands on your mailing lists and financial records. Many organizations have been crippled because the government grabbed all of their membership and financial records.

If you choose to send out a mailing, you will save time and money if, a few days before the meeting, you phone people to remind them of the meeting. If some of those you call express no interest in the organization, then scratch them from your lists, noting the reasons for their lack of interest alongside their name.

Members should be encouraged to recruit friends to come to public meetings. One way to bring in friends and acquaintances is to have members set a goal for the number of people each person will recruit. Encourage competition to see who recruits the largest number of people. Setting mobilizing goals can help people to increase their confidence in organizing, because they see that their technique gets results.

THE NUTS AND BOLTS OF
THE MEETING

Public meetings are not only opportunities for you to recruit, they are also opportunities for training new members in mobilizing techniques. For each area of work try to have a new member work with an old member so that mobilizing skills can be spread out.

Pay attention to little things on organizational work. Appoint one or two people to handle the sign-in at the meeting. Ask people to print, not write, their name, address, phone number, and zip code. Set up a time when the names obtained will be transferred to small file cards. On the back of each card keep a record of the meetings the person has attended. Pay special attention to people who have attended two or more meetings. People who fall in this category indicate that they are interested in the organization. Assign some of your members to talk to these interested persons before they leave the next meeting. Try to arrange a personal meeting at a potential new member's home so you can get better acquainted.

Develop a follow-up plan for your meeting. The follow-up plan may consist of recruiting interested people into the existing organizational program; it may involve encouraging people to attend a demonstration; or it may consist of a personal meeting with the potential new member. Whatever your follow-up plans, make them in advance, and appoint the people who will do the follow-up work.

Select a master of ceremonies, who is a good public speaker, and who will require people to stick to their time limit. Most meetings start late, because they operate on the CPT (Colored People's Time) concept. Once you establish a late pattern, you guarantee that people will keep coming late. Get off on the right foot, and start the meeting on time, even if there are only a few people present. This will encourage more people to get to the meeting on time. Meetings should not only start on time, they should also end on time. Black people generally don't like long drawnout meetings. By keeping your meetings short you will convince more people to come back, especially if the meetings are interesting and relevant.

The Black community has a rich tradition of mobilization, and the Black church is its main mobilizing center. It is such an important mobilizing center that a good organizer would not consider holding a meeting during the time Sunday services are being conducted. Similarily, it would seem that good organizers would learn some lessons from the most effective mobilizers and organizers in the Black community, the Black church.

The Black church knows how to balance preaching with soulful music. Many brothers and sisters go to church to hear a good sermon, and to enjoy some soulful gospel music. The soulful approach to mobilizing is a tradition in the Black community. Yet while it is a tradition, too many Black political organizations ignore tradition. Too many are long on rapping, and short on cultural input. The two need to be balanced. Our meetings have a political objective that requires that we have dynamic speakers who deliver a clear message. The meeting should allow plenty of time for questions and answers as well as audience input. But this is not enough, we need to raise the spirit of the people by blowing some strong songs, poetry, and dance. One of our most powerful cultural arms is the Black political choir. A few movement organizations have developed singing groups or choirs that have combined gospel rhythms with liberation songs. This kind of cultural arm fill a spiritual void in the Black community, and provide an inspiration for struggle.

Avoid cliques by encouraging regular members to sit with members of the audience rather than clustering among themselves. Too often, Black political organizations create a barrier between themselves and the community by separating themselves from community people. Members should be encouraged to sit with community people and strike up conversations. Each member should attempt to establish a personal relationship with potential new members.

MASS MOBILIZATION
BOYCOTTS

Another mobilizing technique is the boycott. Boycotts are of many types. Symbolic boycotts highlight opposition to a particular government or business policy, that supports South Africa, or Israel. These boycotts can be local, national, or international. National boycotts require a national organizational structure, and they also require strong alliances with other national organizations. A national boycott should not be undertaken if your organization does not have the strength to carry it out successfully.

Local boycotts, can be a symbolic type, or economic, or political. Local economic boycotts are organized to stop money from going to racist institutions, which refuse to hire Blacks, or organizations that control political institutions (such as the police) that are oppressing Blacks.   A political boycott usually demands that certain sectors of the business community apply pressure to politicians and police to end police brutality. Which of these two types of boycotts (economic or political) you use will be dictated by your local situation.

ORGANIZING A LOCAL ECONOMIC BOYCOTT

In choosing a target for an economic boycott, research the hiring policies of local businesses. Of those businesses that hire few or no Blacks, select a target that has a large number of Black customers and sells a product that Black people can be persuaded to boycott.

An example of a product that is difficult to boycott is the automobile. Black people are major purchasers of cars, but just because they are big customers does not mean that they will withdraw their money from particular automobile companies. You will have to have an extremely strong and conscious organizational base to persuade Blacks to boycott cars, whether they are Cadillacs or Fords.

Companies that Blacks are likely to boycott are supermarkets, department stores, fresh drink companies, dairies, etc. Department stores that are extremely vulnerable to an economic boycott are those stores that have a large Black clientele. Such stores usually offer bargains that Blacks can afford.

Supermarkets with significant Black patronage are vulnerable to the boycott because they operate on a very small profit margin. A heavy dent in their profits for a prolonged period of time can put some stores out of business or force them to come to terms with your group.

In order for a small organization to boycott a large chain store, or a major product or a large store, it will need allies. The most important ally for major local boycotts is the Black church. The Black church has the base that can make or break a boycott with their support or neutrality. In gaining church support it is best to go to the church federations, i.e., Baptist and Methodist Ministerial Alliances, etc. You should clearly spell out the hiring policies of the company or companies you intend to boycott. Ministers should be included on your negotiating team, and if negotiations break down they should be asked to go to their congregations to tell them not to buy where they can't work.

There are a number of tactical considerations in carrying out a boycott. First, do you want to boycott a single company, or do you want to take on a whole industry (department stores for example)? Sometimes you will find that you only have the strength to take on a single company at a time. However, experience in the San Francisco freedom movement shows that you can force an entire industry to reach a hiring agreement by attacking its weakest link and making an example of it. In San Francisco, the Congress of Racial Equality and the Baptist Minister's Union negotiated with an industry-wide unit for downtown department stores called the Retail Dry Goods Association. When negotiations broke down, we boycotted their weakest link, Penneys and Macy's . Penney's and Macy's was their weakest link because they had an extremely large Black clientele. The boycott took over two months, but it ended with success. The other downtown department stores signed agreements because they did not want to go through what Penneys and Macy's suffered.

This strategy of attacking the weakest link can be applied on a broader level. Once you succeed in setting a few examples and bringing an industry or a few large employers into line, you can enter into negotiations with employers in other industries. Very often you will be able to reach agreements without boycotts or demonstrations because they don't want to be your next target. Sometimes, of course, an employer will be hardnosed, forcing you to beat them into the ground.

Next to picking an employer or employers that you can beat, and having strong allies, the most important thing is that you choose the right time for your boycott. Again, it has been our experience that timing is crucial to the success of an economic boycott. For this reason, you should pick a time of the year when you can choke-off a lion's share of the employer's profits. Christmas is the ideal time for boycotts against department stores, because they make most of their profit during this holiday season. Christmas boycotts against department stores are also effective because during this time of year people are more willing to support struggles for human rights.

In some struggles the question of timing doesn't have to do with the season, but with the campaign build up. In 1964, taking on the Bank of America, the largest bank in the world, we found that the best time to challenge the B of A was when we had successfully defeated the downtown department stores, the dairies, the Sheraton Palace Hotel, Lucky Supermarket, and Auto Row. Some big victories impressed a big enemy. The best timing for a particular boycott will depend upon the type of business you are dealing with and the strengths and weaknesses of your organization and your enemy.

Every phase of the boycott campaign should be well advertised. You should issue press releases, leaflets, and hold public rallies to explain the companies' hiring policies, the results of negotiations, and the type of support you want from the community.

The community should be given alternatives to the company they're boycotting. For instance, if you are boycotting the Five and Dime, then encourage people to shop at Penneys or Sears, since they also sell cheaper products than do most of the other department stores.

Once the boycott starts, an informational picket line should be maintained in front of the store. To highlight your boycott campaign you may want to have a march on the store to focus attention on the boycott. Psychologically, it is impressive if you can show growing support for your boycott. Get community endorsements for the boycott, and issue news releases that show a growing number of community groups and individuals that have endorsed the boycott.

The picket line serves an informational purpose. You should have leaflets to pass out to the public explaining the purpose of the boycott. When community people violate the boycott and cross the picket lines there are a number of things you can do. If you get their names and addresses, you can have a group of people meet with them in their homes to explain the seriousness of the boycott. If they don't come around, you can publish their name and photographs in the Black press, and on leaflets. More drastic methods have been used that are best left to the imagination.

In the very beginning of your protest, plan for success. Plan for follow-up after the boycott succeeds. Advanced follow-up planning is necessary to prevent a paper success and an actual failure. Without a follow-up plan you are left with a paper agreement, which will usually be violated as soon as the heat is off.

A follow-up committee should be organized that has the responsibility for establishing meetings with employers, and monitoring whether the employer has lived up to the agreement. Employers should be informed that your organization is prepared to carry out new boycotts if they violate the agreement. The results of follow-up meetings should be published in the newspaper to praise or criticize employers.

Volunteer organizations are often inconsistent in follow-up work because it is the kind of work that requires a long term commitment. A boycott may take a week, a few months, or even a year or more, but follow-up should take place as long as the company is in business. Of course, if the organization undertaking the boycott is unstable, it may not be around long. If that is the case then the achievement will ultimately erode. A boycott is a long term project, and should only be undertaken when you are prepared to make a long term commitment.

At the very beginning of your project you should develop a recruitment policy based on two alternatives. You can allow the employer to recruit, or you can insist that your organization will pick the employees. If you don't have a base in the Black community, you may not be able to recruit the new employees.

Experience in the Black liberation movement demonstrates that it is a serious error to let the employer pick the Blacks they will hire. This approach is wrong because the people who benefit from Black struggle should participate in the struggle, and have a sense of commitment to the Black community. When you choose conscious people to fill the positions, you will have people who have a sense of responsibility and accountability. If these people turn to white values, then you should conduct boycotts, or pressure the employer to remove them. People you pick should be accountable to you, qualified and serve as a support base. These new people must have an ideological outlook and set of values that will be the basis for consistent commitment to the Black community and your organization.

When the employer picks the employees, he is likely to pick people who have no history of struggle and think that they got the job because they were qualified. This type of person will usually be loyal to the one who butters his or her bread. Today most Blacks who hold jobs, or share other benefits resulting from our people's struggles, think that they got their jobs because they were qualified. Since, in most cases, we did not demand control over the selection process, and because our movements failed to continue, we have to assume the major responsibility for the "I made it because I'm qualified" syndrome.

Another type of boycott is the educational boycott. Educational boycotts are used to change public educational policies. Parents disatisfied with the quality of education, racist teachers, poor facilities, etc., have used boycotts to bring about improvement in the public schools. Boycotts are feared by educational officials because they are effective, they shut off government monies that are provided when students attend school. When students stay out of school on massive levels they knock a big hole in the educational funds.

An example of an effective school boycott, and a creative program of educational reform is provided by the Portland Black community under the leadership of Ron Herndon then chair of the Portland Black United Front. They began to meet with Black community groups to discuss the need for educational reform. Black churches, the NAACP, sororities, fraternities, and labor groups were supportive of a program to improve education for Black students.

A program was developed that included demands for an end to arbitrary busing and the hiring of more Black teachers and principals. Other demands included an end to the policy of suspending Black students, and most importantly, the demand that the curriculum be rewritten by African-American experts selected by the Black community, to accurately reflect African and African-American history and culture, along with an Afro-centric approach to teaching literature, music, science and mathematics.

During the summer of 1979 Portland BUF threatened a school boycott if these demands were not met. Facing broad-based community support, the school board agreed to implement these demands, but then failed to carry out the decision.

An angry Black community responded to the boards hypocrisy by boycotting the schools on Malcolm X's birthday, May 19, 1980. The boycott was 85-90% effective. This strong unity forced the school board to cave in. Since 1980, the Portland Black United Front and a broad grouping of the Black community have been implementing different aspects of this program.

The Black community has moved this far because their leadership has paid special attention to the basics of organizing. The school boycott succeeded because of careful preparation. A lot of time was spent by BUF in individual meetings with community leaders where the state of public education in Portland was discussed and alternatives were put forward. This period of foundation building produced a lot of good ideas on how the school system could provide a relevant education for Black youth.

When the Portland Board of Education came face-to-face with the demands for educational change, the Black community was united behind the movement, and prepared to shut the schools down if their demands were not met. Since the boycott, a group of educational experts under the leadership of Dr. Asa Hilliard has been selected by the Black community, and has written a baseline curriculum. Parents' committees with official authority have been selected by the Black community to monitor the enforcement of the movement's demands.

So economic boycotts and educational boycotts are good ways to apply pressure to these institutions to change their racist economic and educational policies.

OUTDOOR RALLIES AND MARCHES

An excellent way to raise our people's consciousness is with outdoor rallies and marches because they give the community the chance to hear political ideas and take part in struggles that strike out at the common enemy. Outdoor rallies and marches can be called to highlight an international, national, or local issue.

Outdoor rallies should be planned well in advance, at a time of year when the weather is warm. Careful attention should be paid to the development of a program and to entertainment.

Pick a site that is large enough to handle the crowd that you anticipate. The rally site should be a convenient: close to major public transportation systems and familiar to the people.

Once your planning is complete, develop a program budget. Give yourself enough time to implement a fundraising program that will generate enough money to cover your rally expenses: it is a mistake to operate from hand-to-mouth. Low start-up funds mean that either you go without needed materials or you have to drain the financial resources of your membership. For events that are held on a regular basis, fundraising should start a year in advance, so that you have plenty of time to raise the money.

The type of turnout you expect will determine the type of sound system you will need. Get someone who knows sound equipment to shop for your equipment. When shopping for sound equipment select the most appropriate and economical equipment. Try to find a Black sound company to rent your equipment from.

If your organization plans to hold numerous outdoor rallies, then it is advisable to purchase sound equipment, either on your own, or with the assistance of other groups. When the equipment is not in use, you can rent it to other community groups.

Portable stages can be rented, or sometimes you can get them from the local art commission or other public bodies. If you are going to try to get a free stage, then allow yourself plenty of time to see if this approach is feasible. Always have a back-up for any free equipment; be prepared to rent the equipment if the free route fails.

The person you select for master of ceremonies for an outdoor rally should be a person, who is a good speaker and is able to improvise. No matter how well you plan your program there will always be some changes. To the audience, the changed program should appear natural and well planned. So the master of ceremonies has to be able to handle quick changes of program, shifting people from one time slot to another, based on who is available. If the speakers and entertainers are there early, the changes can be reduced or eliminated.

This should be done, but don't expect everyone to be there early or even on time.

The master of ceremonies needs a couple of stage coordinators who will serve as a back-up crew. The back-up crew rounds up those on the program who are away from the stage. The back up crew also makes last minute suggestions to the MC about program changes.

Outdoor rallies should be secured by a well-disciplined security force. If the rally is organized by a coalition, then the security force should be made up of a body that is representative of all the groups taking part in the event. If a single organization is putting on the event, then you can rely on your own members to handle security. If you don't have enough people, recruit some supporters to help out.

The security team should consist of disciplined, mature people, who are confident in their ability to handle emergency situations. The security people should be in good physical condition, and at least some should be trained in martial arts. If the security team is going to secure a large area, they will need walkie-talkies that have the power to project over long distances.

The area you are securing can be broken down into security zones, with a security team being assigned to each zone. A number of rehearsals should be held to review how security will handle different situations. Security people should be instructed to be polite to the participants of the rally. When a problem arises, try to solve it without resorting to force. Usually, the community will honor a polite request to stop gambling, etc. Where a person or group seems intent on disrupting the event, make a show of force, and escort them out of the rally.

There are two views on the visibility of security. Some think that security should be concealed; others think it should be identifiable. Actually, if you have troops, there are advantages to using both approaches. It is good to have an identifiable security force, who wear security tee-shirts, arm bands, etc., because a disciplined force that is visible has the psychological effect of assuring the community that the event is well organized; it also discourages foolishness. On the other hand, unidentified security can mingle more freely with the people, and get a better feel of what is going on. Unidentified security is ideal for protecting specific individuals, because it is harder for anyone who is planning trouble to identify their opposition.

Often, booths are rented to community organizations at outdoor rallies. Booths have their positive and negative aspects. On the positive side, they are an excellent source of funds, and since booth operators talk up the event, they are a source of free advertising. Booths help Black businesses make a profit, so they provide some important allies for your organization. On the negative side, outdoor rallies, which have a large number of booths, can take on a carnival atmosphere, with customers talking and taking more of an interest in the booths than in the program. Some booth operators have little political awareness, and are only at the event to make money.

You have to weigh the positives and negatives to determine how you want to handle the booth issue. If you choose to go ahead with booth rentals, then you will need to establish a booth committee that develops booth rental policies. When you are selling food and other items you will need a city permit. Get your permits early. A mailing should be sent to potential booth operators. Once your responses are received, call a meeting to discuss booth policies.

Establish a late fee for booth operators and enforce it for people who rent their booths late. This reduces the number of late rentals. It is in your interest to keep the number of late rentals to a minimum so you can cut down on last minute work that will detract from your supervision of the rented booths. The booth committee should supervise the booths to see that the operators are living up to the terms of the contract. Booth committee people can always expect that some people will use creative ways to get around the rules.

Outdoor rallies and the supervision of booths is another aspect used for mass mobilizing. The mobilizing techniques used for public meetings, boycotts, conferences and marches may be a part of a mass movement, or they may be separate efforts to raise the consciousness of the community; or they could be a part of a specific campaign. Either way, mobilizing prepares the groundwork for future organizing. The success of our mobilizing efforts depends upon creativity and attention to detail. Whether you are conducting a public meeting, march or boycott, you have to tend to the details of planning, organizing, publicity, and follow-up. Attention to the little things, will produce larger successes.

Ultimately, the local campaigns against racist educational systems, racist employers, etc., have to be hooked up so that we can begin to build a national movement that mobilizes our people for broad change. The rising tide of the mass movement will create the climate and atmosphere for a fired up Black community that will have the enthusiasm to organize solid grass-roots structures. For this era of struggle we must profit from the rich mobilizing experience that precedes us, locally, nationally, and internationally, so that we can raise our struggle to a higher, organized level, with layers and layers of leadership, and a flexible many-sided program of mass mobilization and organization.

When organizing a march, clearly spell out the purpose of the march. Marches that are part of an outdoor rally are usually educational, and are not organized to produce an immediate change in government or corporate policy. Since most marches are educational, even when they are part of a broader campaign, it is important that the march route have a relationship to the purpose of the march. If the march is organized to oppose U.S. policies toward South Africa, then an obvious route would be one that passes the federal government buildings or the South African consulate's office. If the march is organized to protest specific corporate practices, it often helps to have stops along the march route, so that speakers can address the marchers on the march's purpose. March stops should have a symbolic value just as the march routes do.

Once you have selected the march route, arrange a meeting with the police department to obtain a march permit. Give yourself enough time to go through the red tape. Marches that occur without a legal permit are running an unnecessary risk of police conflict a risk that march organizers have no right to expose the participants to. March permits guarantee that you will have a march route and give you the opportunity to have intersections blocked along the route.

If you plan to march on the sidewalk then no march permit is required; marches in the street do require a march permit. March organizers should plan for every conceivable possibility. While most marches remain peaceful, some are disrupted.

March monitors should be appointed to maintain discipline during the march. March monitors should be responsible for securing a particular section of the march, and they should be instructed on how to handle disrupters and other march problems. March monitors should have copies of the march permit, in case they are questioned by the police.

March slogans should be planned in advance. Good slogans fire up the marchers. A lack of slogans takes the spirit and the sense of purpose out of the march. For large marches, some of the march monitors should have bull horns to communicate with the marchers.

Street marches should be considerate of the public. An opening should be made for pedestrians. Encourage members of the community to join the march by passing leaflets as you march through the community. Marches will often attract the press, so march organizers should establish a system for answering the questions of the press. An effective method for handling the press is to appoint one person who will answer all press questions. This person should be well-briefed on the questions the press will probably ask, and they should rehearse their answers.

Marches should have high visibility for community people, and for those against whom the march is directed. Marches, like outdoor rallies, are a way of dramatizing an issue, and increasing the base of community support. Another effective, though little known, mass mobilizing method is the "shop-in."

THE SHOP-IN

The shop-in was a tactic I initiated in the San Francisco Bay Area in 1964, during a campaign against the Lucky supermarket chain. Lucky supermarket had fewer than 1% Black employees at this time; negotiations had produced no change in their hiring policies.

Almost all Lucky supermarkets were located in white communities, so the boycott was not an effective tactic. The shop-in was used to bring the business to a halt, by having demonstrators enter the store and fill up their shopping carts with groceries, only to end up paying for a piece of bubble gum or cheap candy. Shop-ins were carried out for a couple of weeks, and proved to be extremely effective. As previously noted supermarkets operate on a low profit margin, so that an interruption of business for any period of time is very damaging.

After a couple of weeks of shop-ins, Lucky's entered into an agreement with CORE. The agreement provided that for one year 100% of all Lucky's new employees would be Black. An article in the San Francisco Examiner dated February 29, 1964, summarized the achievement of the Lucky Store shop-in campaign:

> Representatives of Lucky Stores and the Congress of Racial Equality reached agreement yesterday on ending the bitter conflict over the hiring of (Black) clerks by the supermarket chain.
>
> All that remained to finally settle the dispute -- and end two weeks of CORE shop-ins and picketing -- was the expected ratification of the agreement today by members of CORE's nine Northern California chapters.
>
> Mayor Shelley called the agreement 'a most satisfactory conclusion' to an affair that began February 15, with CORE and the

San Francisco Baptist Minister's Union, denouncing Lucky for 'clear violation' of an agreement it had signed four months earlier with CORE to hire more (Blacks)...

Lucky officials said they doubted if they'd even try to ascertain what effect the demonstrations may have had on their business although it was substantial.

From CORE's point of view, the demonstrations and especially the shop-ins had been successful.54

The shop-in was successful because it stopped the flow of business and took management by surprise. Because the shop-in was a new tactic, management did not know how to respond to it. While they were scratching their heads, CORE was able to cut into their profit margins. The loss of profit that Lucky officials described as "substantial" forced them to reach agreements with the San Francisco chapter of CORE.

Picket lines should be maintained during the course of a shop-in, so that people are informed of the purpose of the demonstration. Shop-ins are not illegal since you are engaging in the act of buying. It is not your fault that you can't afford to pay for all of those groceries in your cart.

The value of the mass movement should not be underestimated. When a struggle reaches the stage where the people are demonstrating for jobs, better housing, a meaningful education or a change of foreign policy, they have the rulers on the defensive. The economic and political power structure is especially fearful that an awakened people will begin to question the legitimacy of the system itself.

Whatever response the system makes to the demand of the mass movement, the system faces the great likelihood that the people will begin to loose faith in the system. If the system chooses to repress the movement by killing its key leadership, imprisoning and exiling other leaders and militants, then the system exposes its repressive undemocratic face. On the other hand, if the rulers choose to make concessions to the mass movement then it runs the risk of being charged with pursuing a policy of tokenism. Reforms, by their nature, leave more problems unsolved then they answer. The Civil Rights bill and the Voting Rights bill were both reform measures carried out by the government to meet some of the Civil Rights Movement's demands. These reforms had the unintended effect of revealing their failure to provide jobs, adequate housing, adequate health care and real empowerment for the people they were supposed to benefit. In this way, reforms help to radicalize many movement activists. Of course reforms can also cut against the mass movement by co-opting sectors of the people who are pacified through jobs and other benefits.

So the mass movement poses difficult problems for those in power. For the serious organizer the mass movement is the second stage in the organizing process. The first stage has already been described, the stage of developing a core group and winning the support of the people. The stage of the mass movement is important because it allows the people to stand up and shake up employers, school boards, city governments, state governments, national governments, the military, the police, and other sources of power. Even more important, the mass movement provides a collective classroom where the people can discover who they are, and who their enemy is.

CHAPTER TEN

KNOW YOUR COMMUNITY: THE BLACK SOCIAL STRUCTURE

BROADENING YOUR ORGANIZATIONAL BASE:

KNOW YOUR COMMUNITY AND KNOW YOUR ENEMY

To be victorious in the Black liberation movement, it is absolutely necessary that we know ourselves and our enemy. A knowledge of ourselves allows us to shape a strategy of liberation that fits our people hands like a glove. A knowledge of our enemy allows us to tighten our fists into a powerful unified force that will knock over all obstacles in our way. The well fitting glove of liberation is our people's history and culture. A winning strategy of liberation must grow out of the history and culture of our people.

The liberation movements that have succeeded in destroying colonialism have understood the history and social structure of their people. The Guinea Bissau revolution based its strategy of liberation on a thorough knowledge of the history and social structure of Guinea Bissau. Their organizing approach was one of the most scientific if not *the* most scientific organizing method, used by any liberation movement in the twentieth century. This approach, which was based on a detailed knowledge of the people, enabled their party, the PAIGC (Party for the Independence of Guinea Bissau and the Cape Verde Islands), to lead their people to victory over Portuguese colonialism.

CABRAL'S SOCIAL STRUCTURE METHOD

Amilcar Cabral, leader of the revolution in Guinea Bissau, made a careful study of the social structure of his people, which he used to determine which groupings among his people would be supportive, neutral, or in opposition to the national liberation struggle. This knowledge was gained through living with the people, and carefully observing their social structure, cultural traditions, and their relationship to the colonial system.

Cabral's study revealed that a number of groupings were aligned with the Portuguese. These included the Fula chiefs, a section of the African elite, prostitutes, beggars, etc. African ethnic groups which were supportive of the liberation movement followed the traditional religious system did not have a structured leadership system, which could be controlled by the Portuguese. This also promoted equality between men and women, and shared the land communally. Youth, who had moved from the countryside to the cities and were living with their relatives, were aware of the oppression facing Africans in the cities and the conditions of life in the countryside. This group made up the core of the organized cadres of the PAIGC. A sector of the elite, sided with the national liberation movement, and along with the youth, who were literate, made up the leadership of the armed struggle. The dock workers became a highly conscious group, that carried out strikes, and were supportive of the armed struggle.

Cabral took a different view of the farmers (peasants) than had leaders of most revolutions in developing countries. Most revolutions in Asia, Africa and Latin America, identify the farmers as the leading revolutionary force. Cabral saw the farmers as the leading physical force, because they were the overwhelming majority; however, he did not see them as a revolutionary force. This was because the farmers were removed from the whites, and were unable to compare their condition with that of the Portuguese. It was difficult for them to understand that they were oppressed. The PAIGC worked hard to win the farmers over to the armed struggle.

It is interesting that the conscious groups that were easiest to win over to the armed struggle were the youth in the cities who had been exposed to racism through living near the European. Exposure to racism made them conscious of their enemy. This consciousness was the seed out of which sprang a consciousness of national liberation.

KNOW YOUR COMMUNITY'S HISTORY

Most of the history of local Black communities has not been put into writing; most of it is in the heads of our people. You have to go to the people in your community who know the community's history (or a part of it), and tape and write down what they have to say. People who are sources of community history are Black newspaper reporters especially older reporters who have stories on community history in their heads, and in their newspapers. Many Black businessmen and businesswomen have participated in or financed community struggles. Black activists come out of specific struggles, such as former Black Panthers, former members of the UNIA (Universal Negro Improvement Association), etc., and they can give you specific information on specific Black movements. Black ministers, who have been supportive of community struggles, can also give you a lot of information on the community's history. Black writers, who have researched community history or particular community struggles, are also an important source of information. Every community has brothers and sisters who are community historians. These brothers and sisters can give you details about political struggles, and family histories of key community people, along with their strengths and weaknesses. On most blocks, there are elders who have taken a personal interest in the lives of the people on the block. These elders make a good source of information on most of the block's members. They can tell you what particular people are like, what kind of children they were, and what kind of parents they are. The neighborhood historian is watching you, and he/she will be able to tell others what kind of person you are. These historians will be able to tell about the strengths and weaknesses of your group, so make sure that you have got yourself together.

Next to oral sources, which are the richest and most important because they come from observers and participants, are the written sources. Community history can be obtained from books and articles on community struggles, and from newspaper clippings. Newspaper articles written by the white press are the most unreliable sources, since they are usually written from the perspective of the oppressor. These sources should therefore be carefully checked against oral sources and reliable written sources.

Usually movement activists do not learn their community's history through the systematic process outlined above. Most often community history is learned through participation in community struggles. By taking part in community struggles, become acquainted with leading personalities and discover their strengths and weaknesses. While this is the usual approach for learning the community's history, we need to combine this approach with the systematic approach where we seek to know as much about our community as is humanely possible.

You need to study the community by doing active research, and by participating in community struggles, to find out what kind of "political traditions" the community has. If a community has a long tradition of fighting racism, then it will be easier to organize a base for future struggles. If it does not have a fighting tradition then you will have to create one.

BLACK ESTABLISHMENT

In researching the Black community it is important to understand how national Black institutions interact with each other and impact on political decisions in local Black communities.   This is important because power in America is rooted in institutions. Among the national Black organizations there exists a Black establishment. Lerone Bennett in his book *Black Mood*, describes the makeup of this Black establishment.

Bennett shows that the Black establishment is not made up exclusively of Blacks.   Rather, the Black establishment consists of an organized group of Blacks and whites who control national Black institutions. The members of the Black establishment hold the leadership positions in national organizations as executive directors, chairpersons of the board, organizational presidents, and members of the boards of directors. Until fairly recently, the presidents of the national protest and welfare organizations (NAACP and Urban League) have been white. Black bishops of major Black churches, ministers of the largest Black churches, owners of major Black newspapers and magazines, national Black educators, as well as business and professional people, constitute the representatives of the national Black establishment.[55]

The groups within the national Black establishment that have the greatest influence in shaping or approving national racial policies are the leaders of the national protest, improvement, and publishing groups.

There is an establishment within the Black establishment. This group makes up the core group of the Black establishment. The core consists of members who have served on establishment boards over a long period of time. They also accumulate power by holding office on numerous national executive boards. Long-serving board members provide consistency in Black establishment decisions.

Bennett correctly notes that the Black establishment has a shadow cabinet, that consists of the labor, liberal, and Zionist coalition. The United Auto Workers, along with other so-called liberal labor unions, the American Civil Liberties Union, the American Jewish Congress, the race relations departments of the YWCA, YMCA, the National Council of Churches and the American Friends Service Committee make up what Bennett describes as the shadow cabinet of the Black establishment.[56] Key foundations that have a history of financing Black organizations are also a part of this "shadow cabinet."

The "shadow cabinet" supplies the Black establishment with whites who participate on Black establishment boards in leading roles. This shadow cabinet trains Blacks to assume leading roles within the Black establishment. Generally, the shadow cabinet sets the limits for what is appropriate and inappropriate for the Black establishment to consider and act on. In many ways the "shadow cabinet" acts as the neocolonizer does in Africa. They train the elites and have them operate on remote control. The Black elites are so well trained that they know what to think before they are told what to think. The shadow cabinet, like its neocolonial counterparts, brings bankrolls to the table, and their money talks.

The central problem that the Black establishment poses for the community organizer is the establishment's relationship to the Black masses. The Black establishment occupies the position of a buffer between the Black masses and oppressive white establishment community. Black establishment members are removed from the Black masses. This Black elite never lives among the masses, nor does it have an understanding of the thinking of the masses. Even worse the members of this Black elite both fear and have contempt for its own people. The attitude of the Black establishment toward its people is simply a reflection of the values of the white oppressor.

The Black establishment's main role is to do what they can to maintain the status quo. Never, not once, has the Black establishment joined with the masses to organize them for social change. Whenever mass movements have risen from the grassroots, the Black establishment has done their best to beat them back. This was true in the twenties when the Black establishment aligned themselves with the government against the Garvey movement. In the sixties the Black establishment fought the new Civil Rights leadership organizations coming out of the South and the North. The Black establishment attacked Black power and Black studies. One leading Black establishment organization issued directives to its local affiliates instructing them not to give any assistance to Angela Davis.

Today the Black establishment is in a stronger position than it was during the sixties. Black establishment forces have expanded as a result of some of the reform strategies of the sixties. Voting right's legislation has increased the number of Black political representatives at the local, state, and national level. Clearly, the Congressional Black Caucus represents a new addition to the Black establishment.

While the Black establishment has aligned with certain powerful arms of the American Institutional power, it has benefited from the repression carried out against the nationalists and the progressive leadership of the sixties. The removal of Adam Clayton Powell, the assassination of Malcolm X and Martin Luther King, the destruction of the Black Panther Party, along with the splitting of the Nation of Islam, all contributed to a weakening of the nationalists and progressive forces which could only strengthen by default the moderate Black establishment forces. The nationalist forces were further weakened by the ideological splits that occurred within the African Liberation Support Committee and the Congress of African People. At bottom Marxism versus nationalist ideological battles reflected an uncertainty over the programmatic direction that the Black liberation movement should take. Nationalists in the sixties and seventies failed to develop a mass based program (with the exception of the Nation of Islam) that would organize the grass roots for social change. The ideological shootouts reflected the underlying frustrations felt by leadership that could rally people to support African liberation struggles, but could not provide programmatic direction for Black people in the United States.

Today the moderate Black establishment forces dominate the national political scene with well financed organizations and the only visible national organizational presence. Because the nationalists are in disarray the national Black establishment does not feel the heat from the grassroots.

The only political motion coming from the Black establishment, arises from the new establishment forces represented by Jesse Jackson, Trans-Africa, and a few Black politicians who have been able to gain mass support in their struggle to wrest power from white political machines.

The moderate Black establishment continues to issue press releases that condemn Reagan's indifference to the poor and his support for the racist attacks against Blacks and people of color. As in the past the Black establishment has no interest in organizing the grass roots for social change.

As organizers, it is important that we understand how this group operates. Locally, many of the chapters of the establishment organizations play much the same role that their national organizations play. However, in some cases, local affiliates of the Black establishment may be maverick chapters that are willing to support serious grassroots campaigns. An arm of the national Black establishment may be based in some local Black communities. In San Francisco, for example, the Sun Reporter and Metro newspapers, owned by Dr. Carlton Goodlett, play an important role in the life of the Bay Area Black community. Goodlett is one of the Black publishers who is a leader in the national Black establishment. Goodlett is also one of the most radical members of the Black establishment. He has consistently supported progressive community struggles, and has been critical of governmental policies that operate against the interest of the grassroots. Goodlett and other progressives within the Black establishment are allies of the Black liberation movement. As organizers, we should develop working relationships with radical and progressive forces such as these. They can provide valuable assistance in any serious organizing campaign.

For the community organizer the best way to deal with the moderate Black establishment is to develop solid grassroots programs that deal with the peoples basic needs. Our task is to build organizations that serve the needs of the people. To do that we have to take up the basic issues of economic development, education, housing, the Black family, drugs, and crime. These campaigns have to be tied to a cultural program that develops a sense of peoplehood. We have to popularize the idea that "we are an African people." We have to develop bonds of respect and love among our people.

Nationally, we have to work to build a national organizational presence, so we can organize the grassroots around a national agenda. The revolutionary nationalist will only remove the moderate establishment forces when we put forward a program of action that organizes the grassroots for social change and cultural transformation. As we shape such a program we also need to establish selective relationships with the progressive members of the Black establishment. Those members of the Black establishment who support an agenda for social change are isolated from their moderate establishment members. Many of the progressives find themselves periodically under government attack. Most of them lack a well-organized grassroots constituency. They need the support of Black nationalists with this constituency. Black nationalists need the legitimacy that the progressives bring to the political arena. A Ron Dellums brings a level of legitimacy and prestige to our organizations.

The Black establishment nationally and locally draws its recruits from skilled Blacks or members of the Black middle class. It is important that as organizers we understand the makeup and potential of this group.

THE BLACK MIDDLE CLASS

E. Franklin Frazier, in his classic, the *Black Bourgeoisie*, documented the rise of the Black middle class. According to Frazier the economic basis of the Black Bourgeoisie was derived from "the services which they rendered as white collar workers."[57] If we accept this definition of what it means to be a member of the Black middle class then bank tellers, cashiers, secretaries, stenographers, telephone operators, mail carriers, bus drivers, and a host of other service workers would be defined as middle class. While people who work in these areas do not do manual labor, and a few are better paid than some Black professionals, and some may have middle class values, these are not middle class occupations. Whether they are white collar or blue collar occupations, which are in some cases nonunionized, they are still working class jobs that generate prestige in the Black community because of their incomes, job title and, security.

The Black middle class consists of professional Blacks who are schoolteachers, ministers, doctors, dentists, lawyers, college professors, entertainers, embalmers, funeral directors, social workers, nurses, politicians, and architects, engineers, chemists, and business persons.

DuBois' observations about the motivation of this group still remain valid. According to DuBois, Black professionals have the "American ambition to become rich and independent, and to live on income rather than labor."[58] In spite of their bourgeoisie ambitions most middle class Blacks do not command capital, work for whites for a living, and put their income into consumer spending. More important, the Black bourgeoisie is not the primary investor in Black labor; therefore, the Black middle class exploits Black labor very little.

Still, there is a great gulf between poor Blacks and the large majority of the Black middle class. The institutions run by the Black middle class, the protest organization, the Black church and Black improvement organizations have turned their backs on the masses of Black people. Many of these organizations do not provide jobs for the masses, very few provide housing, and most religious institutions don't even offer a relevant theology to the people who make up their membership.

As a result, there is a strong feeling of bitterness felt by poor Blacks towards the more successful Black professionals. This attitude of bitterness expressed towards successful Blacks, is partially based on the contempt that too many Black professionals feel towards their own people. Elite contempt is expressed in many ways including the flight of professional Blacks away from the Black community into the "sugar hills" of America; the attempt made by professional Blacks to "mainstream" and become a part of white society; and Black yuppism, which imitates the make believe lifestyles of the white middle class. At bottom, the disease of the Black middle class is the disease of self-hatred. More than any other segment of the African-American social structure, the majority of the Black middle class hates itself. Carter G. Woodson has defined the cause of self-hatred among the Black middle class as arising from an educational system that has programmed them to worship Europe and to hate Africa. This cultural alienation accounts for the lack of creativity that exists among a majority of this group.

All of this creates severe problems for Blacks as a whole because we need to harness the skills and financial resources of a part of the Black middle class if we are going to achieve liberation in America. The technical skills that this group possess are the most important skills owned by any African people in the world. As organizers, we have to figure out how to tap some of these resources for our peoples' benefit.

Politically, the Black middle class on the local level can be divided into a number of different groups, with varying potential for making a contribution to the Black movement. The Black middle class consists of moderates, progressives, radicals, nationalists, conservatives those who are social in their orientation, and those who are simply concerned about making a living, acquiring money, and if they can, property.

The thing that the Black middle class needs more than anything else is a sense of peoplehood.[59] The sense of self-hatred, which is masked in attitudes of arrogance and contempt for Black people, reflects this group's hatred for itself. As organizers, we have to employ creative strategies to attempt to create a sense of peoplehood and pride among this group. Partially, this can be done through encouraging the middle class nationalists to inject nationalism into various middle class organizations. Black teachers need to be taught African history and culture so they can impart an African-centric perspective to their students. Nationalist ministers need to sharpen the debate around creating an African theology rooted in an updated African religion. Black nationalist organizers need to create political organizations that place power in the hands of poor Blacks and professionals who, working in concert, can use their skills to strengthen the organization. Overall, the central focal point of our organizing must be centered on returning our people as a whole to their historical roots, past and present.

As we develop organizing programs, whether they are providing jobs, housing, education, or political representation, we need to focus on how the different sectors can be organized to support the program. Moderate civil rights organizations on the local level can often be persuaded to endorse a struggle for quality education, jobs, or better housing. All these groups may do is endorse a struggle, but the importance of their endorsement should not be underestimated. If your organization is preparing to boycott the schools, or business, the support of these groups may make the difference between success or failure. The key thing about the moderates is that if we can't get their support, then we should work hard to keep them neutral. Neutrality is always better than open opposition.

Black progressives are those professional Blacks who have a record of fighting for or supporting struggles for better housing, more jobs and a quality education, etc. The progressive does not put forward a program for overturning the system, but the progressive does want to see significant changes in the living conditions of the people. As organizers we should be able to work with progressives around the particular issues we are organizing, or we should support the progressive issues they put forward. The thing about the progressives is that they represent a minority within the Black middle class, yet their consistency and courage in pushing for social change often gives them influence that exceeds their numbers.

Radical members of the Black middle class are in a distinct minority. They are advocates of profound social transformation. Some Black radicals are tied to rigid ideological positions others are not. The organizer should try to gain agreement from individuals in this category to support specific issues and programs that will contribute to social change.

The nationalists grouping has many shades of thought. Some are more cultural, others are more religious, still some are more interested in economics or political action. At this time the nationalist is not a significant political force in most local Black communities, and nationalists are virtually invisible on the national level. As much as possible, we have to selectively work with those nationalists who are willing to support organizing efforts for social change. Some may participate directly in our organizations, others will be willing to provide specialized support as advisors, etc. Some of the creative intellectuals within this group can be asked to shape curriculums for our schools, provide ideas for economic development, along with strategies for strengthening the Black family, and a variety of other ideas. Committed activists from this group will provide many of the forces that will make up the core group of community organizations.

Many Black professionals and Blacks who aspire to be in the "social" middle class, are Blacks whose primary orientation is social. This group of Blacks often has little concern for political issues, instead they occupy their time organizing parties, fashion shows, and other types of social events. Often Black women dominate this area of Black life; however, some social clubs are run by Black men. It is very easy to dismiss these groups as escapist, and turn your backs on them. If you take this course then you will be turning your backs on some very important financial and political support. Black social groups provide a social outlet for the Black community. They are also excellent fundraisers. Social groups can be persuaded to contribute financially to a struggle for better education, more jobs, or better housing. Social clubs can also provide significant political support for organizing campaigns. Many of the sisters who play leading roles in Black social clubs are also leaders in the Black church. They can demand that their church support your organizing efforts.

The Black conservatives are a sad lot who have sold their skills to the highest bidder. Its important to read their writings and speeches, and keep track of their activity. There are some Black conservatives who are willing to provide financial support to your organizations.

The largest group within the Black middle class are those who work for a living, and are interested in acquiring wealth and property. Since this group represents the majority of the Black middle class, they are the primary beneficiaries of the Black movement. Rarely will you find members of this group taking political positions. Their political views, when they have any, are usually expressed behind closed doors. The majority of the Black professionals work for whites for a living and do not want to rock the boat. Some within this group can be moved by self-interest. They may support a struggle when their job is at stake. Others may be willing to quietly support the struggle with information, money, or some other valuable resource. As organizers, we need to draw whatever we can from this group, recognizing that their comfort and values make them extremely reluctant to commit themselves to a serious struggle.

In spite of the arrogance, self-hatred, and isolation from the Black masses experienced by many Black professionals, some are very conscious, committed, and creative. The organizer must realize that we need the technical skills possessed by this group. To win the loyalty of a sufficient number of members of the Black middle class we will have to create a sense of "peoplehood" to return then to their historical roots. At the same time, we must learn a fundamental law of Black political struggle that teaches us to rest our organizations on the majority of our people who work for a living, or are struggling to find work.

BLACK WORKERS

Whether Blacks are working in old line automobile production, in service jobs for Coca- Cola or Macy's as salespersons, delivery people, postal workers, on the waterfront as longshoremen, or at construction sites as carpenters or plumbers, by the nature of their work, they make up a part of Blacks who are members of the Black working class.

It is from this group of Blacks that the rich culture of African-America arose. The Blues, Gospels, Spirituals, Rhythm and Blues, and so-called "Jazz" (Black classical music) were creations of the masses of Blacks who worked from "can see to can't see." This rich culture represented a fusion of African and American elements. Grassroots Blacks held onto a "folk" cultural legacy that was passed on through word of mouth and through song. The African-American singer passed his history, his story through song and feeling.

The sharing patterns, the participation in community decision making, the respect for elders, and the strong sense of spirituality all characterized this strong new African culture that arose from the "Souls of Black Folks," and gave us the inspiration to survive and create.

The agrarian movements of the 19th century, the Garvey movement of the 1920s, the Civil Rights movement, the Black Power movement, the Nation of Islam, and the Black Panther Party were all Black people's movements that were rooted in farmers, the Black working class, and the Black poor. It is because the largest sector of our people decided to back these movements that they gained a mass character and posed a political threat to the established system. No organization among Black people can claim to wield real power if it does not have the support of the Black working class.

As organizers it is crucial that you know the makeup, strengths, and weaknesses of this group so that you can base your organizations on this important foundation. If you fail to root your organization in the Black majority, then ultimately you will become a middle class organization, isolated from your people and probably elitist in attitudes and directions. This is, in fact, a danger that faces too many of our progressive and radical Black organizations that are composed primarily of college-educated Blacks, who have few non-college educated members. Many of these organizations develop programs that serve the ideological taste of their small membership and remain isolated from the majority of Black people.

In understanding the makeup of the Black working class it is important to understand their relationship to the white working class. As DuBois noted, in theory, Black workers are part of the larger working class. Black workers, for example, work alongside white workers sharing the same work place. Still, as DuBois observed, Black workers are not part of the *white* working class. Black workers are not only oppressed by the rulers who are white, but Black workers are oppressed by white workers who hold higher paying, more technically advanced jobs, who have a low unemployment rate because Black workers carry the burden of high unemployment; and Black workers are oppressed by whites who deny them membership in trade unions, while white workers deny Blacks housing and attack Blacks through right wing organizations and right wing politicians.

The reality of slavery and racism has created a caste aspect of the Black/white relationship, whether we are talking about the Black elite, the Black worker, or the Black poor.   In America, color privilege has created the idea that whites should lead and Blacks should follow. Under caste rules the lowest white person has a license to kill or insult Blacks no matter what social category Blacks may come from.   Caste privilege allows a white high school graduate to earn more money than a Black college graduate.

Slavery created the material basis for the economic prosperity of white workers. The tremendous profits gained from slavery not only went into the pockets of businessmen and slave masters, but it provided much of the capital used to launch America and Europe's industrial takeoff. The cotton economy of the South provided the raw material for the textile industry of the North.   Similarily, a large part of northern shipping was engaged in the slave trade. The white worker's standard of living was directly related to the super profits gained from free slave labor that provided part of the capital that paid the white worker's salary.

Today, the white worker is cushioned against hard times by the Black worker; Whites have been able to largely avoid poverty by shifting it onto the backs of Blacks and Hispanics. According to 1978 federal government statistics, 31 per cent of all Blacks in the U.S. are poor, with 22 per cent of Hispanics living in poverty, while only 9 per cent of all whites are poor. Clearly, skin privileges keep most whites out of the category of the poor.

So while Black workers may work alongside whites, Blacks find themselves in a bottom position on the job, in the housing market, on the ladder of poverty, and in the political system in general where they are politically under-represented.

Today, the Black workers position is weakened by structural changes in the economy. As usual racism works to make the Black worker most exposed to the technological changes occurring in the economy. The June 1, 1981, issue of Business Week discussed some very important developments in the American economy. According to this source, the American economy operates on five legs that do not walk together. Growth can occur in one part of the economy, while contraction and even transformation can take place in another part of the economy. This largely accounts for what this edition describes as an economy, which since 1977 "has been far stronger than anyone expected, it has refused to go into recession when predicted, it has been more inflationary than forecast, and has created more new jobs than imagined."[60] The five legged economy means that prosperity could occur in one part of the economy while people are living under depression conditions in one or a number of other sectors of the economy.

The five legs of the American economy are: (1) the old manufacturing industries, which "include automobiles, steel, textiles, appliances, construction, electrical and non-electrical machinery, food and tobacco manufacturers; (2) agriculture, e.g., livestock, vegetables, food grains, forestry, fishery products, cotton and poultry; (3) energy, e.g., coal, oil, natural gas, and utilities; (4) high technology, e.g., semiconductor and computer technology, office machines, aircraft, dental and optical supplies, surgical supplies, radio and television equipment; and (5) services, e.g., finances, personnel, consulting, information processing, education, health care, hotels and apartments, real estate, media, insurance, and other social services."[61]

According to the Business Week article a number of sectors of the American economy are expected to grow over the long term while other parts of the economy will undergo severe cutbacks and transformation. The areas of the economy that Business Week says will do well are energy, high technology, a large part of the services, and agra-businesses and all areas in which Blacks are poorly represented.

Black workers are concentrated in the parts of the economy that are going through crisis, decline, and structural transformation. Black workers are heavily concentrated in the old manufacturing industries; auto and steel where tremendous cutbacks on the workforce have occurred. While Blacks are represented in the government sector (service) this is an area of the economy that faces severe cutbacks. Clearly, Black workers are in the areas of the economy that have been hardest hit by plant closings, the shift of plants abroad and the introduction of computerized technology into the work place. The prospects for the Black worker are dim and are likely to get worse, unless as organizers, we are able to set an agenda that calls for fundamental changes in the economy as a whole.

What makes this situation so serious, is the fact that racism, combined with the five tiered economy, has produced a growing number of permanently unemployed Blacks whose percentage has grown from 8.1% in 1965 to approximately 25-30% in 1987.

Faced with this bleak outlook, what alternatives can the organizer present to the people. First, as stated in the beginning of this book, we need to create a sense of "peoplehood" among our people. We have to see that as African people we stand together or we fall together. Although some members of the Black middle class may think that the fate of the Black working class and the Black poor is not their fate, in truth the Black elite is only a paycheck away from the unemployment lines. More important, the Black elite cannot pass on a secure economic condition to their children who may well make up the ranks of the unemployed.

As a nation of people we must develop a dual approach to the economic question. On the one hand, we need to build up a strong Black economy that will provide jobs for our people. The chapter on economic development puts forward proposals in this area. We have to design a program that operates on a number of fronts. Generally, the problems faced by the American economy have a global dimension. Manufacturing plants that move overseas to take advantage of cheap labor deny jobs to workers in the United States. The labor movement has been unable to fight this move because their leaders have worked in league with big business to rip-off people of color in the U.S. and abroad. Also, the labor movement operates on a national basis while capital operates on a transitional basis.

For labor, especially Black labor, the job crisis will not simply be solved on the national level.   Black labor, and Black people in general, have to develop an international strategy designed to fight big business in the arena of real power, the global level. Organizers have to develop imaginative plansthat will tie Black political support for African and Third world countries to the questions of runaway shops. One demand that we need to put forward is the call for runaway shops to provide higher wages for Third world workers.

On the domestic front, we need to do a number of things. The skill level of many Black workers needs to be upgraded to service the growth areas in the economy. For young Blacks there will have to be structural transformation in the educational system that provides an African-centric history and culture along with an African-centric approach to teaching reading, math, and science. Our youth need to be prepared to manage a nation. They will need a sense of "African" consciousness if they are going to have the desire to prepare for the 21st century.

Politically, we need to raise the question of a guaranteed liveable income for millions of people who cannot work. Here we are not talking about welfare; we are talking about an income that will allow people to live with dignity and self respect. Certainly if corporations can live lavishly off government funds, then the poor have the right to share in the nations wealth. We also need to push for a guaranteed job for all adults who are able to work.

Beyond this, there is a more serious question of a different kind of structural transformation of the economy. Ideally, we need to fashion an agenda that calls for the collective ownership of the wealth of this country, so that wealth can be used for public rather than private benefit. Unfortunately, racism makes this a particularly difficult if not impossible objective to achieve; for as long as white workers have a racist Euro-centric worldview, they will seek to keep Blacks on the bottom of even a publicly-owned economy.

Whether the mentality of whites change or not, the organizer must push for self-help organizing strategies for the internal Black economy, while at the same time organize a broader social agenda that calls for change in the larger economy and political system. In doing this, the organizer needs to understand the institutional structure of the Black and white community.

THE SOCIAL STRUCTURE OF THE BLACK COMMUNITY

Active organizing and careful research will help you determine which forces have been actively supportive of community struggles, in opposition, or neutral. You also want to know the relationship between Black community leaders and the downtown economic and political power structure. All of this information is part of knowing the social class and political structure of your community. This knowledge is extremely important because it tells you where your potential support and potential opposition lies. For example, if you determine that certain social clubs in the Black community have not taken political stands, but have provided financial support to a number of political struggles, then you know not to attack them because they have not been politically active, instead you should try to gain financial support from them. If, on the other hand, you find that a particular community leader has taken a number of progressive stands on community issues, but has occasionally made political deals with the white political structure, you will be mindful of the limits of the person's political support.

THE BLACK PRESS

One of the things you are trying to do is to make a power analysis of your community. You want to know what newspapers have influence in the Black community. What kind of news do they push? What is their philosophical orientation? Generally, most Black community newspapers are owned by professional Blacks, but others are conservative. How much support can you get from your local community press? Since personal relationships usually override political philosophy, you often get more out of a

Black newspaper if you have established a good personal relationship with its editor and publisher.

THE BLACK CHURCH

In analyzing your local community you want to determine which are the most influential Black churches. What kind of stands have they taken on particular political issues? If they have taken some progressive stands, why? Are there key individuals in that church which influence the minister to take particular progressive stands? If so, you will need to establish a relationship with those individuals and the minister.

The Black church is the strongest organizational arm in the Black community, yet most Black churches are involved in praying and begging. Most are Not politically active in community struggles. Your job is to identify the few that are, and form ties with them It is a serious mistake for a Black political organization to isolate itself from the Black church community. Similarily ties should be maintained with the ministerial organizations: Baptist minister unions, Methodist ministerial alliances, interdominational alliances, and other denominations. The nature of the ties you will be able to form will depend upon your knowledge of the Black church community, your personal relationships in that community, and your personal creativity.

BLACK WOMEN

Black women are the most active organizational force in the Black community. The majority of the members of the Black church are made up of Black women. Increasingly, Black women's political groups are having a strong impact on the Black community. You should check out the Black women's organizations in your community to see what kinds of stands they take on community issues, and to better understand their strength in the Black community. The ties you form with these groups will be determined by your personal relationships with them, and your ability to define some common areas for work.

COMMUNITY ORGANIZATIONS

A very important part of the social structure of every Black community is formed by the local community organizations. Community organizations vary from drug counseling centers, youth organizations, educational institutions, service agencies, Black nationalist groups, Black marxist groups, Black historical societies, welfare rights groups, social clubs, block organizations, and many others. The Black community has a lot of organizations. Your job is to develop relationships with these different groups and to find ways that you can be mutually supportive. Again, effectiveness in this area depends upon your personal creativity. One way you can develop positive ties with other community organizations is to agree to promote each other's functions, and not to hold conflicting events. Another way is by publicizing certain groups in your organization's newspaper or newsletter. the support relationships you can develop are endless; you just have to use your creativity to develop them.

OPPOSITION LEADERSHIP

In every community there will be those forces that will oppose your efforts. Some for personal reasons, others out of loyalty to the enemy, still some because they see your group as a threat to their leadership. This Black leadership, often with the aid of the white power structure, will attempt to discredit you and steal your thunder. When they can, they will try to create diversions to take the communities attention away from noncompromising struggle. If they can, they will infiltrate your movement, serving as a fifth column, pretending to be your friends, while they are working to divert and dismantle the movement. Sometimes they will capture the leadership of progressive organizations just to guarantee that they do nothing.

The mission of this group is to see that nothing happens on the grass roots front. It is a serious, serious mistake to underestimate this group.   Often they will come as individuals, offering help, creating diversions, or smearing your movement and its leadership. It is a natural tendency for you to think that you are dealing with weak, isolated individuals.   Usually you are dealing with people who have exercised leadership in the Black community, and have strong ties with the white power structure. In some cases the white power structure has sent them into your group to capture it or divert it. In other cases they are acting on their own to remove competing leadership, and/or to impress downtown with their responsible behavior so that they can be appointed to a judgship or to a political position.

FRESNO MODEL

If the community in which such disruption has occurred is extremely conservative, and these destructive tactics have been successful then you will have to be very careful in how you go about organizing a base.   A case in point is the Fresno Black community.   This is a Black community that exists in the heart of the agro-business organization, yet Blacks today live in the city of Fresno and do not work in agriculture or in the canning business.   Most Blacks work for the city, state or federal government, or they are on relief. A Black elite exists in Fresno that grew out of a group of Blacks who supervised the work of Black agricultural workers for white land owners. This group of Blacks was able to buy a little land ans send their children to college. Until recently, they have controlled the leadership positions in the Black community. They headed up the poverty program and infiltrated and destroyed the only successful grass roots movement in Fresno. More recently they have been challenged by a new group of professional Blacks who are more progressive and include Pan African Nationalists.

The nationalists were aware of the history of Fresno's Black community, and they knew that this elite group had the capacity to knock off progressive Black groups. The strategy that nationalists in Fresno used was to forge relationships with key leaders in the Black community. After creating these relationships, they joined most of the Black community and political groups, and took the leadership of some key community institutions (including a community center where one of the Pan African leaders, Kehinde, chairs the board of directors and supervises the work of the director, who is the chairman of the local NAACP chapter). In addition, the nationalist organization writes a newspaper column for the local Black newspaper, and places its editor on the city council, on a Pan African Nationalist platform.

This is an example of some sophisticated organizing, where Pan Africanists have turned the tables on some establishment Negroes, who had successfully prevented other progressive Black organizations from getting off the ground. Their technique was to entrench themselves into the strategic institutions in the Black community, where they have been able to wield power over establishment employment and influence community attitudes through utilizing the Black media. Also, they have become a basic part of community life by joining and aligning with the community organizations. This strategy makes it difficult for the elite group to disrupt the Pan African Secretariat chapter, because it is a vital part of the total community.

Of course, each community is different, so you will have to develop a strategy that suits your community. In situations where Black people are dispersed into a number of communities in the same city, you should pick a specific community in which to locate your organization. Where possible, pick a Black community that has a tradition of political struggle, rather than one that does not have such a tradition. For example, in San Francisco, Black people live in a number of Black communities, including Bay View Hunter's Point, Lakeview, Portrero Hill, and the Fillmore. Of all of these communities the Fillmore has been the center of political struggle and political consciousness. In the forties, it was the center of "Don't buy where you can't work" campaigns. In the sixties, the major civil rights organizations (CORE and NAACP) were based there, along with the Nation of Islam. Today, redevelopment has destroyed most Black businesses in the

Fillmore, and the Black removal campaign has destroyed much of the moderate income housing, replacing it with expensive condos. Still, the bulk of the nationalist and progressive groups are based in the Fillmore, including Marcus' Bookstore, the Pan African Peoples Organization, the NAACP, three extremely progressive Black churches, Third Baptist Church, New Liberation Church, and Bethel AME Church. In addition, the Fillmore serves as the base of operations for the *Sun Reporter* Newspaper, the speaker of the state Assembly, Willie Brown, and the Wajumbe Dance Troupe, along with a number of other progressive Black organizations. These organizations provide a base of support for progressive Black political activity. Their work has generated a consciousness which Black political organizations can draw from in their organizing work.

A good organizer knows that knowledge of the Black community cannot be separated from a knowledge of the enemy. You have to possess a thorough knowledge of the white power structure that oppresses your community and uses its resources to make your organizing activities ineffective.

KNOW THE ENEMY:
RESEARCHING THE ENEMY
THE WHITE POWER STRUCTURE

A knowledge of the white power structure is gained through study and political struggle. The very concept of "power structure" became popular when Black people took to the streets in the 50's and 60's and began to identify a group of white people who controlled economic, political, and military power. As we began to identify members of the "white power structure," many of its members tried to hide behind the smokescreen that the white power structure didn't exist. Political leaders, who were forced to convene meetings of economic and political leaders to redress Black grievances, often did so saying that these leaders did not represent a power structure.

Why did the members of the white power structure deny their own existence? Ralph Ellison provides an insight into this interesting question in his book, *Shadow and Act.* He says that part of the hypocritical tradition of America is expressed through the "rich man pretending to be poor," and the "wise man pretending to be dumb." Powerful people have tried to hide their power and wealth behind silence, mystery, and a smokescreen of being common folks. This pretense of poverty has been designed to free the power structure of charges of living in luxury created by the labor of the masses. The power elite has done its best to avoid charges of being the "new robber barons," and the manipulators of those exercising political power. Also, America's democratic pretense has made it necessary for the

American power structure to take on a democratic worker's pretense. This is expressed by American skyscrapers that are plain and free of the artistic adornment of Victorian aristocratic architecture. Similarily, the big estates and the luxurious consumption of the elite are hidden from the public view.

Hidden though this elite may be, it exists, and its decisions affect the amount of taxes you pay, whether your community is a target for urban (Black) renewal (removal), whether you face the draft and war, and whether you are in or out of work. Knowing this power structure is an organizer's responsibility. The usual way you find out about the white power structure is through political contest or political struggle. Through demonstrations, boycotts, political campaigns, struggles for control of schools, efforts to end the drug traffic in the Black community, and working with established community leaders, you discover the nature, strengths, and weaknesses of this power group. Struggles against a single department store for more jobs, may suddenly expose an association of department stores, which shapes a unified policy.

As you begin to negotiate, and later struggle against this kind of corporate association, you may find the mayor or other public officials trying to mediate the dispute. The struggle then teaches you that the corporation has influence over key local politicians.

Similarly, if you take on a statewide, or national economic institution, you may find that this national institution influences newspaper and television editorial policy, and can even move a governor to act against you. This kind of activity shows you how major economic institutions influence the state and national political institutions. An example of the pervasive power of economic institutions is shown by a 1964 secret meeting of top state and local officials, who were meeting to devise ways to stop the San Francisco Civil Rights movement.

Governor Edmund G. Brown served notice last night that State Officials "cannot and will not tolerate any further disruptive mass demonstrations such as that held last week at the Sheraton Palace Hotel. In the event of any future violations there will be prosecutions," the Governor said. "There is no doubt about that."

The statement was made after the Governor emerged from a closely guarded summit meeting on civil rights demonstrations at City Hall with Mayor John F. Shelley and other top state and city officials.

Plain clothesmen patrolled the corridors to Shelley's office as

Attorney General Stanley Mosk, Police Chief Thomas Cahill, District Attorney Thomas Lynch, U.S. Attorney Cecil Poole and San Francisco Police Commission Members slipped into the inner chambers for the Meeting.

The summit meeting was convened shortly after a delegation of leading downtown business executives closeted themselves with the Mayor for almost an hour on the demonstration picture here. The group led by Human Rights Director, James P. Mitchell, was tight-lipped as it filed out of Shelly's office.

Almost immediately police closed in on the Mayor's chambers and in an unprecedented move hustled City Hall reporters into the outside corridor.

Governor Brown's appearance was wholly unannounced. He first lightly dismissed his presence as being occasioned by his traditional St. Patrick's Day golf date here tomorrow, then acknowledged that he was to discuss the growing racial tensions with Shelly. Others in the late hour meeting included City Attorney Thomas O'Connor and Edward Howden, head of the Sate Fair Employment Practices Commission. Earlier in the day Negro leaders announced that more mass demonstrations could be expected in San Francisco, starting with renewed picketing at the Cadillac motor cars showrooms on Van Ness Avenue. The San Francisco chapter of the NAACP, bolstered by sympathizers from other civil rights groups, has been picketing the Cadillac agency since Monday. The NAACP accuses the agency of refusing to hire Negroes except for menial jobs....

On other fronts it was a day of conferences and public appearances devoted to the picketing question....

Chairman Bill Bradley (the author of this book) of the Congress of Racial Equality said the Bank of America spoke too soon in announcing its refusal to "capitulate to illegal pressures" -- mostly because CORE has not planned as yet to picket the world's largest bank chain. The chairman of CORE said it has entered 357 employment agreements without demonstrations. A conference with Bank of America officials is scheduled at 5 p.m. Monday, Bradley said, "and is still on as far as I know."

While Mayor John F. Shelley conferred in private with a group of business and industrial leaders in City Hall, his police chief, Thomas Cahill, declared he would enforce all injunctions and prevent disruption of business during future demonstrations. "Obstructionists will be removed," he said.[62]

Mass struggle is the best teacher; it teaches you who your enemies and friends are. At the time of the secret meeting described above I was chairman of the San Francisco Chapter of the Congress for Racial Equality. Along with the NAACP under the leadership of Dr. Burbride and the Ad Hoc Committee under the leadership of Tracey Simms, we unleashed a mass movement, involving thousands of people, on the economic power structure. Thousands of demonstrators marched on the Sheraton Palace Hotel, Auto Row, and the Bank of America.

As the momentum increased, leading members of the San Francisco financial community began to meet with the Mayor to lay out a strategy for breaking up the movement. The power of these financial figures was so great (especially the Bank of America, then the world's largest bank) that they were able to bring together the Governor, State Attorney-General, U.S. Attorney, and other leading law enforcement officials.

Mass struggle is a classroom that teaches how power is organized in this country and in the world. As you deal with different arms of this white power structure you may come to see that racism is an inseparable part of their operating policies. The power structure you are dealing with comes to be seen not only as an economic power structure, but as a racial power structure, which deals with Blacks as "those people," who are threatening their (white's) orderly "civilized world."

At the same time conflicts with the economic power structure may bring you into contact with mayors and governors, city and state politicians, who reveal the corrupt, slick, racist nature of the American political system. Political struggle is worth more than all of the textbooks on political science, because political struggle tells it like it really is. Through taking political actions, you discover the nature of your enemy. You begin to identify his vital points, and you learn the importance of refining your organizing approaches so that you attack his weaknesses while avoiding the strengths.

POWER STRUCTURE RESEARCH

So if you want to know your enemy locally and nationally, then get involved in mass political struggle. At the same time that your eyes begin to open up, you will begin to ask many questions, such as who are the major employers in the city I live in? What are their assets and liabilities? How does the economic power structure hook-up locally, state-wide, and nationally? What influence do various businesses have over the local, state-wide, or national political system? Where are Black people concentrated in the local economy? What relationships exist between the economic power structure and local Black community leaders? What's the business community's input into the redevelopment agency's policy? What kind of plan does downtown have for your Black community? What kind of support do they have for that plan within the Black community?

An important area of power structure research is the growing national rivalry between old northeastern wealth and new southwestern wealth. It is important to determine how this struggle affects the presidency, foreign policy, military, and economic policies. As an organizer you want to ask, what forces Bush, Reagan, Carter, or their successors represent? How do their economic priorities affect the position of Blacks on welfare, in public education, federal employment, and in industry?

Alongside this question of new wealth versus old wealth, is the question of the role of groups like the Trilateral Commission, the Council on Foreign Relations, the Brookings Institution, and the Hoover Institution.

RESEARCH SOURCES

Some good sources for power structure research are: the yearly issue of the *FORTUNE 500*, which lists the leading 500 corporations in the United States; the August 1979 issue of *FORBES* magazine, which lists the 400 richest Americans; *THE POWER ELITE*, and *WHITE COLLAR*, by C. Wright Mills, books that break down the makeup of the United States power elite and the growth of white collar jobs; *TRAGEDY AND HOPE, A HISTORY OF THE WORLD IN OUR TIME*, by W. Quigley, a book that examines the rise of the southwestern rich. *IMPERIAL BRAIN THRUST*, by Shoup and Minter, Monthly Review Press, N.Y., and London, is an excellent study of the Trilateral Commission and the Council on Foreign Relations. *BETWEEN TWO AGES, AMERICA'S ROLE IN THE TECHNETRONIC ERA*, by Zbigniew Brezenzinski, 1970, was written by Carter's National Security Council advisor and analyzes the impact of new technology, and service work on the culture, political structure, and economic system of America. *THE YANKEE COWBOY WAR*, by Carl Oglesby, Berkeley Publishing Corporation, is an analysis of the conflict between new southwestern wealth versus old southeastern wealth. *TRILATERALISM, THE TRILATERAL*

COMMISSION edited by Holly Sklar, Southend Press, is a study of the Trilateral Commission. *THE ROBBER BARONS*, by Matthew Josephson, 1934, a Harvest Book, which is a classic study of how America's power elite accumulated their wealth; *THE CRISIS OF DEMOCRACY*, Michael J. Crozier, Samuel Huntington, and Joji Watanuki, N.Y., University Press, 1975, a study of the political crisis besetting the western political system. *IN SEARCH OF ENEMIES, A CIA STORY*, 1978, W.W. Norton and Company, by John Stockwell, former chief of the CIA's Angola Task Force. This book is an account of CIA intervention in Angola. *WHO'S WHO IN AMERICA*, is a book published every two years (*WHO'S WHO* also has regional studies for the east, midwest, south, southwest, and west); Poors and Dun and Bradstreet itemize who are the corporate directors of the power structure; the *U.S. GOVERNMENT ORGANIZATION MANUAL* lists agencies and officials of all three branches of government on a yearly basis. Another good piece on researching the national power structure is a phamplet entitled "*Researching the Governing Class of America,*" William Domhoff, New England Free Press, 791 Tremont Street, Boston. And finally, by the O.M. Collective, *THE ORGANIZER'S MANUAL*, 1971, Bantum Books.

Sources for research on your local power structure can be obtained from newspapers. A good source is the local business section of the newspaper, which regularly runs stories on the status of local businesses. Other good sources are the local chamber of commerce, the redevelopment agency, and the microfilm section at City Hall, which lists the owners of local property. Your organization should maintain files on the power structure.

To be successful as organizers you must know your people and your enemy. This requires that organizers must have a theoretical understanding of their peoples history and the history of the enemy. Theoretical knowledge must be combined with practical organizing skills. The complexity of America demands that organizers in the Black liberation movement be theoretical organizers who can take history, political, cultural, and economic ideas and bring them down to earth in the form of practical programs.

When your organization defines a programmatic thrust, whether it be around education, economic development, jobs, housing or campaigns to end drug addiction, then you can take your program and apply it to the different social and economic groupings in the Black community. Remember, your goal is to organize a whole community. When you understand the interest and motivations of different sectors of the Black community then you will be able to win over different elements of your community to your program. This theoretical organizing approach enables you to define a role for every segment of the Black community.

Conclusion

Ultimately, the art of organizing is the art of organizing people. People are both the product of their social organization (the family, the community and the nation), and they are the motive force of organization. People are influenced by the organizations of society and they a shapers of their organizations and society.

Volume II will cover other aspects of organization including approaches to winning the minds of people, and ways to transform attitudes, thoughts and behaviors from negative to positive patterns. In addition, volume II will cover public relations campagins and mass organizing approaches, including Black organizing.

Finally and most importantly, volume II will critically analyze the most sophisticated strategies used by the government (low intensity operarations) to disrupt and destroy organizations. Volume II will offer creative strategies for counteracting these campagins.

APPENDIX

1. Sample lesson plan, course outline, school job description and bylaws for independent Black School and pre-school.

2. Ajili Hodari's "Proposal for Development of Promotion and Persuasion Campaignfor the Pan African Center for Progressive Education."

3. Political Education materials:

   a.Orientation Schedule

   b.Cycles of African Consciousness

   c.Introductory Reading List

   d.Basic Family Bibliography onAfrican and African-AmericanHistory and Culture (compiled by Dr.Asa Hilliard)
   e. Black Political Struggles Reading List

   f. Sample Cadre Training Outline

4. Intelligence Section

President Reagan's Memorandum onIntelligence Activities

COURSE OUTLINE:
BLS 320 BLACK POLITICS MASS MOVEMENTS
AND LIBERATION THEMES

COURSE CONTENT

The political values, structure and behavior of Blacks in the United States. Theories, problems, issues relating to Black political behavior.

COURSE DESCRIPTION

The course Black Politics will examine Black political movements which developed during the "Golden Age" of Black political struggle, the 1960s. The following mass movements and leaders of the sixties will be analyzed; the Montgomery Bus Boycott; the Student Sit-ins; the Monroe Self Defense Movement; the Freedom Rides; the Albany Movement; the Birmingham Movement; the San Francisco Civil Rights movement; the March on Washington; Martin Luther King; C.O.R.E., and S.N.C.C. This course will also cover the transformation of the Civil Rights movement to Black nationalism by examining the role of

Malcolm X, the Nation of Islam, the OAAU, the Urban Rebellions; Black Power, the Black Panthers, and the San Francisco State University Strike.

EVALUATION

Midterm	25%
Final Examination	30%
Team research Project	20%
Oral Report	15%
Attendance and Class Participation	10%

REQUIRED TEXTS

Clayborne Carson, *In Struggle, SNCC and the Black Awakening of the 1960's*, Cambridge, Massachusetts, and London, England: Harvard University Press, 1981.

Oba T'Shaka, *The Political Legacy of Malcolm X*, Chicago: Third World Press, 1984.

Oba T'Shaka, *The San Francisco State Strike, A Study of the First Black Studies Strike in the United States*, San Francisco: S.F. State Black Studies Department, 1982, pg. 15-23.

COURSE SYLLABI:

FIRST WEEK

Counterrevolution of the 70s the campaign to convince Blacks that revolutionary struggle was useless through the media, COINTELPRO, drugs, eastern religion materialism, health food, jogging, and the breakdown of Black culture.

SECOND WEEK

The Black political reality in America. Movements for reform and nationalist's movements for independence. Historical consolidation, the path to Black liberation.

Oba T'Shaka, *The Art of Leadership*, Chapter One, San Francisco.

THIRD WEEK

Background for the Black political movements of the fifties and sixties. The connection between the expanding post World War II economy and the Black political movements of the 1950s and 1960s.

The impact of economic expansion on reformist post World War II movements.

Transformation of Black lifestyles and hopes.

The Black Cultural Revolution of the 40s, 50s and 60s.

The significance of "Be-Bop" as a revolt against and acceptance of Western values; Charlie Parker as a symbol of Black revolt.

John Coltrane and Black nationalism in music.

Rhythm and Blues and trends in Black thinking during the sixties.

Leroi Jones, *Blues People*, New York: William Morrow and Company, 1963. pp. 188-235.

G.O. Simpkins, *Coltrane A Biography*, New York: Herndon House Publishers, pp. 1-255.

FOURTH WEEK

The Montgomery Bus Boycott. E.D. Nixon, Rosa Parks and Martin Luther King.

Howell Raines, *My Soul is Rested the Story of the Civil Rights Movement in the Deep South*, New York: 1977, pp. 37-70.

Robert Brisbane, *Black Activism, Racial Revolution in the United States 1954-1970*, Valley Forge: 1974, pp. 21-72.

FIFTH WEEK

Robert Williams and the Monroe movement for self-defense.

SIXTH WEEK

Greensboro and the student sit-ins. The beginning of the Southern wide movement. The transformation of Southern Black students from a social consciousness to a militant political consciousness.

The formation of the Student Non-Violent Coordinating Committee.

Clayborne Carson, *In Struggle SNCC and the Black Awakening of the 1960's*, Cambridge, Massachusetts, and London England: 1981, pp. 9-30.

Howell Raines, *My Soul is Rested in the Story of the Civil Rights Movement in the Deep South*, New York, New York: 1977, pp. 71-108.

SEVENTH WEEK

The Freedom Rides and the Albany movement.

Clayborne Carson, *In Struggle SNCC and the Awakening of the 1960's*, Cambridge, Massachusetts, and London England: 1981, pp. 31-44.

My Soul is Rested, pp. 109-130.

EIGHTH WEEK

The Birmingham movement, and the March on Washington. The reaction of the Kennedy administration, and the liberal labor Zionist forces to the march on Washington. The shift of the national Civil Rights movement to the local level - an assessment of King's leadership.

In Struggle, pp. 83-95.

My Soul is Rested, pp. 139-186.

NINTH WEEK

The San Francisco Civil Rights Movement. C.O.R.E.; N.A.A.C.P. and the Ad Hoc Committee.

TENTH WEEK

Mid-term, reading and lecture: Oba T'Shaka *The Political Legacy of Malcolm X*, Chicago: Third World Press, 1984.

Malcolm's contribution to the Nation of Islam.

Malcolm's break with the NOI, and the formation of the Muslim Mosque Inc., and the Organization of Afro-American Unity.

Malcolm's international program.

COINTELPRO attack against Malcolm X and the Black nationalist movement.

ELEVENTH WEEK

Reading and Lectures: Robert H. Brisbane, *Black Activism*, Valley Forge, Judson Press, pp. 193-223.

Black nationalism within SNCC and CORE, and the emergence of Black Power.

The emergence of the Black Panther Party.

The strengths and weaknesses of armed self-defense.

TWELFTH WEEK

Reading Ibid, pp. 193-223.

Black Panther philosophy, from Black nationalism to Marxism, Leninism, Mao Tse Tung thought.

Critique of the BBP program.

FBI war against the BPP.

THIRTEENTH WEEK

Reading ibid, pp. 223-245; Oba T'Shaka, *The San Francisco State Strike*, San Francisco Journal of Black Studies, 1982.

The S.F. State strike, a revolt for Black Studies.

The impact of national Black political struggles on the Negro Student Association, and the Black Students Union.

The history program philosophy and objectives of the NSA.

The transformation of the NSA into the Black Students Union.

The BSU and the tutorial program.

Organizing the strike; the BSU on campus and off campus organizing strategy.

George Murray and the BSU demands.

The Strike and its achievements and shortcomings.

FOURTEENTH WEEK

Lectures and discussion; the "Urban Rebellion," a struggle against police repression.

FIFTEENTH WEEK

Lectures and discussions; the Republic of New Africa, and the Pan African People's Organization.

SIXTEENTH WEEK

Summation of lessons learned from the Black liberation movement.

Planned versus spontaneous movements.

Correcting the theoretical deficiencies of the past.

Clarifying the long range objective.

Alliances and coalitions versus independent organizing efforts.

Building the mass organizational base for liberation.

SEVENTEENTH WEEK

FINAL EXAMINATION.

BIBLIOGRAPHY FOR COURSE OUTLINE:

Allen, Robert, *Black Awakening in Capitalist America*, N.Y., Anchor Books, Double Day and Company.

Brisbane, Robert H. *Black Activism*, Judson Press, Valley Forge, 1974.

Carson, Clayborne *In Struggle, SNCC and the Black Awakening of the Sixties*, Cambridge,Massachusetts, and London England: Harvard University Press, 1981

Crozier, Michael T. Samuel P. Huntington, Joji Wantanuki, *The Crises of Democracy*, New York, N.Y., New York University Press, 1975.

James Forman, *The Making of Black Revolutionaries*, N.Y., The MacMillan Company, 1972.

Leroi Jones, *Blues People*, N.Y. William Morrow and Company, 1963.

Howell Raines, *My Soul is Rested*, New York, New York: 1977.

G.O. Simpkins, *Coltrane A Biography*, New York: Herndon House Publishers, pp. 1-255.

Oba T'Shaka, *Learn From the Past: Unite Theory with Practice to Build the National Black United Front*, Black Scholar Magazine, February-March, 1982.

Oba T'Shaka, *Strategies and Tactics for Building a Mass Based Black United Front*, Patrice Lumumba Publishers, S.F. 1980.

Oba T'Shaka, *The Political Legacy of Malcolm X*, Chicago: Third World Press, 1984.

Malcolm X, *By Any Means Necessary*, N.Y., Pathfinder Press, 1970.

PAN AFRICAN CENTER FOR
PROGRESSIVE EDUCATION

STAFF OBLIGATIONS

ADMINISTRATOR

*Responsible for hiring and firing staff.
*Responsible for supervising staff work.
*Responsible for organizing and
   coordinating staff training.
*Responsible for chairing staff meetings.
*Responsible for maintaining and
   establishing budget/finances.
*Responsible for paying salaries.
*Responsible for ordering supplies and
   equipment.
*Responsible for establishing work schedules.
*Responsible for developing work
   relationship with other African schools.
*Responsible for advertising the school.
*Responsible for interviewing new parents.
*Responsible for chairing parent meetings.
*Responsible for classroom assistance in
   emergencies.
*Responsible for effective record keeping.
*Responsible for maintenance and security
   of building.

*Responsible for adhering to the philosophyof revolutionary Pan African nationalism.

PAN AFRICAN CENTER FOR PROGRESSIVE EDUCATION/ TEACHERS

*Responsible for instruction of all school students.
*Responsible for maintaining weekly lesson plans and quarterly syllabi.
*Responsible for supervising children at all times.
*Responsible for attending all staff meetings.
*Responsible for attending all parent meetings.
*Responsible for assuming an equal workload in maintenance and equipment areas.
*Responsible for teacher training participation.
*Responsible for incorporation of teacher training techniques into the classroom.
*Responsible for maintaining an open and positive relationship with parents.
*Responsible for releasing children only to authorized person(s).
*Responsible for administering discipline to children when required.
*Responsible for maintaining a positive (African) example to all students and staff.
*Responsible for transmitting a revolutionary

Pan African Nationalist ideology to all students,parents and staff.

BY-LAWS OF THE PAN AFRICAN CENTER FOR PROGRESSIVE EDUCATION

I

Statement of Purpose. Our school is one concrete step (of many) in African nation building. We are a "domestic colony" struggling for independence. Institutional power is an important base for freedom and independence. Through African institutions we are able to organize ourselves in order to meet our basic needs. The Pan African school is a vital institution in nation building, because it prepares our youth for the "responsibility" of building a new society. The Pan African school is not preparing African youth to be cogs in American society; cogs who occupy the bottom ladder of the society as 20th century slaves. Unlike the public school, we are not preparing our youth to fit into the places that this society has prepared for us as maids, janitors, or white collar flunkies. We are preparing our youth to make a place for themselves in a society of our own. So the Pan African school seeks to develop the Pan African awareness that moves us to unify with our African brothers and sisters throughout the world in a common struggle for independence and freedom. The Pan African school seeks to equip our youth with the skills of science and technology, African languages, agriculture, and skills that prepare the race to rely on itself for freedom and self-respect. These skills must be used to build up institutions (cooperatives, hospitals, schools) among our people in the colony of America. In using these skills for our people here in America, we are building institutions in order to wage a struggle for independence from America.

Our youth are also being trained to provide their skills for the nations of Africa. The Pan African school has a vital role to play in helping to develop Africa. This is important because the future of Black people in America is tied to the liberation of Africa. A free and independent Africa means that Africa will be a base of freedom for Africans throughout the world. In carrying this goal out, it is important for independent African states to recognize independent Pan African institutions as skill supplying centers for Africa.

In struggling to build a new society, the Pan African school must shape a new African. New Africans who will commit their lives to serving our people, to meet our people's basic needs. The Pan African school is a character building institution. Our character is shaped through our day to day work with our people, in organizing, learning, and sharing with our people. The new African is born on the field of collective struggle. Through working with our classmates, teachers, parents, and elders for liberation, we learn the meaning of self respect and self love.

Through listening to our people we learn the meaning of self respect. Through a day-to-day struggle we learn the meaning of selflessness, the meaning of self love.

Character building is a basic part of nation building. Through instilling strong African principles in our youth, we are building a strong foundation for our future African nation.

As the old African proverb says, "Children are the reward of life." The Pan African school is the reward for African children.

II

P.A.C.P.E. is a partnership between parents and P.A.P.O. Both assume major responsibilities in financing and working in the school. Therefore the organizational structure of the Parents Committee should reflect this fact. All offices in the Parents Committee should be dual, i.e., Co-Chairman, Co-Secretary, etc. One chairman should be a parent, the other should be a member of P.A.P.O. This already exists. The organizational structure will reflect a cooperative relationship between parents and members of P.A.P.O.

III

Parents who have withdrawn their children from P.A.C.P.E. These parents are no longer members of the Parents Committee. Since membership of the Parents Committee requires that a person either be a parent of a child in the school or a member of P.A.P.O.

IV

Decisions of the Parents Committee will be by consensus. But where a consensus cannot be obtained; decisions shall be made by a majority vote. Each parent has the obligation of working on the Parents Committee, paying tuition and attending Parents Committee meetings.

V

P.A.C.P.E. is a self reliant African institution. It relies on African people for direction and financial support. It will under <u>n o</u> circumstances accept government grants or money from any <u>white source</u>. This dependence would only compromise the school.

In order to maintain the self reliance of the Pan African Center for Progressive Education and ensure its proper management, each family must be responsible for the Pan African Center for Progressive Education's financial well-being and security. Therefore, each must be pursuant to the following:

1. Each family is responsible for paying tuition the first calendar day of every month.

2. Tuitions paid after the third calendar

day of a said month will be assessed a
an additional $2.50 per day.

3. In the event that any said family does
    not pay tuition by the tenth calendar
    day, the child/ren of that family are
    subject to be dismissed from the Pan
    African Center for Progressive Education.

4. Prior to entry of a child of a family into the
    Pan African Center for Progressive
    Education tuition is due.

5. The first month's tuition of any said family
    is not refundable.

6. If a tuition check is returned marked
    "insufficient funds" then that tuition is
    considered not paid for the said
    month and an additional five dollars
    will be assessed for bank service
    charges.

7. Each family who has a child/ren at
    the Pan African Center for Progressive
    Education is responsible for a minimum
    of $40, in addition to tuition, per quarter.
    Each family shall be free to raise
    additional monies by the method(s)
    of their choice.

VI

On discipline we need to recognize that
there are correct and incorrect views. One
view stems from individualism and is a

hangover from the public schools. This view says that no teacher can lay his/her hands on my child. This position was correct in the public school, where the teacher abused our children. It was also, unfortunately, correct during the period of disorganization in our school. However, at this time when the school's organization has improved, when learning and self discipline has improved, and when in fact the classroom is an extended family, with every student being a brother and a sister; with the teacher being the parent, then we have to understand that the teacher must build character and skills just as parents in the home must. Therefore, discipline is not oppressive and the teacher is not an oppressor! The teacher is looking out for the well being of the child. From time-to-time this may mean that the teacher will have to spank a child or the student council may have to discipline a child, When this happens the goal is to correct a child; it is done because we care enough about the child to discipline him/her.

VII

P.A.C.P.E. seeks to build character and a new African personality within our youth. This means physically as well as mentally and spiritually. Proper care of the body and teeth through good health and eating habits is necessary if our youth·are to be prepared for learning. Each student will be requested to have at least (1) one full Medical check-up and (1) one visit to a dental physician during the school year.

Health

I.   Each family shall act in a manner to ensure the health of that family's child/ren hence, assuring the health of others.

II. Physical examinations. Each child and instructor shall have proof of having had a recent complete physical examination (within two months) before admittance to the Pan African Center for Progressive Education.

III. Children who have productive coughs, fevers or rashes due to communicable diseases - (but not allergies) such as, chickenpox, measles or mumps, should be encouraged to stay home until such conditions have satisfactorily cleared.

IV. Children and other family members of the Pan African Center for Progressive Education should receive immunizations as are needed to ensure the prevention of communicable diseases whenever possible.

   A Each child should receive a tuberculin
      skin test once a year.

V. Health related materials should be included in the lesson plans of various subjects to ensure that adequate knowledge of health concepts as they are related to daily living, science, math and

African history and are developed in the minds of the students of the Pan African Center for Progressive Education.

VI. Basic hygiene of students at the Pan African Center for Progressive Education must be encouraged.

VII. Instructors and parents are also expected to maintain themselves both physically and mentally in a manner benefitting the setting of good examples of African strength and values.

VIII.

   A a "Learning Center" for health related materials will be developed and in general use at the Pan African Center for Progressive Education by 1975.

   B. an Advisory Committee for Health shall be developed by September 1974.

IX. Each family shall have an Emergency Card on file before its child/ren begin attendance at the Pan African Center for Progressive Education. Emergency information should include: (1) the name of a relative or close friend, (2) the name of a physician or medical facility of the family's choice, and (3) signature giving permission for transportation and treatment at a medical center.

COMMUNICATIONS

I. Each parent must strive to overcome the barriers of communication between parent and parent; parent and instructor; instructor and student, that have been a hindrance to the proper function of the Pan African Center for Progressive Education in the past.

II. Each parent should expect to attend two meetings per month. In the event that attendance at monthly or semi-monthly meetings is not possible due to work or illness, then that parent(s) must submit a brief explanation in writing to the Parent's Corresponding Secretary.

III. The Parents of the Pan African Center for Progressive Education must elect a Corresponding Secretary.

The duties of the Corresponding Secretary shall be:

A. to inform parents of regular and emergency meetings.

B. to inform parents of large fundraising events.

C. to coordinate efforts leading to the publication of a monthly CALENDAR OF EVENTS NEWSLETTER.

IV. A "Buddy-System" of communication shall be adopted by parents to keep each other informed.

A. special efforts should be made through the Buddy-System, to keep new families(parents) informed of events of the Pan African Center for Progressive Education.(New parents should be contacted by old parents at least once every two weeks.)

V. All parents must be familiar with the by-laws and other guiding principles of the Pan African Center for Progressive Education, before entering their children in the school.

VI. An emergency support system by and for the parents shall be developed by February, 1975.

PROPOSAL FOR DEVELOPMENT
OF PROMOTION AND PERSUASION
CAMPAIGN FOR THE PAN
AFRICAN CENTER FOR
PROGRESSIVE EDUCATION

SUBMITTED BY:
AJILI HODARI

INTRODUCTION

In order for any promotional campaign to be successful, a clear understanding of the specific group of persons to be reached is absolutely necessary.
Nothing should be taken for granted. Research must be developed to prove or disprove assumptions about this target group.

RESEARCH

Research should answer some basic questions about parents who are: (1) interested (2) uninformed (3) unconcerned.

In more detail we need to answer: (for above questions)

Who

Why

Where they are

When

Working

Welfare

Unemployed

Age

Married

Average number of children

Average income

Level of education

Student

Leval of nationalist awareness

Attitude toward education: public, private, or independent Black schools.

These are but a few of the particulars that may seem trivial but can strengthen a cadres persuasive pitch, as factual information. These obviously can be expanded or limited. With adequate research we can properly aim our promotional campaign and "sales" pitch in the right direction.

UNIQUENESS

Out of the information gathered from polls, questionnaires, phone data, etc., a uniqueness will begin to appear. Something about a particular segment of parents, from data gathered, that stands out. Once this "particular" is confirmed it becomes the center of promotion, advertising, leafleting, etc. Secondary target segments are added arounf this group, and appealed to, relative to anticipated return. If this uniqueness is true, then all that remains is an appeal to it, through the most effective medium (also cost effective).

METHODS OF PROMPTION

Our principle aim here is to reach as many parents, in an around our target, as possible. Charts, graphs and tables should be used to evaluate the effectiveness of our medium. A random sample should be taken to reflect the means by which people become aware of the PACPE.

TYPES OF MEDIA

Medium	Advantages	Limitations
Leaflets	cost effective, easy to read, simple distribution	May not be distributed properly, inadequate printing quantity

Brochures	can be more informative, return for future reference	preparation time cost to print/to get maximum return
Posters	mass appeal, mass distribution, eye catching	vandalism/ improper placement
Radio	large audience, responses, can be built in, fast exposure	aired not in peak hours/days
Television	same as radio, but greater numbers reached	same as radio
Phone Ads	selective parents, personal appeal, etc. re-affirm interest	too personal, too fast
*Door-to-Door	detailed information, feedback from prospective parent,eval. your approach quickly	improper, inability to answer questions or listen to parent

Pins,	campaign	limited to
Buttons,	seems large, all	distribution
Flags, T-	encompassing	
Shirts, etc.		

* If door-to-door approach is used, it can be the most effective means of reaching those parents to which it is aimed. Seminars and workshops should be programmed into cadre training to achieve the maximum effect while in a potential parent's home.

KEY AREAS TO FOCUS UPON

While in the homes of parents, care should be given not to intimidate parents. Questions should be asked to guage, more clearly, the parents understanding of nationalist education, skills they see as important, and commitment to any existing independent self help type programs. Always be flexible in your approach, but do not offer anything that can not be delivered (at least not planned for in future development). Try to be as warm as possible without overdoing it. There should be something about the parent, home or child, that you can identify with. Once a friendly atmosphere is established your pitch should begin.

PERSUASION PITCH

I. History of Black Education
   A Educators
   B. Schools
   C. Graduates accomplishments

II. Independent Schools
   A Successes
   B. Failures
   C. Causes for both

III. Public School
   A History (slavery/post slave periods)
   B. 1950's North/South
   C. Present

IV. Comparison Between
     Public/Private/Black
   A Ability to impart skills
   B. Self pride
   C. Achievement levels

V. National Independent Black Institutions
   A CIBI
   B. Oakland Community School
   C. Others

VI. Local Institutions
   A Panthers
   B. Muslims
   C. Others

VII. Educational Movement

A Creation of atmosphere
B. March/Rally
C. Workshops/planning/development

VIII. Pan African Center for Progressive Education
A Teachers
B. Curriculum
C. Students
D. Environment
E. Track records/GED/College Entrance
  1. reading improvement (show data)
  2. math achievement level
  3. problem areas
F. Parent/teacher committee
G. Tuition Fees
H. Accredidation

IX. Enrollment
A Why/when/how
B. Physical Exam
C. Entrance Exam
D. Semester schedules
E. Holidays/vacations etc.

X. Other
A Discipline
B. Withdrawal
C. Transfer

XI. Social Functions/Fundraisers

VISUAL/AUDIO AIDS FOR
PRESENTATION

In developing a "sales" pitch, visual and audio aids, can enhance your presentation and make PACPE more acceptable. Slides, movies, video tapes, cassette recordings, brochures, photos and booklets will give a complete picture of PACPE. Remember to always center visual aids around the students and audio aids around their voices, this can be catchy and warming.

CLOSING

Try to get a response, promise or commitment. Don't push too hard! Let them decide. be humble if you must, without being passive. Try and solicit for other potential parents, (names, addresses etc.) be as appreciative as need be.

ARRANGING PARENT HOME PRESENTATIONS

Try and make large presentations for more than one parent, smaller less detailed presentations may be better during a one-to-one session. The home presentation is the "big gun" it should be fired to put the clincher on a potential parent. The cadre participating should have a thorough briefing before, not last minute "come along for the ride." Parents, teachers and possibly students, if the hour is right should also take part in presentations.

SUGGESTED DISTRIBUTION PONTS

For Leaflets, Brochures, Pamphlets

College and High School Black Student Unions
Welfare offices
Food stamp outlets
Health care clinics
Gynecologist/Obstetrician offices
Pediatric waiting rooms
Unemployment offices
College information stations
Shopping centers and malls
Local corner stores
laundry houses
Fast food restaurants (and Soul food sit downs)
Churches (bulletin boards, Sunday announcements)
Program advertisements (church, sporting events)
Movie (theater) lines
Beauty parlors and barber shops
Record stores
Drug stores
Entertainment spots (boarding house, Cow Palace, Circle Star, etc.)
Housing projects
Downtown bus stops
Parked cars (windshields)
Buses, streetcars, trolleys
Airports
Bus stations, barns and benches
Black nightclubs

Black owned businesses

RADIO SPOTS   TV SPOTS

Stations	Show	Chan.
KDIA	Black Renaissance	Ch. 44
KPOO	All Together Now	Ch. 5
KPFA	Public TV (Black Perspectives)	Ch. 9
KJAZ	Vibrations for a People	Ch. 5
KSOL	BET Cable Channel	Ch. 34
KRE		
KSFX		

NEWSPAPER ADS

Sun Reporter (metro section)
Classified Flea Market (East Bay)
Afrikan Awakener
California Voice
Chronicle/Examiner
Oakland Post
Bay Guardian
San Francisco Progress
Oakand Tribune
San Francisco Advertiser
Campus Newspaper
Richmond Independent
Berkley Barb

SPEAKING ITINERARY
Women's groups
Black social clubs
Churches
Press conferences
Women's (and other) crisis organizations
Community groups
Afrikan Liberation Day

MEDIA BUDGET

(projected expenditures)

This budget will be projected over a one-year period

Newspaper	$ 300.00
Television	FREE
Radio	FREE (100.00)
Leaflets	200.00
Brochures	400.00
Posters	600.00
T-shirts, Buttons	200.00
Travel expenses	100.00
Phone Expenses	300.00
Miscellaneous	400.00

TOTAL BUDGET   2,500.00
(possible radio minimum 100.00)

INCOME FOR MEDIA BUDGET

(projected resources)

From Fundraisers

Miscellaneous Donations, Personal Grants
   $2,500.00

Dinner sales	$ 300.00
Pins, Buttons, Flags, T-shirts, etc.	450.00
Car washes	150.00
Garage sales	200.00
Parties	300.00
Bake sales	150.00
Raffles, Auctions, Flea Markets	200.00
Street soliciting	200.00
Cultural events, Bazaars	250.00
Miscellaneous Donations, Personal Grants	200.00
ALD Booths	<u>400.00</u>
TOTAL INCOME	2,800.00

ORIENTATION SCHEDULE

I. First Meeting

Discussion of the purpose of political education, the history of PAPO and the Pan Afrikan Secretariat. Explanation of the structure and rules of PAPO. Discussion of the history of the Black United Front. Show slides on PAPO and ALD. Assign reading of Pan Afrikan values, and cycles of Afrikan consciousness. Reading material to be discussed at send meeting.

II. Second Meeting

Discussion of the Assimilation and the Survival Sould Cultural Awareness stages of consciousness. Discussion of the Pan AfricanValues paper. Discussion of how this material applies to our experiences with assimilation, or the survival soul consciousness stage of awareeness.

III. Third Meeting

Application of the Disturbance and Exposure stage of consciousness to our own personal experiences.

V. Fourth Meeting

Discussion of the transformation process we are undergoing through the Nationalist stage of consciousness. What specific weaknesses are we working on.

V. Fifth Meeting

Discussion of Afrikan Manhood and Womanhood. The matrilneal family and the Black family in slavery. The status of the Black family today. Causes for the breakdown in Black families. Discussion of how this applied to your family situation. Tie this into Herbert G. Gutman, *The Black Family In Slavery & Freedom, 1750-1925*, New York, Pantheon Books, and Cheikh Anta Diop, *The Cultural Unity of Black Africa*, Chicago, Third World Press, 1959.

VI. Sixth Meeting

Discussion of Afrikan Manhood and Womanhood. Stages in the development of a relationship. Responsibilities in a relationship. Developing support systems including building extended families, family advice systems, child rearing support systems, mediation systems, and value sharing systems.

Examination of Afrikan carryovers in the Black family today. Keys to building non-exploitative loving relationships. Divisions of reponsibilities in the family. The family as the foundation unit for the nation. development of sisters in the family and organization.

VII. Seventh Meeting

Definition of Revolutionary Pan Afrikan Nationalism. Application of the Revolutionary Pan Afrikan Nationalists stage of consciousness to our personal political development. Theorectical summing up of Black political movements i.e., King, SNCC, CORE, the historical development of the civil rights movement. Play taped interview with CLR James on the "Meaning of Pan Afrikanism." Readings include, Clayborne Carson, *In Struggle SNCC and the Black Awakening of the 1960's*, Cambridge Massachussets, Harvard University Press, 1981. Robert Brisbane, *Black Activism*, Valley Forge, Judson Press, 1974, pp. 43-105.

VIII. Eighth Meeting

Analyze in a theorectical way the significance of Malcolm, the NOI, the OAAU, Black Power, the Urban rebellions, The Balck Panther Party, and Cultural Nationalism. Analysis of COINTELPRO strategies. Assessments of strengths and weaknesses, and application to our strguules today.

IX. Ninth Meeting

Analysis of the S.F. State Strike, Congress of Afrikan People, Afrikan Liberation Support Committee and Black Political Assembly.

Examination of causes behind their break up. Analysis of Strategies and Tactics for Black Liberation.

Readings include, William H. Orrick, Jr., "Shut It Down! A College in Crisis", San Francisco State Colege, October 1968 - April 1969, June 1969. Oba T'Shaka, *Strategies and Tactics for Building a National Mass Based Black United Front*, San Francisco, March 1980. Oba T'Shaka, "The San Francisco Strike, A Study of the First Black Studies Strike in the U.S." S.F. 1977.

X. Tenth Meeting

Self Defense, Soul and Creativity, and Afrikan Nationhood. Focus on Afrikan Nationhood. What do we mean by nationhood? Examination of various positions on the land question, including the PAS position.

Tape on the land panel, third Black United Front Convention: Oba T'Shaka, "Analysis of the Black Belt South Position", 1982.

XI. Eleventh Meeting

Continuation of the discussion on the land question. Discussion of a youth organization project.

XII. Twelfth Meeting

Discussion of areas of work for new members, meeting dates. Evaluation of prospective members.

I

BASIC BIBLIOGRAPHY ON AFRICAN AND AFRICAN-AMERICAN HISTORY AND CULTURE

by Dr. Asa G. Hilliard III
Georgia State University

Following is a list of recommended basic books on African and African-American history and culture. These are books which should be available on order through most bookstores. Unfortunately, few bookstores, including many African-American bookstores, do not maintain a complete stock of the most significant books in African and African-American history. However, the following books are well worth any temporary inconveniences which may be caused due to a short wait.

The following books should be thought of as a basic reference list, primarily for parents. However, some of the material may be suitable for older children, especially the stories in Joel Rogers' *World's Great Men of Color.*

Armah, A.K. *Two Thousand Seasons.* Chicago: Third World Press, 1979.

Counter, A. and, Evans, D.L. *I Sought My Brother: An Afro-American Reunion.* Cambridge,Massachussets: MIT Press, 1981.

Diop, C.A. *The African Origin of Civilization: Myth or Reality?* New York: Lawrence Hill, 1974.

Diop, C.A. *The Cultural Unity of Black Africa.* Chicago: Third World Press, 1959.

DuBois, W.E.B. *Black Reconstruction in America: An Essay Toward a History of the Part Which Black Folk Played in the Attempt to Reconstruct Democracy in America, 1860-1880.* New York: Athaeneum, 1973.

Garvey, A.J. *Garvey and Garveyism.* New York: Collier Books, 1968.

Hansberry, W.L. *Africa and Africans as Seen by Classical Writers: The William Leo Hansberry African History Notebooks,* Vol. 2 (J.E. Harris, Ed.). Washington, D.C.: Howard University Press, 1977.

Hansberry, W.L. *Pillars in Eithiopian History: The William Leo Hansberry African History Notebooks,* Vol. 1 (J.E. Harris, Ed.). Washington, D.C.: Howard University Press, 1974.

Herskovits, M.J. *The Myth of the Negro Past.* Boston: Beacon Press, 1958.

Jackson, J.G. *Introduction to African Civilization.* Secaucus, New Jersey: Citadel Press, 1974.

James, G. G.M. *Stolen Legacy.* San Francisco: Julian Richardson, 1976.

Jones, L. *Blues People.* New York: William Morrow,1963.

Korngold, R. *Citizen Toussaint.* New York: Hill & Wang, 1965.

Price, R. (Ed.). *Maroon Societies: Rebel Slave Communities in the Americas.* New York: Anchor Books, 1973.

Redmond, E.B. Drum Voices: *The Mission of Afro-American Poetry.* New York: Anchor Books, 1976.

Rodney, W. *How Europe Underdeveloped Africa.* Washington, D.C.: Howard University Press, 1974.

Rogers, J.A. *World's Great Men of Color, Vols. 1 and 2.* New York: Collier Books, 1972.

Smitherman, G. *Talkin and Testifyin: The Language of Black America.* Boston: Houghton Mifflin, 1977.

Turner, L. *Africanisms in the Gullah Dialect.* New York: Arno Press, 1969.

Van Sertima, I. *They Came Before Columbus.* New York: Random House, 1976.

Vass, C.W. *The Bantu Speaking Heritage of the United States.* Los Angeles: Center for Afro-American Studies, University of California, 1979.

Williams, C. *The Destruction of Black Civilization: Great Issues of the Race from 4500 B.C. to 2000 A.D.* Chicago: Third World Press, 1974.

Woodson, C.G. *The Miseducation of the Negro.* Washington, D.C.: Associated Publishers, 1969. First published 1933.

JOURNALS

The Journal of African Civilizations. I. Van Sertima, Ed. New Brunswick, New Jersey: Douglass College, Rutgers University.

Black Books Bulletin. H.R. Madhubuti, Ed. Chicago: The Institute for Positive Education, 7524 South Cottage Grove Avenue, Chicago, Illinois 60619

Selected bookstores where some of these materials may be purchased:

The Aquarian Bookstore, Los Angeles

Mamie Clayton's Third World and Ethnic Books, Los Angeles
Marcus Books, San Francisco, Oakland
Liberation Bookstore, Harlem, New York City
The Black Book, Baltimore
Amistad Bookplace, Houston
Hakim's Bookstore, Atlanta
The Shrine of the Black Madonna, Atlanta
Ellis Books, Chicago
The Talking Drum Bookstore, Portland, Oregon
Liberation Information, Washington, D.C.

II

EVIDENCE FOR THE AFRICAN ORIGIN OF
THE EARLIEST RECORDED CIVILIZATION,
FOR THE ANCIENT AFRICANS AS BEING BLACK
PEOPLE, AND FOR THE EXISTENCE OF
CIVILIZATIONS THROUGHOUT AFRICA BEFORE
EUROPEAN COLONIALISM

Adams, William. *Nubia: Corridor to Africa.*
Princeton: Princeton University Press, 1977.

Alfred, C. *Art in Ancient Egypt.* London: Alec
Tiranti, 1969.

Bain, Mildred and Lewis, Ervin (Eds.). *From
Freedom to Freedom: African Roots in
American Soil.* New York: Random
House, 1977.

Battuta, Ibn. *Travels in Asia and Africa 1325-
1354.* New York: Augustus M. Kelley, 1969.

Bell, H. Idris. *Cults and Creeds in Graeco-
Roman Egypt.* Chicago: Aries, 1957.

Ben-Jochanan, Yosef. *Africa, Mother of
Western Civilization.* New York: Alkebu-Lan
Books, 1970.

Ben-Jochanan, Yosef. *A Chronology of the
Bible: Challenge to the Standard Version.*
New York: Alkebu-Lan Books, 1973.

Ben-Jochanan, Yosef. *African Origin of the Major "Western Religions"*. New York: Alkebu-Lan Books, 1970.

Ben-Jochanan, Yosef. *Black Man of the Nile*. New York: Alkebu-Lan Books, 1972.

Ben-Jochanan, Yosef. *The Black Man's North and East Africa*. New York: Alkebu-Lan Books, 1971.

Ben-Jochanan, Yosef. *The Black Man's Religion: Excerpts and Comments from the Holy Black Bible*. New York: Alkebu-Lan Books, 1970.

Blavatsky, H.P. *Isis Unveiled: A Master Key to the Mysteries of Ancient and Modern Science and Theology*. Pasadena, California: University Press, 1972.

Bovill, E.Q. *The Golden Trade of the Moors*. New York: Oxford University Press, 1980.

Breasted, James Henry. *The Dawn of Conscience*. New York: Charles Scribner, 1978.

Breasted, James Henry. *A History of Egypt from Earliest Times to the Persian Conquest*. New York: Charles Scribner & Sons, 1937. First published 1909.

Brent, Peter. *Black Nile: Mungo Park and the Search for the Niger*. New York: Gordon Cremonisi, 1977.

British Museum. *The Rosetta Stone.* London: British Museum Publications, 1974.

Budge, E.A. Wallis. *Amulets and Talismans.* New York: Collier, 1970. First published 1930.

Budge, E.A. Wallis. *The Book of the Dead, The Papyrus of Ani.* New York: Dover Publications, 1967. First published 1895.

Budge, E.A. Wallis. *The Dwellers on the Nile.* New York: Dover 1977. First published 1926.

Budge, E.A. Wallis. *The Egyptian Heaven and Hell.* Lasalle, Illinois: Open Court Press, 1974. First published 1905.

Budge, E.A. Wallis. *Egyptian Magic.* Secaucus, N.J.:Citadel Press, 1978. First published 1899.

Budge, E.A. Wallis. *Egyptian Religions.* Secaucus, NJ: University Books, 1959. First published 1899.

Budge, E.A. Wallis. *The Gods of the Egyptians: Or, Studies in Egyptian Mythology,* Vols. I and II. New York: Dover, 1969. First published 1904.

Budge, E.A. Wallis. *Osirus and the Egyptian Resurrection.* New York: Dover, 1973. First published 1911.

Carruthers, Jacob H. Maat: *The African Universe.* Unpublished Manuscript.

Carruthers, Jacob H. *Orientation and Problems in the Redemption of Ancient Egypt.* Unpublished Manuscript.

Carruthers, Jacob H. *Tawi: The United Two Lands.* Unpublished Manuscript.

*Churchward, Albert. *The Signs and Symbols of Primordial Man: The Evolution of Religious Doctrines from the Eschatology of the Ancient Egyptians.* Westport, Connecticut: Greenwood Press, 1978. First published 1913.

Clark, J. Desmond. *The Prehistory of Africa.* New York: Praeger, 1971.

Collins, Robert O. *Problems in African History.* Englewood Cliffs: Prentice-Hall, 1968.

Cooley, W.D. *The Negroland of the Arabs Examined and Explained: An Inquiry into the Early History and Geography of Central Africa.* Frank Cass and Co., Ltd., 1966.

Cottrell, Leonard. *Lady of Two Lands: Five Queens of Ancient Egypt.* New York: Bobbs-Merrill, 1967:

Cox, Georgia O. *African Empires and Civilizations.* Washington, D.C.: African Heritage Publishers, 1974.

Davidson, Basil. *African Kingdoms.* New York: Time-Life Books, 1971.

Davidson, Basil. *Discovering Our African Heritage.* Boston: Ginn and Co., 1971.

Davidson, Basil. *Old Africa Rediscovered.* London: Victor Gollancz Ltd., 1970.

*Diop, C.A. *The African Origin of Civilization: Myth or Reality?* New York: Lawrence Hill and Co., 1974. First Published 1955.

*Diop, C.A. *The Cultural Unity of Black Africa.* Chicago: Third World Press, 1978. Originally published 1959.

Doane, T.W. *Bible Myths and Their Parallels in the World's Major Religions: Being a Comparison for the Old and New Testament Myths and Miracles with Those of Heathen Nations of Antiquity, Considering also Their Origins and Meaning.* New York: Truth Seeker Press, 1882. Reprinted 1948.

Dubois, Felix. *Timbuktu the Mysterious.* Longmans, Green & Co., 1896.

DuBois, W.E.B. *The World and Africa: An Inquiry into the Part Which Africa Has Played in World History.* New York: International Publishers, 1972. Originally published 1946.

Emery, Walter B. *Lost Land Emerging.* New York: Charles Scribner, 1967.

Fage, J.D. and Oliver, R.A. *Papers in African Prehistory.* Cambridge: The University Press, 1970.

Fazzini, R.A. *Art from the Age of Akhnaton.* Brooklyn, New York: Brooklyn Museum Press, 1973.

Fell, Barry. America B.C.: *Ancient Settlers in the New World.* New York: Wallaby, 1976.

*Fleming, Beatrice J. & Pryde, Marian J. *Distinguished Negroes Abroad.* Washington, D.C.: Associated Publishers, 1946.

Frankfort, Henri. *Ancient Egyptian Religions.* New York: Harper Torchbooks, 1961. First published 1948.

Frankfort, Henri. *Kingship and the Gods: A Study of Ancient Near Eastern Religion as the Integration of Society and Nature.* Chicago: University of Chicago Press, 1978. First Published 1948.

Frankfort, Henri, Frankfort, H.A., Wilson, J.A., Jacobsen, T., & Irwin, W.A. *The Intellectual Adventure of Ancient Man: An Essay on Speculative Thought in the Ancient Near East.* Chicago: University of Chicago Press, 1977. First published 1946.

Frazer, P.M. *Ptolemaic Alexandria.* Oxford at the Clarendon Press, 1972.

Freud, Sigmund. *Moses and Monotheism.* New York: Vintage, 1967. First published 1939.

Graves, Anna Melissa. *Africa: The Wonder and the Glory.* Baltimore: Black Classic Press, P.O. Box 13414, Baltimore, MD 21203, 1961.

Graves, Kersey. *The World's Sixteen Crucified Saviors: Or Christianity Before Christ.* New York: Truth Seeker Press, 1975. First published 1875.

Griule, Marcel. *Conversation with Ogotemmeli: An Introduction to Dogon Religious Ideas.* Oxford University Press, 1972.

Hall, Manly P. *Free Masonry of the Ancient Egyptians.* Los Angeles: Philosophical Research Society, Inc., 1971. First Published 1937.

Hapgood, Charles H. *Maps of the Ancient Sea Kings: Evidence of Advanced Civilization in the Ice Age.* New York: E.P. Dutton, 1979.

Harris, Joseph E. (Ed.). *Africa and Africans as Seen by Classical Writers: The William Leo Hansberry African History Notebook, Volume II.* Washington, D.C.: Howard University Press, 1977.

Harris, Joseph E. *Africans and Their History.* New York: Mentor, 1972.

Higgins, Godfrey. Anacalypsis: *An Attempt to Draw Aside the Veil of the Saitic Isis: Or an Inquiry into the Origin of Languages, Nations and Religions.* London: Longmen, Rees, Oras, Brown, Green, Longman, Paternoster Row, 1836. Reprinted 1972 by Health Research, Mokelume Hill, California.

Hull, Richard W. *African Cities and Towns Before the European Conquest.* New York: W.W. Norton & Co., 1976.

Hurry, Jamieson B. *Imhotep: The Vizier and Physician of King Zoser and Afterwards the Egyptian God of Medicine.* Oxford University Press, 1928.

Hutchinson, Louise D. *Out of Africa: From WestAfrican Kingdoms to Colonization.* Washington, D.C.: Smithsonian Institution Press, 1979.

Ions, Veronica. *Eqyptian Mythology.* London: Hamlyn, 1965.

Jackson, John G. *Introduction to African Civilizations.* NJ: The Citadel Press, 1974. First Published 1970.

*Jackson, John G. *Man, God and Civilization.* New York: University Books, Inc., 1972.

Jairazbhoy, R.A. *Ancient Egyptians and Chinese in America.* Totowa, NJ: Roman and Littlefield, 1974.

James, George G.M. *Stolen Legacy.* San Francisco: Julian Richardson, 1976. First published 1954.

Johnson, Samuel. *The History of the Yorubas: From Earliest Times to the Beginning of the British Protectorate.* Lagos, Nigeria: CSS Bookshops, P.O. Box 174, 50 Broad Street, Lagos, Nigeria, 1976. First published 1921.

Jones, Edward L. Black Zeus: African Mythology and History. Seattle: Edward L. Jones, Frayn Printing Co., 2518 Western Avenue, Seattle, WA 98121, 1977.

*Jones, Edward L. *Profiles in African Heritage.* Seattle: Edward L. Jones, Frayn Printing Co., 2518 Western Avenue, Seattle, WA 98121, 1972.

*Jones, Edward L. *Tutankhamen.* Edward L. Jones and Associates, 5517 17th Avenue, N.E., Seattle, WA 98105, 1978 Library of Congress Card #78-61436.

July, Robert W. *A History of the African People.* New York: Charles Scribner & Sons, 1974.

Kandi, Baba Kumasi. *Down the Nile.* Detroit: A Greater Visions Classic, P.O. Box 21606, Detroit, Michigan, 1978.

Leakey, L.S.B. *By the Evidence: Memoirs 1932-1951.* New York: Harcourt Brace Jovanovich, 1974.

Leslau, Wolf. *Falasha Anthology: The Black Jews of Ethiopia.* (Translated from Ethiopic Sources). New York: Schocken, 1951.

Lugard, Lady. *A Tropical Dependency: An Outline of the Ancient History of the Western Sudan with an Account of the Modern Settlement of Northern Nigeria.* Frank Cass & Co. Ltd., 1964.

MacKenzie, Norman. *Secret Societies.* New York: Crescent, 1967.

Maquet, Jacques. *Civilizations of Black Africa.* New York: Oxford University Press, 1972.

Massey, Gerald. *A Book of the Beginnings: Containing an Attempt to Recover and Reconstitute the Lost Origins of the Myths and Mysteries, Types and Symbols, Religion and Language, with Egypt for the Mouthpiece and Africa as the Birthplace.* Secaucus, NJ: University Books, 1974. First published 1881.

Massey, Gerald. *Ancient Egypt, the Light of the World: A Work of Reclamation and Restitution in Twelve Books.* New York: Samuel Weiser, Inc., 1973. Originally published 1907.

*Massey, Gerald. *The Natural Genesis: Or Second Part of a Book of the Beginnings, Containing an Attempt to Recover and Reconstitute the Lost Origins of the Myths and Mysteries, Types and Symbols, Religion and Language, With Egypt for the Mouthpiece and Africa as the Birthplace.* Samuel Weiser, Inc., 1974.

McEvedy, Colin. *The Penguin Atlas of African History.* New York: Penguin Books, 1980.

Means, Sterling M. *Black Egypt and Her Negro Pharaohs.* Baltimore: Black Classic Press, P.O. Box 13414, Baltimore, Maryland, 1978.

Means, Sterling M. *Ethiopia and the Missing Link in African History.* Harrisburg, PA: The Atlantis Publishing Co., 1980. First published 1945.

Morrell, E.D. *The Black Man's Burden: The White Man in Africa from the Fifteenth Century to World War I.* New York: Modern Reader Paperbacks, 1969. First published 1920.

Murphy, E. Jefferson. *The Bantu Civilization of Southern Africa.* New York: Thomas Y. Crowell, 1974.

Murphy, E. Jefferson. *History of African Civilization.* New York: Dell, 1972.

Nyane, D.T. Sundiata: *An Epic of Old. Mali.*

Obadele, I. and Obadele, A. *Civilization Before the Time of Christ.* New York: Dell, 1972.

Olda, Henry. *From Ancient China to Ancient Greece.* Atlanta: Black Heritage Corporation and The Select Publishing Company, 1981.

Oliver, Roland and Fagin, Brian. *Africa in the Iron Age: c. 500 B.C. to A.D. 1400.* Cambridge: Cambridge University Press, 1975.

Oliver, R. and Oliver Carolyn (Eds.). *Africa in the Days of Exploration.* Englewood Cliffs: Prentice-Hall, 1965.

Osei, J.A., Nwabara, S.N., & Odunsi, A.T.O. *A Short History of West Africa A.D. 1000 to the Present.* New York: Hill and Wang, 1973.

Osei, G.K. *African Contribution to Civilization.* London: The African Publication Society, 1973.

Osei, G.K. *The African: His Antecedents, His Genius, His Destiny.* New Hyde Park: University Books, 1971.

Parker, George Wells. *The Children of the Sun.* The Hamitic League of the World, 1918.

Piankoff, Alexandre, & Rambova, N. *The Shrines of Tut-Ankh-amon.* Princeton, NJ: Princeton University Press, 1977.

Rogers, Joel A. *Africa's Gift to America.* New York: Helga M. Rogers, 1270 Fifth Avenue, New York 10029, 1956.

Rogers, Joel A. *The World's Great Men of Color.* New York: Collier MacMillan, 1972.

Rout, Leslie B., Jr. *The African Experience in Spanish America: 1502 to the Present Day.* Cambridge: Cambridge University Press, 1976.

Samkange, S. African Saga: *A Brief Introduction to African History.* New York: Abingdon Press, 1971.

Samkange, S. *The Origins of Rhodesia.* New York: Praeger, 1968.

Snowden, Frank M., Jr. *Blacks in Antiquity: Ethiopians in the Graeco-Roman Experience.* Cambridge: Harvard University Press, 1971.

Sweeting, Earl, & Lez, Edmond. *African History.* New York: African-American International Press, P.O. Box 775, Flushing, New York 11352, 1973.

UNESCO. *"The Historiography of Southern Africa: Proceedings of the Experts' Meeting*

Held at Gaborone, Botswana, from 7 to 11 March 1977." Paris: UNESCO, 1980.

UNESCO. "The Peopling of Ancient Egypt and the Deciphering of Meroitic Script: Proceedings of the Symposium Held in Cairo from 28 January to 3 February 1974." Paris: UNESCO, 1978.

Uya, Okon Edet. *African History: Some Problems in Methodology and Perspective.* Cornell University African Studies and Research Center, 1974.

Volney, C.F. *The Ruins or Meditation on the Revolution of Empires and the Law of Nature.* New York: Truth Seeker Co., 1950. First published 1793.

Walsh, M. *The Ancient Black Christians.* San Francisco: Julian Richardson, 1969.

Weatherwax, John M. *The African Contribution:* Parts I and II. Los Angeles: The John Henry and Mary Louisa Dunn Bryant Foundation, 1968.

Wiener, Leo. *Africa and the Discovery of America.* New York: Kraus Reprint Co., 1971. Originally published 1920.

*Williams, Chancellor. *The Destruction of Black Civilization: Great Issues of A Race 4500 B.C. to 2000 A.D.* Chicago: Third World Press, 1974.

*Williams, John A. (Ed.). *Y'Bird,* Volume 1, No. 2 1978.

Windsor, R.S. *From Babylon to Timbuktu: A History of the Ancient Black Races Including the Black Hebrews.* New York: Oxford University Press, 1966.

Woodson, Carter G. *African Heroes and Heroines.* Washington, D.C.: The Associated Publishers, Inc., 1969.

X, Malcolm. *On African-American History* New York: Pathfinder Press, 1967.

III

EVIDENCE FOR AFRICAN ANCESTRY IN EUROPEAN
POPULATIONS AND FOR THE CONTINUOUS INTERACTION OF AFRICANS AND EUROPEANS FROM EARLIEST TIMES

Read, Jan. *The Moors in Spain and Portugal.* London: Faber and Faber, 1974.

*Rogers, Joel, A. *Nature Knows No Color Line: Research Into the Negro Ancestry in the White Race.* New York: Helga M. Rogers, 1270 Fifth Avenue, New York, 1952.

*Rogers, Joel A. *Sex and Race,* Vols. 1, 2, 3. New York: Helga M. Rogers, 1270 Fifth Avenue, New York.

Scobie, Edward. *Black Britannia: A History of Blacks in Britain.* Chicago: Johnson, 1972.

Shyllon, Folarin. *Black People in Britain, 1555 to 1833.* London: Oxford University Press, 1977.

IV

EVIDENCE FOR THE AFRICAN PRESENCE IN AMERICA BEFORE COLUMBUS, AND EVEN BEFORE CHRIST

Clegg, Legrand H. *The Beginning of the African Diaspora: Black Men in Ancient and Medieval America.* Los Angeles: Unpublished manuscript, 1977.

*Van Sertima, Ivan. *They Came Before Columbus.* New York: Random House, 1976.

Von Wuthenau, A. *Unexpected Faces in Ancient America: 1500 B.C. to 1500 A.D., The Historical Testimony of Pre-Columbian Artists.* New York: Crown Publishers, 1975.

V

EVIDENCE FOR HOW EUROPE UNDERDEVELOPED
AFRICA WHICH IN MANY PLACES WAS MUCH MORE HIGHLY DEVELOPED THAN EUROPE AT THE TIME OF HER EXPLORATIONS

Ayandale, E.A. *The Missionary Impact on Modern Nigeria, 1914-1942: A Political and Social Analysis.* London: Longman, 1966.

Chineweizu. *The West and the Rest of Us: White Predators, Black Slavers and the African Elite.* New York: Vintage Books, 1975.

Fanon, Frantz. *A Dying Colonialism.* New York: Evergreen, 1965.

Fanon, Frantz. *Black Skin, White Masks.* New York: Grove, 1967.

Farrant, Leda. *Tippu Tip and the East African Slave Trade.* New York: St. Martins Press.

Hallett, Robin (Ed.). *Records of the African Association: 1788 to 1831.* London: Thomas Nelson and Sons, Ltd., 1964.

Mannix, D.P. and Crowley, M. *Black Cargoes: A History of the Atlantic Slave Trade 1518-1865.* New York: Viking, 1962.

Memmi, Albert. *The Colonizer and the Colonized.* Boston: Beacon, 1965.

Morell, E.D. *The Black Man's Burden: The White Man in Africa from the Fifteenth Century to World War I.* New York: Modern Reader Paperbacks, 1969.

Nkrumah, Kwame. *Neo-Colonialism: The Last Stage of Imperialism.* New York: International Publishers, 1965.

*Rodney, Walter. *How Europe Underdeveloped Africa.*Washington: Howard University Press, 1974.

Rotberg, Robert I. (Ed.). *Africa and Its Explorers: Motives, Methods and Impact.* Cambridge: Harvard University Press, 1973.

XI

READING LIST ON BLACK
POLITICAL STRUGGLES BY OBA T'SHAKA

Allen, Robert. *Black Awakening in Capitalist America.* New York: Anchor Books, 1969.

Anthony, Earl. *Picking Up the Gun.* New York: Pyramid Books, 1970.

Asante, SKB. *Pan African Protest: West Africa and The Italo-Ethiopian Crises 1934-1941.* Britain: Longman Group, Ltd., 1977.

August, John H. Meier, and Elliot, Rudwick and Francis, Broderick L. *Black Protest Thought in the Twentieth Century,* Second Edition. Indianapolis and New York: The Bobs-Merrill Company, Inc.1965.

August, John H. Meier, and Elliot, Rudwick. *CORE: A Study of the Civil Rights Movement 1942-1968.* New York: Oxford University Press, 1978.

Barlow, William and Shapiro, Peter. *An End to Silence The San Francisco State Student*

Movement in the 60's. New York: Bobbs-Merrill Company, Inc. Publishers, 1971.

Bennett, Lerone. *The Negro Mood, and Other Essays.* Chicago: Johnson Publishing Co., Inc., 1964.

Berube, Maurice, and Gitteou, Marilyn. *Confrontation at Ocean Hill Brownsville.* New York: Frederick A. Praeger, 1969.

Bracey, J.R., August, John H. Meier, and Elliot, Rudwick. *Black Nationalism in America.* New York and Indianapolis: The Bobbs-Merrill Company, Inc. 1970.

Brisbane, Robert H. *Black Activism Racial Revolution In the United States 1954-1970.* Valley Forge, Judson Press, 1974.

Brotz, Howard. *Negro Social and Political Thought 1850-1920, Representative Texts.* New York: Basic Books, Inc. Publishers, 1966.

Carmichael, Stokely. *Stokley Speaks: Black Power Back to Pan Africanism. New York: Vintage Books. 1965.*

Chambers, Bradford. *Chronicles of Black Protest.* New York: New American Library, 1968.

Chrisman, Robert, and Hare, Nathan. *Contemporary Black Thought: The Best from The Black Scholar.* New York: Bobbs-Merrill, 1973.

Chrisman, Robert, and Hare, Nathan. *Pan Africanism.* New York: The Bobbs-Merrill Company, Inc. 1974.

Clayborne, Carson. *In Struggle SNCC and the Black Awakening of the 1960's.* Cambridge and London : Harvard University Press, 1981.

Cohen, Carl Robert. *Black Crusader, A Biography of Robert Franklin Williams.* Secaucus, NJ: Lyle Stuart, Inc., 1972.

Criminal Code Reform Act of 1977, Washington, D.C.: U.S. Government Printing Office: November 15, 1977.

Foner, Philip S. *The Black Panthers Speak.* Philadelphia, New York: J.B. Lippincott Company, 1970.

Forman, James. *The Making of Black Revolutionaries.* New York, New York: The MacMillan Company, 1972.

Garrett, James. *The Struggle for Black Education 1968-1971.* Washington, D.C.: Drum andSpear Press, 1972.

Garrow, David. *The FBI and Martin Luther King, Jr. From "Solo" to Memphis.* New York, London: W.W. Norton Company, 1981.

Martin Luther King., Jr., Security Assassination Investigations. Washington, D.C. U.S.

Government Printing Office, January 11, 1977.

Hall, Raymond. *Separatism in the United States.* New England: Hanover, University Press of New England, 1978

Harding, Vincent. *There is a River The Black Struggle for Freedom in America.* New York and London: Harcourt Brace Jovanovich Publishers, 981.

Haywood, Harry. *Negro Liberation.* Chicago, IL: Liberation Press, 1976.

Holly James, Theodore, and Harris, Dennis. *Black Separatism and the Caribbean 1860.* Ann Arbor: The University of Michigan Press, 1970.

Jackson, George. *Blood in My Eye.* New York: Random House, 1972.

Jackson, George. *Soledad Brothers, The Prison Letters of George Jackson.* New York: Bantam Books, 1976.

James, C.L.R. A History of the *Pan African Revolt.* Washington: Drum and Spear Press, 1969.

Karenga, M. Ron. *Essays on Struggle: Position and Analysis.* San Diego, CA: Kawaida Publications, 1978.

Karenga, Maulana. *Kawaida Theory: An Introductory Outline.* Inglewood, CA: Kawaida Publications, 1980.

Killens, John Oliver. *The Trial Record of Denmark Vesey.* Boston: Beacon Press, 1970.

Lane, Mark, Gregory, Dick. *Code Name Zorro.* New York: Pocket Books, 1977.

Lester, Julius. *Revolutionary Notes.* New York: Grove Press, Inc. 1960.

Lomax, Lewis. *The Negro Revolt.* New York: Harper & Row, 1962.

Madhubuti, Haki. *Enemies The Clash of Races.* Chicago: Third World Press, 1978.

Masotti, Louis and Corsi, Jerome. *Shoot-Out in Cleveland Black Militants and the Police: July 23, 1968.* Washington: U.S. Government Printing Office, May 1969.

Millard, Arnold. *The Testimony of Steve Biko His Beliefs About Black Consciousness, In His Own Words Recorded at a Political Trial.* Britain: Maurice Temple Smith, 1978.

Obadele, Abubakari Imari. *Foundations of the Black Nation.* Detroit, Michigan, San Francisco: The House of Songhay and Julian Richardson Associates, 1975.

Obadele, Abubakari Imari. *War in America the Malcolm X Doctrine.* Detroit, Michigan: The Malcolm X Society, August 1968.

Orrick, William J.R. *Shut It Down! A College In Crisis.* San Francisco State College, October 1968-April 1969. U.S. Government Printing Office June 1969.

Painter, Irvin Nell. *Exodusters: Black Migration to Kansas After Reconstruction.* New York: Alfred A. Knopf, 1977.

Painter Irvin, Nell. *The Narrative of Hosea Hudson, His Life as a Negro Communist in the South.* Cambridge, Massachusetts: Harvard University Press, 1979.

Pearsall Brainard, Robert. *The Symbionese Liberation Army.* Amsterdam: Rododi, 1974.

Redkey, Edwin. *Black Exodus Black Nationalist and Back to Africa Movements, 1850-1910.* New Haven and London: Yale University Press, 1969.

Riots, Civil and Criminal Disorders. Part 11 (1968), Part 17 (1969), Part 19 (1969), Part 21 (1969) Washington, D.C.: U.S. Government Printing Office.

Sellers, Cleveland, Terrell, Robert. *The River of No Return The Autobiography of a Black Militant and the Life and Death of S.N.C.C.* New York: William Morrow and Company, Inc., 1973.

Stuckey, Sterling. *The Ideological Origins of Black Nationalism.* Boston: Beacon Press, 1972.

Supplementary Detailed Staff Reports on Intelligence Activities and the Rights of Americans, Book III Washington, D.C. U.S. Government Printing Office. April 27, 1976.

T'Shaka, Oba. *Assessing the Lull in the Black Liberation Struggle.* Chicago: Black Books Bulletin, Vol. 6 No. 1 Spring.

T'Shaka, Oba. *Make the Past Serve the Present: Strategies for Black Liberation.* San Francisco: The Black Scholar Journal of Black Studies and Research, Jan-Feb, 1983.

T'Shaka, Oba. *Marcus Garvey The Father of Revolutionary Black Nationalism.* San Francisco: Journal of Black Poetry.

T'Shaka, Oba. *Strategies and Tactics for Building A Mass Based Black United Front.* San Francisco: National Black United Front Position Paper, 1980.

T'Shaka, Oba. *The Political Legacy of Malcom X.* Chicago: Third World Press, 1983.

T'Shaka, Oba. *The San Francisco Movement for Dignity and Freedom.* San Francisco: Black Dialogue Magazine, 1965.

T'Shaka, *Oba. The San Francisco State Strike, A Study of the First Black Studies Strike in the United States.* San Francisco: San Francisco State University's Black Studies Department, 1982.

Thompson, Vincent Bakpetu. *Africa and Unity: The Evolution of Pan Africanism.* Britain: Longman, 1969.

Udom, Essien E.U. *Black Nationalism A Search for an Identity in America.* Chicago: University of Chicago Press, 1962.

Williams, Robert. *Negroes With Guns.* New York: Marzani & Munsell, Inc., 1962.

BIBLIOGRAPHY FOR THE ART OF LEADERSHIP

Berube, Maurice and Tittell, Marilyn. *Confrontation at Ocean Hill, Brownsville, New York.* New York: Penguin Books, 1977.

Breitman, George. *The Last Year of Malcolm X. The Evolution of a Revolutionary.* New York: Merit Publishers, 1967.

Cabral, Amilcar. *Revolution in Guinea: Selected Texts.* New York and London: Monthly Review Press, 1969.

Carruthers, Jacob. *The United Two Lands.* Chicago: unpublished manuscript, Winter 1979.

Challand, Gerard. *Revolution in the Third World.* Middlesex and New York: Penguin Books, 1976.

Clarke, John Henrik. *Malcolm X The Man and His Times.* New York: Collier Books, 1969.

_____. *Marcus Garvey and The Vision of Africa.* New York: Vintage Books, 1974.

O.M. Collective. *The Organizer's Manual.* New York: Bantum Books, 1971.

Counter, S. Allen and Evans, David L. *I Sought My Brother.* Cambridge and London: The MIT Press, 1981.

Cruse, Harold. *The Crisis of the Negro Intellectual.* New York: William Morrow and Company, 1967.

DuBois, W.E.B. *Dusk of Dawn.* New York: Shocken Books, 1968.

Fanon, Frantz. *Black Skin White Masks.* New York: Grove Press, 1967.

_____. *Studies In A Dying Colonialism.* New York: Monthly Review Press, 1959.

_____. *The Wretched of the Earth.* New York: Grove Press, 1963.

_____. *Toward the African Revolution.* New York: Grove Press, 1967.

Fax, Elton C. *Garvey The History of A Pioneer Black Nationalist.* New York: Dodd, Mead and Company, 1972.

Garvey, A. Jacques. *Garvey and Garveyism.* Kingston: 1963.

Garvey, Marcus. *Philosophy and Opinions of Marcus Garvey or Africa for the Africans,* Vols. I and II. New York: The Universal Publishing House, 1925 and 1926.

Gendzier, Irene L. *Frantz Fanon A Critical Study.* New York: Pantheon Books, 1973.

Goldman, Peter. *The Death and Life of Malcolm X.* New York, Evanston, San Francisco, London: Harper and Row Publishers, 1965.

Guinea-Bissau: Toward Final Victory, Selected Speeches and Documents from PAIGC. Canada: LSM Information Center, 1974.

Haley, Alex. *The Autobiography of Malcolm X.* New York: Grove Press, 1964.

Hare, Nathan and Hare, Julia. *The Endangered Black Family. Coping with Unisexualization and Coming Extinction of the Black Race.* San Francisco: Black Think Tank, 1984.

Hill, Robert A. Editor, *The Marcus Garvey and Universal Negro Improvement Association Papers,* Vols. I-III. Los Angeles: University of California Press.

Kahn. Si. *Organizing.* New York: McGraw-Hill Book Company, 1982.

Killens, John Olliver. *The Trial Record of Denmark Vessey.* Boston: Beacon Press, 1970.

Kitson, Frank. *Low Intensity Operations, Subversions, Insurgency, Peace-Keeping.* London: Archon Books, 1971.

Malcolm X Speaks, Selected Speeches and Statements. London: Secker and Warburg, 1965.

Martin, Tony. *Race First.* Westport and London: Greenwood Press, 1976.

Morris, Albert B. *The Origin of the Civil Rights Movement.* New York and London: Free Press, 1984.

Quandt, William B. *Revolution and Political Leadership: Algeria 1954-1968.* Cambridge and London: The M.I.T. Press, 1969.

Raines, Howell. *My Soul Is Rested.* New York: Penguin Books, 1977.

Rudebeck, Lars. *Guinea-Bissau A Study of Political Mobilization.* Sweden: Africana Publishing Company, 1974.

Sowing the First Harvet, National Reconstruction in Guinea-Bissau. Oakland: LSM Information Center, 1978.

Stedman, John Gabriel. *Narrative of an Expedition Against the Revolted Negroes of Surinam.* Holland: University of Massachusetts Press, 1971.

Sun Zis Art of War Principles of Conflict, Recompilation and New English Translation with Annotation on Sun Zis *Art of War.* San Rafael, 1969.

T'Shaka, Oba. *The Political Legacy of Malcolm X.* Chicago: Third World Press, 1983.

Tolbert, Emory J. *The UNIA and Black Los Angeles.* Los Angeles: Center for Afro-American Studies, 1980.

Urdang, Stephanie. *Fighting Two Colonialisms Women in Guinea Bissau.* New York and London: Monthly Review Press, 1979.

Vincent, Theodore G. *Black Power and the Garvey Movement .* Berkeley: Ramparts Press.

X, Malcolm. *By Any Means Necessary.* New York: Pathfinder Press, 1970.

INDEX

A-K

Adam Clayton Powell 291

Footnotes

1   Chiekh Anta Diop, *Precolonial Black Africa* (Westport, Connecticut: Lawrence Hill & Company, 1987), p. 63.

2   Ibid., pp. 43-44

3   Chancellor Williams, *The Destruction of Black Civilization* (Chicago: Third World Press, 1976) p. 180.

4   Nell Irvin Painter, *Exodusters Black Migration to Kansas After Reconstruction* (New York: Alfred A. Knopf, 1977), p. 22.

5   Ibid., p. 25.

6   Ibid., p. 25.

7   Ibid., p. 27.

8   Ibid., p. 28.

9   Ibid., p. 28.

10   Jacob H. Carruthers, *Race Vindication The Spirit of the Haitian Revolution* , unpublished manuscript, 1981, p. 136.

11   Clayborne Carson, *In Struggle SNCC and the Black Awakening of the 1960's* (Cambridge and London: Harvard University Press, 1981), p. 20.

12   Ibid., p. 20.

13   Jacob Carruthers, *The United Two Lands* (Chicago: unpublished manuscript, Winter 1979), lecture.

14   *Mdu Ntr Text of the Eloquent Peasant,* 1 A De Buck Egyptian Reading Book, p. 98.

15   Hierocles, *The Golden Verses of Pythagoras* (London, Concord: Grove Press, 1983), p. 34.

16   Ibid., p. 34.

17   Gerard Chaliand, *Revolution in the Third World* (Dallas: Penguin Books, 1977), p. 76.

18 Sun Zi, *Art of War Principles of Conflict*,
    Recompilation and New English Translation with
    Annotation of Sun Zi's *Art of War* (San Rafael, 1969),
    p. 74.

19 Carl Oglesby, *The Yankee and Cowboy War*
    (Berkeley: Berkeley Publishing Company, 1976), p.
    28.

20 Ibid., p. 31.

21 Ibid., p. 31.

22 Ibid., p. 32.

23 Kirkpatrick Sale, *Power Shift The Rise of the
    Southern Rim   and it's Challenge to the Eastern
    Establishment* (New   York: Random House,
    1975), p. 5.

24 Ibid., p. 5.

25 Ibid., p. 5.

26 Vyacheslan Nikitin, *The Ultras in the USA* (Moscow:
    Progress Publishers, 1971), p. 243.

27 Ibid., p. 244.

28 Kirkpatrick Sale, *The Power Shift* (New York:
    Random House, 1975), pp. 25-6.

29 Vyacheslan Nikitin, *The Ultras in the USA* (Moscow:
    Progress Publishers, 1971), p. 244.

30 Russell Means, "For the World to Live, Europe Must
    Die Fighting Words on the Future of the Earth,"
    (Mother Jones, 1980), p. 26.

31 Lerone Bennett, Jr., *The Negro Mood* (Chicago:
    Johnson Publishing Company, 1964), pp. 50-1.

32 Julius Lester, *The Seventh Son The Thoughts and
    Writings of W.E.B. Du Bois*, Vol I (New York:
    Random House, 1971), p. 255.

33 Nell Irvin Painter, *Exodusters* (New York: Alfreda
    Knopf, 1977), p. 101.

34 Harold Cruse, *The Crisis of the Negro Intellectual*
    (New York: William Morrow and Company, 1967), p.
    90.

35 Dr. Asa Hilliard, "Remarks from the 1988 Atlanta Urban League Conference."

36 Nathan Hare and Julia Hare, *The Endangered Black Family Coping with Unisexualization and Coming Extinction of the Black Race* (San Francisco: Black Think Tank, 1984), pp. 49-50.

37 Ibid., p. 50.

38 Ibid., p. 53.

39 John Oliver Killens, *The Trial Record of Denmark Vesey,* (Boston: Beacon Press, 1970), p. xiii Introduction.

40 The O.M. Collective, *The Organizer's Manual,* (New York: Bantum Books, 1971), p. 5.

41 Le Duan, *This Nation and Socialism are One* (Chicago: Vanguard Books, 1976), pp. 64-5.

42 A. Jacques Garvey, *Garvey and Garveyism* (Kingston: Amy Jacques Garvey, 1963), pp. 85-6.

43 Oba T'Shaka "Black Resistance in America and Grenada, One Struggle Many Fronts." (San Francisco: Journal of Black Studies, San Francisco State University, Black Studies Department, Fall/Winter 1983), pp. 31-2.

44 David R. Hampton, *Contemporary Management,* (New York: McGraw Hill Book Company, 1977), p. 67.

45 Ibid., p. 68.

46 Ibid., p. 68.

47 Ibid., pp. 68-9.

48 Oba T'Shaka, "The San Francisco State Strike, A Study of the First Black Studies Strike in the United States (San Francisco: Journal of Black Studies, San Francisco State University), Vol. I 1969, p. 16.

49 Maurice R. Berube and Marilyn Tittell, *Confrontation at Ocean Hill Brownsville* (New York, Washington, London: Frederick Parager, 1969), pp. 64-72.

50 W.E.B. Du Bois, *Dusk of Dawn* (New York: Shocken Books, 1968), pp. 210-11.